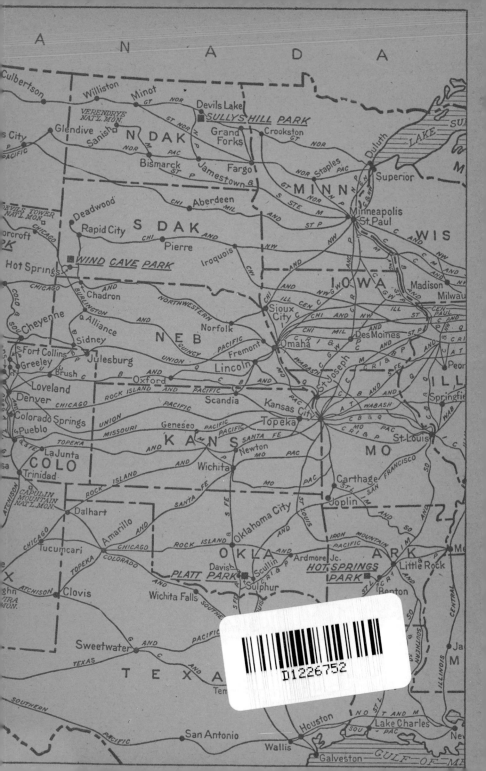

THE BOOK OF
THE NATIONAL PARKS

From the painting by Chris Jorgenson

ZOROASTER FROM THE DEPTHS OF THE GRAND CANYON

Nature's greatest example of stream erosion

THE BOOK OF
THE NATIONAL PARKS

BY

ROBERT STERLING YARD

CHIEF, EDUCATIONAL DIVISION, NATIONAL PARK SERVICE, DEPARTMENT
OF THE INTERIOR
AUTHOR OF "THE NATIONAL PARKS PORTFOLIO"
"THE TOP OF THE CONTINENT," ETC.

WITH MAPS AND ILLUSTRATIONS

NEW YORK
CHARLES SCRIBNER'S SONS
1919

TO
STEPHEN T. MATHER

PREFACE

In offering the American public a carefully studied outline of its national park system, I have two principal objects. The one is to describe and differentiate the national parks in a manner which will enable the reader to appreciate their importance, scope, meaning, beauty, manifold uses and enormous value to individual and nation. The other is to use these parks, in which Nature is writing in large plain lines the story of America's making, as examples illustrating the several kinds of scenery, and what each kind means in terms of world building; in other words, to translate the practical findings of science into unscientific phrase for the reader's increased profit and pleasure, not only in his national parks but in all other scenic places great and small.

At the outset I have been confronted with a difficulty because of this double objective. The rôle of the interpreter is not always welcome. If I write what is vaguely known as a "popular" book, wise men have warned me that any scientific intrusion, however lightly and dramatically rendered, will displease its natural audience. If I write the simplest of scientific books, I am warned that a large body of warm-blooded, wholesome, enthusiastic Americans, the very ones above all others whose keen enjoyment

I want to double by doubling their sources of pleasure, will have none of it. The suggestion that I make my text "popular" and carry my "science" in an appendix I promptly rejected, for if I cannot give the scientific aspects of nature their readable values in the text, I cannot make them worth an appendix.

Now I fail to share with my advisers their poor opinion of the taste, enterprise, and intelligence of the wide-awake American, but, for the sake of my message, I yield in some part to their warnings. Therefore I have so presented my material that the miscalled, and, I verily believe, badly slandered "average reader," may have his "popular" book by omitting the note on the Appreciation of Scenery, and the several notes explanatory of scenery which are interpolated between groups of chapters. If it is true, as I have been told, that the "average reader" would omit these anyway, because it is his habit to omit prefaces and notes of every kind, then nothing has been lost.

he keen inquiring reader, however, the reader who wants to know values and to get, in the eloquent phrase of the day, all that's coming to him, will have the whole story by beginning the book with the note on the Appreciation of Scenery, and reading it consecutively, interpolated notes and all. As this will involve less than a score of additional pages, I hope to get the message of the national parks in terms of their fullest enjoyment before much the greater part of the book's readers.

The pleasure of writing this book has many times

repaid its cost in labor, and any helpfulness it may have in advancing the popularity of our national parks, in building up the system's worth as a national economic asset, and in increasing the people's pleasure in all scenery by helping them to appreciate their greatest scenery, will come to me as pure profit. It is my earnest hope that this profit may be large.

A similar spirit has actuated the very many who have helped me acquire the knowledge and experience to produce it; the officials of the National Park Service, the superintendents and several rangers in the national parks, certain zoologists of the United States Biological Survey, the Director and many geologists of the United States Geological Survey, scientific experts of the Smithsonian Institution, and professors in several distinguished universities. Many men have been patient and untiring in assistance and helpful criticism, and to these I render warm thanks for myself and for readers who may benefit by their work.

CONTENTS

xii CONTENTS

THE SEDIMENTARY NATIONAL PARKS

XII. ON SEDIMENTARY ROCK IN SCENERY 247

XIII. GLACIERED PEAKS AND PAINTED SHALES . . . 251

XIV. ROCK RECORDS OF A VANISHED RACE 284

XV. THE HEALING WATERS 305

THE GRAND CANYON AND OUR NATIONAL MONUMENTS

XVI. A PAGEANT OF CREATION 328

XVII. THE RAINBOW OF THE DESERT 352

XVIII. HISTORIC MONUMENTS OF THE SOUTHWEST . . 367

XIX. DESERT SPECTACLES 385

XX. THE MUIR WOODS AND OTHER NATIONAL MON-
UMENTS 404

ILLUSTRATIONS

xiii

ILLUSTRATIONS

MAPS AND DIAGRAMS

AT END OF VOLUME

THE BOOK OF THE NATIONAL PARKS

The Book of the National Parks

ON THE APPRECIATION OF SCENERY

TO the average educated American, scenery is a pleasing hodge-podge of mountains, valleys, plains, lakes, and rivers. To him, the glacier-hollowed valley of Yosemite, the stream-scooped abyss of the Grand Canyon, the volcanic gulf of Crater Lake, the bristling granite core of the Rockies, and the ancient ice-carved shales of Glacier National Park all are one —just scenery, magnificent, incomparable, meaningless. As a people we have been content to wonder, not to know; yet with scenery, as with all else, to know is to begin fully to enjoy. Appreciation measures enjoyment. And this brings me to my proposition, namely, that we shall not really enjoy our possession of the grandest scenery in the world until we realize that scenery is the written page of the History of Creation, and until we learn to read that page.

The national parks of America include areas of the noblest and most diversified scenic sublimity easily accessible in the world; nevertheless it is their chiefest glory that they are among the completest expressions of the earth's history. The American people is waking rapidly to the magnitude of its scenic possession; it has yet to learn to appreciate it.

Nevertheless we love scenery. We are a nation of sightseers. The year before the world war stopped all things, we spent $286,000,000 in going to Europe. That summer Switzerland's receipts from the sale of transportation and board to persons coming from foreign lands to see her scenery was $100,000,000, and more than half, it has been stated apparently with authority, came from America. That same year tourist travel became Canada's fourth largest source of income, exceeding in gross receipts even her fisheries, and the greater part came from the United States; it is a matter of record that seven-tenths of the hotel registrations in the Canadian Rockies were from south of the border. Had we then known, as a nation, that there was just as good scenery of its kind in the United States, and many more kinds, we would have gone to see that; it is a national trait to buy the best. Since then, we have discovered this important fact and are crowding to our national parks.

"Is it true," a woman asked me at the foot of Yosemite Falls, "that this is the highest unbroken waterfall in the world?"

She was the average tourist, met there by chance. I assured her that such was the fact. I called attention to the apparent deliberation of the water's fall, a trick of the senses resulting from failure to realize height and distance.

"To think they are the highest in the world!" she mused.

I told her that the soft fingers of water had carved

this valley three thousand feet into the solid granite, and that ice had polished its walls, and I estimated for her the ages since the Merced River flowed at the level of the cataract's brink.

"I've seen the tallest building in the world," she replied dreamily, "and the longest railroad, and the largest lake, and the highest monument, and the biggest department store, and now I see the. highest waterfall. Just think of it!"

If one has illusions concerning the average tourist, let him compare the hundreds who gape at the paint pots and geysers of Yellowstone with the dozens who exult in the sublimated glory of the colorful canyon. Or let him listen to the table-talk of a party returned from Crater Lake. Or let him recall the statistical superlatives which made up his friend's last letter from the Grand Canyon.

I am not condemning wonder, which, in its place, is a legitimate and pleasurable emotion. As a condiment to sharpen and accent an abounding sense of beauty it has real and abiding value.

Love of beauty is practically a universal passion. It is that which lures millions into the fields, valleys, woods, and mountains on every holiday, which crowds our ocean lanes and railroads. The fact that few of these rejoicing millions are aware of their own motive, and that, strangely enough, a few even would be ashamed to make the admission if they became aware of it, has nothing to do with the fact. It's a wise man that knows his own motives. The fact that still fewer, whether aware or not of the reason of their happiness, are capable of making the least expression of it, also has nothing to do with the fact. The tourist woman whom I met at the foot of Yosemite Falls may have felt secretly suffocated by the filmy grandeur of the incomparable spectacle, notwithstanding that she was conscious of no higher emotion than the cheap wonder of a superlative. The Grand Canyon's rim is the stillest crowded place I know. I've stood among a hundred people on a precipice and heard the whir of a bird's wings in the abyss. Probably the majority of those silent gazers were suffering something akin to pain at their inability to give vent to the emotions bursting within them.

I believe that the statement can not be successfully challenged that, as a people, our enjoyment of scenery is almost wholly emotional. Love of beauty spiced by wonder is the equipment for enjoyment of the average intelligent traveller of to-day. Now add to this a more or less equal part of the intellectual pleasure of comprehension and you have the equipment of the average intelligent traveller of to-morrow. To hasten this to-morrow is one of the several objects of this book.

To see in the carved and colorful depths of the Grand Canyon not only the stupendous abyss whose terrible beauty grips the soul, but also to-day's chapter in a thrilling story of creation whose beginning lay untold centuries back in the ages, whose scene covers three hundred thousand square miles of our wonderful southwest, whose actors include the greatest forces of nature, whose tremendous episodes shame the imagination of Doré, and whose logical end invites suggestions before which finite minds shrink—this is to come into the presence of the great spectacle properly equipped for its enjoyment. But how many who see the Grand Canyon get more out of it than merely the beauty that grips the soul?

So it is throughout the world of scenery. The geologic story written on the cliffs of Crater Lake is more stupendous even than the glory of its indigo bowl. The war of titanic forces described in simple language on the rocks of Glacier National Park is unexcelled in sublimity in the history of mankind. The story of Yellowstone's making multiplies many times the thrill occasioned by its world-famed spectacle. Even the simplest and smallest rock details often tell thrilling incidents of prehistoric times out of which the enlightened imagination reconstructs the romances and the tragedies of earth's earlier days.

How eloquent, for example, was the small, water-worn fragment of dull coal we found on the limestone slope of one of Glacier's mountains! Impossible companionship! The one the product of forest, the other of submerged depths. Instantly I glimpsed the distant age when thousands of feet above the very spot upon which I stood, but then at sea level, bloomed a Cretaceous forest, whose broken trunks and matted foliage decayed in bogs where they slowly turned to coal; coal which, exposed and disintegrated during intervening ages, has long since—all but a few small fragments like this—washed into the headwaters of the Saskatchewan to merge eventually in the muds of Hudson Bay. And then, still dreaming, my mind leaped millions of years still further back to lake bottoms where, ten thousand feet below the spot on which I stood, gathered the pre-Cambrian ooze which later hardened to this very limestone. From ooze a score of thousand feet, a hundred million years, to coal! And both lie here together now in my palm! Filled thus with visions of a perspective beyond human comprehension, with what multiplied intensity of interest I now returned to the noble view from Gable Mountain!

In pleading for a higher understanding of Nature's method and accomplishment as a precedent to study and observation of our national parks, I seek enormously to enrich the enjoyment not only of these supreme examples but of all examples of world making. The same readings which will prepare you to enjoy to the full the message of our national parks will invest your neighborhood hills at home, your creek and river and prairie, your vacation valleys, the landscape through your car window, even your wayside ditch, with living interest. I invite you to a new and fascinating earth, an earth interesting, vital, personal, beloved, because at last known and understood!

It requires no great study to know and understand the earth well enough for such purpose as this. One does not have to dim his eyes with acres of maps,

THE RAINBOW NATURAL BRIDGE, UTAH

Cut out of red and yellow sandstone by alternate heat and cold, by sand-laden winds, and
by stream erosion

or become a plodding geologist, or learn to distinguish schists from granites, or to classify plants by table, or to call wild geese and marmots by their Latin names. It is true that geography, geology, physiography, mineralogy, botany and zoology must each contribute their share toward the condition of intelligence which will enable you to realize appreciation of Nature's amazing earth, but the share of each is so small that the problem will be solved, not by exhaustive study, but by the selection of essential parts. Two or three popular books which interpret natural science in perspective should pleasurably accomplish your purpose. But once begun, I predict that few will fail to carry certain subjects beyond the mere essentials, while some will enter for life into a land of new delights.

Let us, for illustration, consider for a moment the making of America. The earth, composed of countless aggregations of matter drawn together from the skies, whirled into a globe, settled into a solid mass surrounded by an atmosphere carrying water like a sponge, has reached the stage of development when land and sea have divided the surface between them, and successions of heat and frost, snow, ice, rain, and flood, are busy with their ceaseless carving of the land. Already mountains are wearing down and sea bottoms are building up with their refuse. Sediments carried by the rivers are depositing in strata, which some day will harden into rock.

We are looking now at the close of the era which

geologists call Archean, because it is ancient beyond knowledge. A few of its rocks are known, but not well enough for many definite conclusions. All the earth's vast mysterious past is lumped under this title.

The definite history of the earth begins with the close of the dim Archean era. It is the lapse from then till now, a few hundred million years at most out of all infinity, which ever can greatly concern man, for during this time were laid the only rocks whose reading was assisted by the presence of fossils. During this time the continents attained their final shape, the mountains rose, and valleys, plains, and rivers formed and re-formed many times before assuming the passing forms which they now show. During this time also life evolved from its inferred beginnings in the late Archean to the complicated, finely developed, and in man's case highly mentalized and spiritualized organization of To-day.

Surely the geologist's field of labor is replete with interest, inspiration, even romance. But because it has become so saturated with technicality as to become almost a popular bugaboo, let us attempt no special study, but rather cull from its voluminous records those simple facts and perspectives which will reveal to us this greatest of all story books, our old earth, as the volume of enchantment that it really is.

With the passing of the Archean, the earth had not yet settled into the perfectly balanced sphere which Nature destined it to be. In some places the rock was more compactly squeezed than in others, and these denser masses eventually were forced violently into neighbor masses which were not so tightly squeezed. These movements far below the surface shifted the surface balance and became one of many complicated and little known causes impelling the crust here to slowly rise and there to slowly fall. Thus in places sea bottoms lifted above the surface and became land, while lands elsewhere settled and became seas. There are areas which have alternated many times between land and sea; this is why we find limestones which were formed in the sea overlying shales which were formed in fresh water, which in turn overlie sandstones which once were beaches—all these now in plateaus thousands of feet above the ocean's level.

Sometimes these mysterious internal forces lifted the surface in long waves. Thus mountain chains and mountain systems were created. Often their summits, worn down by frosts and rains, disclose the core of rock which, ages before, then hot and fluid, had underlain the crust and bent it upward into mountain form. Now, cold and hard, these masses are disclosed as the granite of to-day's landscape, or as other igneous rocks of earth's interior which now cover broad surface areas, mingled with the stratified or water-made rocks which the surface only produces. But this has not always been the fate of the under-surface molten rocks, for sometimes they have burst by volcanic vents clear through the crust of earth, where, turned instantly to pumice and lava by release from pressure, they build great surface cones, cover broad plains and fill basins and valleys.

Thus were created the three great divisions of the rocks which form the three great divisions of scenery, the sediments, the granites, and the lavas.

During these changes in the levels of enormous surface areas, the frosts and water have been industriously working down the elevations of the land. Nature forever seeks a level. The snows of winter, melting at midday, sink into the rocks' minutest cracks. Expanded by the frosts, the imprisoned water pries open and chips the surface. The rains of spring and summer wash the chippings and other débris into rivulets, which carry them into mountain torrents, which rush them into rivers, which sweep them into oceans, which deposit them for the upbuilding of the bottoms. Always the level! Thousands of square miles of California were built up from ocean's bottom with sediments chiselled from the mountains of Wyoming, Colorado, and Utah, and swept seaward through the Grand Canyon.

These mills grind without rest or pause. The atmosphere gathers the moisture from the sea, the winds roll it in clouds to the land, the mountains catch and chill the clouds, and the resulting rains hurry back to the sea in rivers bearing heavy freights of soil. Spring, summer, autumn, winter, day and night, the mills of Nature labor unceasingly to produce her level. If ever this earth is really finished to Nature's liking, it will be as round and polished as a billiard ball.

From a photograph by Bailey Willis

MIDDLE FORK OF THE BELLY RIVER, GLACIER NATIONAL PARK

Very ancient shales and limestone fantastically carved by glaciers. The illustration shows
Glenns Lake, Pyramid Peak, Chaney Glacier, and Mount Kipp

Years mean nothing in the computation of the prehistoric past. Who can conceive a thousand centuries, to say nothing of a million years? Yet either is inconsiderable against the total lapse of time even from the Archean's close till now.

And so geologists have devised an easier method of count, measured not by units of time, but by what each phase of progress has accomplished. This measure is set forth in the accompanying table, together with a conjecture concerning the lapse of time in terms of years.

The most illuminating accomplishment of the table, however, is its bird's-eye view of the procession of the evolution of life from the first inference of its existence to its climax of to-day; and, concurrent with this progress, its suggestion of the growth and development of scenic America. It is, in effect, the table of contents of a volume whose thrilling text and stupendous illustration are engraved immortally in the rocks; a volume whose ultimate secrets the scholarship of all time perhaps will never fully decipher, but whose dramatic outlines and many of whose most thrilling incidents are open to all at the expense of a little study at home and a little thoughtful seeing in the places where the facts are pictured in lines so big and graphic that none may miss their meanings.

Man's colossal egotism is rudely shaken before the Procession of the Ages. Aghast, he discovers that the billions of years which have wrought this earth from star dust were not merely God's laborious preparation

PROGRESS OF CREATION

Chart of the Divisions of Geologic Time, and an Estimate in Years based on the assumption that a hundred million years have elapsed since the close of the Archean Period, together with a condensed table of the Evolution of Life from its Inferred Beginnings in the Archean to the Present Time. Read from the bottom up. Read the footnote upon the opposite page concerning the Estimate of Time.

ERA	PERIOD	EPOCH	LIFE DEVELOPMENT	ESTIMATED TIME
CENOZOIC Era of Recent Life	Quaternary	Recent / Pleistocene (Ice Age)	THE AGE OF MAN Animals and plants of the modern type. First record of man occurs in the early Pleistocene.	6 millions of years.
	Tertiary	Pliocene / Miocene / Oligocene / Eocene	THE AGE OF MAMMALS Rise and development of the highest orders of plants and animals.	
MESOZOIC Era of Intermediate Life	Cretaceous		THE AGE OF REPTILES Shellfish with complex shells. Enormous land reptiles. Flying reptiles and the evolution therefrom of birds. First palms. First hardwood trees. First mammals.	16 millions of years.
	Jurassic			
	Triassic			
	Carboniferous	Permian / Pennsylvanian / Mississippian	THE AGE OF AMPHIBIANS. THE COAL AGE Sharks and sea animals with nautilus-like shells. Evolution of land plants in many complex forms. First appearance of land vertebrates. First flowering plants. First cone-bearing trees. Club mosses and ferns highly developed.	
PALEOZOIC Era of Old Life	Devonian		THE AGE OF FISHES Evolution of many forms. Fish of great size. First appearance of amphibians and land plants.	45 millions of years.
	Silurian		Shell-fish develop fully. Appearance and culmination of crinoids or sea-lilies, and large scorpion-like crustaceans. First appearance of reef-building corals. Development of fishes.	
	Ordovician		Sea animals develop shells, especially cephalopods and mollusk-like brachiopods. Trilobites at their height. First appearance of insects. First appearance of fishes.	
	Cambrian		More highly developed forms of water life. Trilobites and brachiopods most abundant. Algae.	
PROTEROZOIC	Algonkian		The first life which left a distinct record. Very primitive forms of water life, crustaceans, brachiopods and algae.	33 millions of years.
ARCHEOZOIC	Archean		No fossils found, but life inferred from the existence of iron ores and limestones, which are generally formed in the presence of organisms.	

of a habitation fit for so admirable an occupant; that
man, on the contrary, is nothing more or less than the
present master tenant of earth, the highest type of
hundreds of millions of years of succeeding tenants
only because he is the latest in evolution.

Who can safely declare that the day will not come
when a new Yellowstone, hurled from reopened volcanoes, shall found itself upon the buried ruin of the
present Yellowstone; when the present Sierra shall
have disappeared into the Pacific and the deserts of
the Great Basin become the gardens of the hemisphere; when a new Rocky Mountain system shall
have grown upon the eroded and dissipated granites
of the present; when shallow seas shall join anew Hudson Bay with the Gulf of Mexico; when a new and
lofty Appalachian Range shall replace the rounded
summits of to-day; when a race of beings as superior
to man, intellectually and spiritually, as man is superior to the ape, shall endeavor to reconstruct a picture

---

NOTE EXPLANATORY OF THE ESTIMATE OF GEOLOGIC TIME IN THE
TABLE ON THE OPPOSITE PAGE

The general assumption of modern geologists is that a hundred million
years have elapsed since the close of the Archean period; at least this is
a round number, convenient for thinking and discussion. The recent
tendency has been greatly to increase conceptions of geologic time over
the highly conservative estimates of a few years ago, and a strong disposition
is shown to regard the Algonkian period as one of very great length, ex-
tremists even suggesting that it may have equalled all time since. For the
purposes of this popular book, then, let us conceive that the earth has
existed for a hundred million years since Archean times, and that one-third
of this was Algonkian; and let us apportion the two-thirds remaining
among succeeding eras in the average of the proportions adopted by Professor Joseph Barrell of Yale University, whose recent speculations upon
geologic time have attracted wide attention.

of man from the occasional remnants which floods
may wash into view?

Fantastic, you may say. It is fantastic. So far
as I know there exists not one fact upon which definite
predictions such as these may be based. But also
there exists not one fact which warrants specific denial
of predictions such as these. And if any inference
whatever may be made from earth's history it is the
inevitable inference that the period in which man
lives is merely one step in an evolution of matter,
mind and spirit which looks forward to changes as
mighty or mightier than those I have suggested.

With so inspiring an outline, the study to which
I invite you can be nothing but pleasurable. Space
does not permit the development of the theme in the
pages which follow, but the book will have failed if it
does not, incidental to its main purposes, entangle the
reader in the charm of America's adventurous past.

I

THE NATIONAL PARKS OF THE UNITED STATES

THE National Parks of the United States are areas of supreme scenic splendor or other unique quality which Congress has set apart for the pleasure and benefit of the people. At this writing they number eighteen, sixteen of which lie within the boundaries of the United States and are reached by rail and road. Those of greater importance have excellent roads, good trails, and hotels or hotel camps, or both, for the accommodation of visitors; also public camp grounds where visitors may pitch their own tents. Outside the United States there are two national parks, one enclosing three celebrated volcanic craters, the other conserving the loftiest mountain on the continent.

I

The starting point for any consideration of our national parks necessarily is the recently realized fact of their supremacy in world scenery. It was the sensational force of this realization which intensely attracted public attention at the outset of the new movement; many thousands hastened to see these wonders, and their reports spread the tidings throughout the land and gave the movement its increasing impetus.

The simple facts are these:

The Swiss Alps, except for several unmatchable individual features, are excelled in beauty, sublimity and variety by several of our own national parks, and these same parks possess other distinguished individual features unrepresented in kind or splendor in the Alps.

The Canadian Rockies are more than matched in rich coloring by our Glacier National Park. Glacier is the Canadian Rockies done in Grand Canyon colors. It has no peer.

The Yellowstone outranks by far any similar volcanic area in the world. It contains more and greater geysers than all the rest of the world together; the next in rank are divided between Iceland and New Zealand. Its famous canyon is alone of its quality of beauty. Except for portions of the African jungle, the Yellowstone is probably the most populated wild animal area in the world, and its wild animals are comparatively fearless, even sometimes friendly.

Mount Rainier has a single-peak glacier system whose equal has not yet been discovered. Twenty-eight living glaciers, some of them very large, spread, octopus-like, from its centre. It is four hours by rail or motor from Tacoma.

Crater Lake is the deepest and bluest accessible lake in the world, occupying the hole left after one of our largest volcanoes had slipped back into earth's interior through its own rim.

Yosemite possesses a valley whose compelling beauty the world acknowledges as supreme. The

GENERAL GRANT TREE
It has a National Park all to itself

valley is the centre of eleven hundred square miles of high altitude wilderness.

The Sequoia contains more than a million sequoia trees, twelve thousand of which are more than ten feet in diameter, and some of which are the largest and oldest living things in the wide world.

The Grand Canyon of Arizona is by far the hugest and noblest example of erosion in the world. It is gorgeously carved and colored. In sheer sublimity it offers an unequalled spectacle.

Mount McKinley stands more than 20,000 feet above sea level, and 17,000 feet above the surrounding valleys. Scenically, it is the world's loftiest mountain, for the monsters of the Andes and the Himalayas which surpass it in altitude can be viewed closely only from valleys from five to ten thousand feet higher than McKinley's northern valleys.

The Hawaii National Park contains the fourth greatest dead crater in the world, the hugest living volcano, and the Kilauea Lake of Fire, which is unique and draws visitors from the world's four quarters.

These are the principal features of America's world supremacy. They are incidental to a system of scenic wildernesses which in combined area as well as variety exceed the combined scenic wilderness playgrounds of similar class comfortably accessible elsewhere. No wonder, then, that the American public is overjoyed with its recently realized treasure, and that the Government looks confidently to the rapid development of its new-found economic asset. The

American public has discovered America, and no one who knows the American public doubts for a moment what it will do with it.

II

The idea still widely obtains that our national parks are principally playgrounds. A distinguished member of Congress recently asked: "Why make these appropriations? More people visited Rock Creek Park here in the city of Washington last Sunday afternoon than went to the Yosemite all last summer. The country has endless woods and mountains which cost the Treasury nothing."

This view entirely misses the point. The national parks are recreational, of course. So are state, county and city parks. So are resorts of every kind. So are the fields, the woods, the seashore, the open country everywhere. We are living in an open-air age. The nation of outdoor livers is a nation of power, initiative, and sanity. I hope to see the time when available State lands everywhere, when every square mile from our national forest reserve, when even many private holdings are made accessible and comfortable, and become habited with summer trampers and campers. It is the way to individual power and national efficiency.

But the national parks are far more than recreational areas. They are the supreme examples. They are the gallery of masterpieces. Here the visitor enters in a holier spirit. Here is inspiration. They are also the museums of the ages. Here nature is still creating the earth upon a scale so vast and so plain that even the dull and the frivolous cannot fail to see and comprehend.

This is no distinction without a difference. The difference is so marked that few indeed even of those who visit our national parks in a frivolous or merely recreational mood remain in that mood. The spirit of the great places brooks nothing short of silent reverence. I have seen men unconsciously lift their hats. The mind strips itself of affairs as one sheds a coat. It is the hour of the spirit. One returns to daily living with a springier step, a keener vision, and a broader horizon for having worshipped at the shrine of the Infinite.

III

The Pacific Coast Expositions of 1915 marked the beginning of the nation's acquaintance with its national parks. In fact, they were the occasion, if not the cause, of the movement for national parks development which found so quickly a country-wide response, and which is destined to results of large importance to individual and nation alike. Because thousands of those whom the expositions were expected to draw westward would avail of the opportunity to visit national parks, Secretary Lane, to whom the national parks suggested neglected opportunity requiring business experience to develop, induced Stephen T. Mather, a Chicago business man with mountain-top enthusiasms, to undertake their preparation for the unaccustomed throngs. Mr. Mather's vision embraced a correlated system of superlative scenic areas which should become the familiar playgrounds of the whole American people, a system which, if organized and administered with the efficiency of a great business, should even become, in time, the rendezvous of the sightseers of the world. He foresaw in the national parks a new and great national economic asset.

The educational and other propaganda by which this movement was presented to the people, which the writer had the honor to plan and execute, won rapidly the wide support of the public. To me the national parks appealed powerfully as the potential museums and classrooms for the popular study of the natural forces which made, and still are making, America, and of American fauna and flora. Here were set forth, in fascinating picture and lines so plain that none could fail to read and understand, the essentials of sciences whose real charm our rapid educational methods impart to few. This book is the logical outgrowth of a close study of the national parks, beginning with the inception of the new movement, from this point of view.

How free from the partisan considerations common in governmental organization was the birth of the movement is shown by an incident of Mr. Mather's inauguration into his assistant secretaryship. Secretary Lane had seen him at his desk and had started

THE GIANT GEYSER—GREATEST IN THE WORLD
Yellowstone National Park

back to his own room.   But he returned, looked in at the door, and asked:

"Oh, by the way, Steve, what are your politics?"

This book considers our national parks as they line up four years after the beginning of this movement.   It shows them well started upon the long road to realization, with Congress, Government, and the people united toward a common end, with the schools and the universities interested, and, for the first time, with the railroads, the concessioners, the motoring interests, and many of the public-spirited educational and outdoor associations all pulling together under the inspiration of a recognized common motive.

Of course this triumph of organization, for it is no less, could not have been accomplished nearly so quickly without the assistance of the closing of Europe by the great war.   Previous to 1915, Americans had been spending $300,000,000 a year in European travel.   Nor could it have been accomplished at all if investigation and comparison had not shown that our national parks excel in supreme scenic quality and variety the combined scenery which is comfortably accessible in all the rest of the world together.

To get the situation at the beginning of our book into full perspective, it must be recognized that, previous to the beginning of our propaganda in 1915, the national parks, as such, scarcely existed in the public consciousness.   Few Americans could name more than two or three of the fourteen existing parks.   The Yosemite Valley and the Yellowstone alone were gen-

erally known, but scarcely as national parks; most of
the school geographies which mentioned them at all
ignored their national character. The advertising
folders of competing railroads were the principal
sources of public knowledge, for few indeed asked for
the compilation of rates and charges which the Government then sent in response to inquiries for information. The parks had practically no administra-
tion. The business necessarily connected with their
upkeep and development was done by clerks as minor
and troublesome details which distracted attention
from more important duties; there was no one clerk
whose entire concern was with the national parks.
The American public still looked confidently upon the
Alps as the supreme scenic area in the world, and
hoped some day to see the Canadian Rockies.

IV

Originally the motive in park-making had been
unalloyed conservation. It is as if Congress had said:
"Let us lock this up where no one can run away with
it; we don't need it now, but some day it may be valu-
able." That was the instinct that led to the reservation of the Hot Springs of Arkansas in 1832, the
first national park. Forty years later, when official
investigation proved the truth of the amazing tales
of Yellowstone's natural wonders, it was the instinct
which led to the reservation of that largely unexplored area as the second national park. Seventeen
years after Yellowstone, when newspapers and sci-

entific magazines recounted the ethnological importance of the Casa Grande Ruin in Arizona, it resulted in the creation of the third national park, notwithstanding that the area so conserved enclosed less than a square mile, which contained nothing of the kind and quality which to-day we recognize as essential to parkhood. This closed what may be regarded as the initial period of national parks conservation. It was wholly instinctive; distinctions, objectives, and policies were undreamed of.

Less than two years after Casa Grande, which, by the way, has recently been re-classed a national monument, what may be called the middle period began brilliantly with the creation, in 1890, of the Yosemite, the Sequoia, and the General Grant National Parks, all parks in the true sense of the word, and all of the first order of scenic magnificence. Nine years later Mount Rainier was added, and two years after that wonderful Crater Lake, both meeting fully the new standard.

What followed was human and natural. The term national park had begun to mean something in the neighborhoods of the parks. Yellowstone and Yosemite had long been household words, and the introduction of other areas to their distinguished company fired local pride in neighboring states. "Why should we not have national parks, too?" people asked. Congress, always the reflection of the popular will, and therefore not always abreast of the moment, was unprepared with reasons. Thus, during 1903 and

1904, there were added to the list areas in North Dakota, South Dakota, and Oklahoma, which were better fitted for State parks than for association with the distinguished company of the nation's noblest.

A reaction followed and resulted in what we may call the modern period. Far-sighted men in and out of Congress began to compare and look ahead. No hint yet of the splendid destiny of our national parks, now so clearly defined, entered the minds of these men at this time, but ideas of selection, of development and utilization undoubtedly began to take form. At least, conservation, as such, ceased to become a sole motive. Insensibly Congress, or at least a few men of vision in Congress, began to take account of stock and figure on realization.

This healthy growth was helped materially by the public demand for the improvement of several of the national parks. No thought of appropriating money to improve the bathing facilities of Hot Springs had affected Congressional action for nearly half a century; it was enough that the curative springs had been saved from private ownership. Yellowstone was considered so altogether extraordinary, however, that Congress began in 1879 to appropriate yearly for its approach by road, and for the protection of its springs and geysers; but this was because Yellowstone appealed to the public sense of wonder. It took twenty years more for Congress to understand that the public sense of beauty was also worth appropriations. Yosemite had been a national park for

From a photograph by Pillsbury

THE YOSEMITE FALLS—HIGHEST IN THE WORLD

From the brink of the upper falls to the foot of the lower falls is almost half a mile

nine years before it received a dollar, and then only when public demand for roads, trails, and accommodations became insistent.

But, once born, the idea took root and spread. It was fed by the press and magazine reports of the glories of the newer national parks, then attracting some public attention. It helped discrimination in the comparison of the minor parks created in 1903 and 1904 with the greater ones which had preceded. The realization that the parks must be developed at public expense sharpened Congressional judgment as to what areas should and should not become national parks.

From that time on Congress has made no mistakes in selecting national parks. Mesa Verde became a park in 1905, Glacier in 1910, Rocky Mountain in 1915, Hawaii and Lassen Volcanic in 1916, Mount McKinley in 1917, and Lafayette and the Grand Canyon in 1919. From that time on Congress, most conservatively, it is true, has backed its judgment with increasing appropriations. And in 1916 it created the National Park Service, a bureau of the Department of the Interior, to administer them in accordance with a definite policy.

V

The distinction between the national forests and the national parks is essential to understanding. The national forests constitute an enormous domain administered for the economic commercialization of the nation's wealth of lumber. Its forests are handled scientifically with the object of securing the largest annual lumber output consistent with the proper conservation of the future. Its spirit is commercial. The spirit of national park conservation is exactly opposite. It seeks no great territory—only those few spots which are supreme. It aims to preserve nature's handiwork exactly as nature made it. No tree is cut except to make way for road, trail or hotel to enable the visitor to penetrate and live among nature's secrets. Hunting is excellent in some of our national forests, but there is no game in the national parks; in these, wild animals are a part of nature's exhibits; they are protected as friends.

It follows that forests and parks, so different in spirit and purpose, must be handled wholly separately. Even the rangers and scientific experts have objects so opposite and different that the same individual cannot efficiently serve both purposes. High specialization in both services is essential to success.

Another distinction which should be made is the difference between a national park and a national monument. The one is an area of size created by Congress upon the assumption that it is a supreme example of its kind and with the purpose of developing it for public occupancy and enjoyment. The other is made by presidential proclamation to conserve an area or object which is historically, ethnologically, or scientifically important. Size is not considered, and

THE NATIONAL PARKS AT A GLANCE

[Number, 18; total area, 10,739 square miles]

NATIONAL PARKS IN ORDER OF CREATION	LOCATION	AREA IN SQUARE MILES	DISTINCTIVE CHARACTERISTICS
Hot Springs, 1832	Middle Arkansas	1½	46 hot springs possessing curative properties—Many hotels and boarding houses—20 bath-houses under public control.
Yellowstone, 1872	Northwestern Wyoming	3,348	More geysers than in all rest of world together—Boiling springs—Mud volcanoes—Petrified forests—Grand Canyon of the Yellowstone, remarkable for gorgeous coloring—Large lakes—Many large streams and waterfalls—Greatest wild bird and animal preserve in world.
Sequoia, 1890	Middle eastern California	252	The Big Tree National Park—12,000 sequoia trees over 10 feet in diameter, some 25 to 36 feet in diameter—Towering mountain ranges—Startling precipices—Large limestone cave.
Yosemite, 1890	Middle eastern California	1,125	Valley of world-famed beauty—Lofty cliffs—Romantic vistas—Many waterfalls of extraordinary height—3 groves of big trees—High Sierra—Waterwheel falls.
General Grant, 1890	Middle eastern California	4	Created to preserve the celebrated General Grant Tree, 35 feet in diameter—6 miles from Sequoia National Park.
Mount Rainier, 1899	West central Washington	324	Largest accessible single peak glacier system—28 glaciers, some of large size—48 square miles of glacier, 50 to 500 feet thick—Wonderful subalpine wild flower fields.
Crater Lake, 1902	Southwestern Oregon	249	Lake of extraordinary blue in crater of extinct volcano—Sides 1,000 feet high—Interesting lava formations.
Wind Cave, 1903	South Dakota	17	Cavern having many miles of galleries and numerous chambers containing peculiar formations.
Platt, 1904	S. Oklahoma	1½	Many sulphur and other springs possessing medicinal value.
Sullys Hill, 1904	North Dakota	1⅛	Small park with woods, streams, and a lake—Is an important wild animal preserve.
Mesa Verde, 1906	S. W. Colorado	77	Most notable and best preserved prehistoric cliff dwellings in United States, if not in the world.
Glacier, 1910	Northwestern Montana	1,534	Rugged mountain region of unsurpassed Alpine character—250 glacier-fed lakes of romantic beauty—60 small glaciers—Sensational scenery of marked individuality.
Rocky Mountain, 1915	North middle Colorado	398	Heart of the Rockies—Snowy range, peaks 11,000 to 14,250 feet altitude—Remarkable records of glacial period.
Hawaii, 1916	Hawaiian Islands	118	Three separate volcanic areas—Kilauea and Mauna Loa on Hawaii; Haleakala on Maui.
Lassen Volcanic, 1916	Northern California	124	Only active volcano in United States proper—Lassen Peak 10,465 feet—Cinder Cone 6,879 feet—Hot springs—Mud geysers.
Mount McKinley, 1917	South central Alaska	2,200	Highest mountain in North America—Rises higher above surrounding country than any other mountain in world.
Grand Canyon, 1919	North central Arizona	958	The greatest example of erosion and the most sublime spectacle in the world—One mile deep and eight to twelve miles wide—Brilliantly colored.
Lafayette, 1919	Maine Coast	8	The group of granite mountains on Mount Desert Island.

development is not contemplated. The distinction is often lost in practice. Casa Grande is essentially a national monument, but had the status of a national park until 1918. The Grand Canyon, from every point of view a national park, was created a national monument and remained such until 1919.

THE GRANITE NATIONAL PARKS

GRANITE'S PART IN SCENERY

THE granite national parks are Yosemite, Sequoia, including the proposed Roosevelt Park, General Grant, Rocky Mountain, and Mount McKinley. Granite, as its name denotes, is granular in texture and appearance. It is crystalline, which means that it is imperfectly crystallized. It is composed of quartz, feldspar, and mica in varying proportions, and includes several common varieties which mineralogists distinguish scientifically by separate names.

Because of its great range and abundance, its presence at the core of mountain ranges where it is uncovered by erosion, its attractive coloring, its massiveness and its vigorous personality, it figures importantly in scenery of magnificence the world over. In color granite varies from light gray, when it shines like silver upon the high summits, to warm rose or dark gray, the reds depending upon the proportion of feldspar in its composition.

It produces scenic effects very different indeed from those resulting from volcanic and sedimentary rocks. While it bulks hugely in the higher mountains, running to enormous rounded masses below the level of the glaciers, and to jagged spires and pinnacled walls upon the loftiest peaks, it is found also in many regions of hill and plain. It is one of our commonest American rocks.

Much of the loftiest and noblest scenery of the world is wrought in granite. The Alps, the Andes, and the Himalayas, all of which are world-celebrated for their lofty grandeur, are prevailingly granite. They abound in towering peaks, bristling ridges, and terrifying precipices. Their glacial cirques are girt with fantastically toothed and pinnacled walls.

This is true of all granite ranges which are lofty enough to maintain glaciers. These are, in fact, the very characteristics of Alpine, Andean, Himalayan, Sierran, Alaskan, and Rocky Mountain summit landscape. It is why granite mountains are the favorites of those daring climbers whose ambition is to equal established records and make new ones; and this in turn is why some mountain neighborhoods become so much more celebrated than others which are quite as fine, or finer—because, I mean, of the publicity given to this kind of mountain climbing, and of the unwarranted assumption that the mountains associated with these exploits necessarily excel others in sublimity. As a matter of fact, the accident of fashion has even more to do with the fame of mountains than of men.

But by no means all granite mountains are lofty. The White Mountains, for example, which parallel our northeastern coast, and are far older than the Rockies and the Sierra, are a low granite range, with few of the characteristics of those mountains which lift their heads among the perpetual snows. On the contrary, they tend to rounded forested summits and knobby peaks. This results in part from a longer subjection of the rock surface to the eroding influence of successive frosts and rains than is the case with high ranges which are perpetually locked in frost. Besides, the ice sheets which planed off the northern part of the United States lopped away their highest parts.

There are also millions of square miles of eroded granite which are not mountains at all. These tend to rolling surfaces.

The scenic forms assumed by granite will be better appreciated when one understands how it enters landscape. The principal one of many igneous rocks, it is liquefied under intense heat and afterward cooled under pressure. Much of the earth's crust was once underlaid by granites in a more or less fluid state. When terrific internal pressures caused the earth's crust to fold and make mountains, this liquefied granite invaded the folds and pushed close up under the highest elevations. There it cooled. Thousands of centuries later, when erosion had worn away these mountain crests, there lay revealed the solid granite core which frost and glacier have since transformed into the bristling ramparts of to-day's landscape.

II

YOSEMITE, THE INCOMPARABLE

YOSEMITE NATIONAL PARK, MIDDLE EASTERN CALIFORNIA.
AREA, 1,125 SQUARE MILES

THE first emotion inspired by the sight of Yosemite is surprise. No previous preparation makes the mind ready for the actual revelation. The hardest preliminary reading and the closest study of photographs, even familiarity with other mountains as lofty, or loftier, fail to dull one's first astonishment.

Hard on the heels of astonishment comes realization of the park's supreme beauty. It is of its own kind, without comparison, as individual as that of the Grand Canyon or the Glacier National Park. No single visit will begin to reveal its sublimity; one must go away and return to look again with rested eyes. Its devotees grow in appreciative enjoyment with repeated summerings. Even John Muir, life student, interpreter, and apostle of the Sierra, confessed toward the close of his many years that the Valley's quality of loveliness continued to surprise him at each renewal.

And lastly comes the higher emotion which is born of knowledge. It is only when one reads in these inspired rocks the stirring story of their making

36

that pleasure reaches its fulness. The added joy of
the collector upon finding that the unsigned canvas,
which he bought only for its beauty, is the lost work
of a great master, and was associated with the romance
of a famous past is here duplicated. Written history
never was more romantic nor more graphically told
than that which Nature has inscribed upon the walls
of these vast canyons, domes and monoliths in a language which man has learned to read.

I

The Yosemite National Park lies on the western
slope of the Sierra Nevada Mountains in California,
nearly east of San Francisco. The snowy crest of the
Sierra, bellying irregularly eastward to a climax among
the jagged granites and gale-swept glaciers of Mount
Lyell, forms its eastern boundary. From this the park
slopes rapidly thirty miles or more westward to the
heart of the warm luxuriant zone of the giant sequoias.
This slope includes in its eleven hundred and twenty-
five square miles some of the highest scenic examples
in the wide gamut of Sierra grandeur. It is impossible
to enter it without exaltation of spirit, or describe it
without superlative.

A very large proportion of Yosemite's visitors see
nothing more than the Valley, yet no consideration is
tenable which conceives the Valley as other than a
small part of the national park. The two are insepara-
ble. One does not speak of knowing the Louvre who

has seen only the Venus de Milo, or St. Mark's who has looked only upon its horses.

Considered as a whole, the park is a sagging plain of solid granite, hung from Sierra's saw-toothed crest, broken into divides and transverse mountain ranges, punctured by volcanic summits, gashed and bitten by prehistoric glaciers, dotted near its summits with glacial lakes, furrowed by innumerable cascading streams which combine in singing rivers, which, in turn, furrow greater canyons, some of majestic depth and grandeur. It is a land of towering spires and ambitious summits, serrated cirques, enormous isolated rock masses, rounded granite domes, polished granite pavements, lofty precipices, and long, shimmering waterfalls.

Bare and gale-ridden near its crest, the park descends in thirty miles through all the zones and gradations of animal and vegetable life through which one would pass in travelling from the ice-bound shores of the Arctic Ocean the continent's length to Mariposa Grove. Its tree sequence tells the story. Above timber-line there are none but inch-high willows and flat, piney growths, mingled with tiny arctic flowers, which shrink in size with elevation; even the sheltered spots on Lyell's lofty summit have their colored lichens, and their almost microscopic bloom. At timber-line, low, wiry shrubs interweave their branches to defy the gales, merging lower down into a tangle of many stunted growths, from which spring twisted pines and contorted spruces, which the winds curve to leeward or bend at sharp angles, or spread in full development as prostrate upon the ground as the mountain lion's skin upon the home floor of his slayer.

Descending into the great area of the Canadian zone, with its thousand wild valleys, its shining lakes, its roaring creeks and plunging rivers, the zone of the angler, the hiker, and the camper-out, we enter forests of various pines, of silver fir, hemlock, aged hump-backed juniper, and the species of white pine which Californians wrongly call tamarack.

This is the paradise of outdoor living; it almost never rains between June and October. The forests fill the valley floors, thinning rapidly as they climb the mountain slopes; they spot with pine green the broad, shining plateaus, rooting where they find the soil, leaving unclothed innumerable glistening areas of polished uncracked granite; a striking characteristic of Yosemite uplands. From an altitude of seven or eight thousand feet, the Canadian zone forests begin gradually to merge into the richer forests of the Transition zone below. The towering sugar pine, the giant yellow pine, the Douglas fir, and a score of decidu-ous growths—live oaks, bays, poplars, dogwoods, maples—begin to appear and become more frequent with descent, until, two thousand feet or more below, they combine into the bright stupendous forests where, in specially favored groves, King Sequoia holds his royal court.

Wild flowers, birds, and animals also run the gamut of the zones. Among the snows and alpine

flowerets of the summits are found the ptarmigan
and rosy finch of the Arctic circle, and in the summit
cirques and on the shores of the glacial lakes whistles
the mountain marmot.

The richness and variety of wild flower life in
all zones, each of its characteristic kind, astonishes
the visitor new to the American wilderness. Every
meadow is ablaze with gorgeous coloring, every copse
and sunny hollow, river bank and rocky bottom, becomes painted in turn the hue appropriate to the
changing seasons. Now blues prevail in the kaleidoscopic display, now pinks, now reds, now yellows.
Experience of other national parks will show that the
Yosemite is no exception; all are gardens of wild
flowers.

The Yosemite and the Sequoia are, however, the
exclusive possessors among the parks of a remarkably
showy flowering plant, the brilliant, rare, snow-plant.
So luring is the red pillar which the snow-plant lifts a
foot or more above the shady mould, and so easily is
it destroyed, that, to keep it from extinction, the government fines covetous visitors for every flower picked.

The birds are those of California—many, prolific,
and songful. Ducks raise their summer broods fear-
lessly on the lakes. Geese visit from their distant
homes. Cranes and herons fish the streams. Every
tree has its soloist, every forest its grand chorus. The
glades resound with the tapping of woodpeckers. The
whirr of startled wings accompanies passage through
every wood. To one who has lingered in the forests

to watch and to listen, it is hard to account for the wide-spread fable that the Yosemite is birdless. No doubt, happy talkative tourists, in companies and regiments, afoot and mounted, drive bird and beast alike to silent cover—and comment on the lifeless forests. "The whole range, from foothill to summit, is shaken into song every summer," wrote John Muir, to whom birds were the loved companions of a life-time of Sierra summers, "and, though low and thin in winter, the music never ceases."

There are two birds which the unhurried traveller will soon know well. One is the big, noisy, gaudy Clark crow, whose swift flight and companionable squawk are familiar to all who tour the higher levels. The other is the friendly camp robber, who, with encouragement, not only will share your camp luncheon, but will gobble the lion's share.

Of the many wild animals, ranging in size from the great, powerful, timid grizzly bear, now almost extinct here, whose Indian name, by the way, is yo-semite, to the tiny shrew of the lowlands, the most fre-quently seen are the black or brown bear, and the deer, both of which, as compared with their kind in neighborhoods where hunting is permitted, are unterri-fied if not friendly. Notwithstanding its able pro-tection, the Yosemite will need generations to recover from the hideous slaughter which, in a score or two of years, denuded America of her splendid heritage of wild animal life.

Of the several carnivora, the coyote alone is occasionally seen by visitors. Wolves and mountain lions, prime enemies of the deer and mountain sheep, are hard to find, even when officially hunted in the winter with dogs trained for the purpose.

II

The Yosemite Valley is the heart of the national park. Not only is it the natural entrance and abiding place, the living-room, so to speak, the central point from which all parts of the park are most comfortably accessible; it is also typical in some sense of the Sierra as a whole, and is easily the most beautiful valley in the world.

It is difficult to analyze the quality of the Valley's beauty. There are, as Muir says, "many Yosemites" in the Sierra. The Hetch Hetchy Valley, in the northern part of the park, which bears the same relation to the Tuolumne River that the Yosemite Valley bears to the Merced, is scarcely less in size, richness, and the height and magnificence of its carved walls. Scores of other valleys, similar except for size, abound north and south, which are, scientifically and in Muir's meaning, Yosemites; that is, they are pauses in their rivers' headlong rush, once lakes, dug by rushing waters, squared and polished by succeeding glaciers, chiselled and ornamented by the frosts and rains which preceded and followed the glaciers. Muir is right, for all these are Yosemites; but he is wrong, for there is only one Yosemite.

It is not the giant monoliths that establish the incomparable Valley's world supremacy; Hetch Hetchy, Tehipite, Kings, and others have their giants, too. It is not its towering, perpendicular, serrated walls; the Sierra has elsewhere, too, an overwhelming exhibit of titanic granite carvings. It is not its waterfalls, though these are the highest, by far, in the world, nor its broad, peaceful bottoms, nor its dramatic vistas, nor the cavernous depths of its tortuous tributary canyons. Its secret is selection and combination. Like all supremacy, Yosemite's lies in the inspired proportioning of carefully chosen elements. Herein is its real wonder, for the more carefully one analyzes the beauty of the Yosemite Valley, the more difficult it is to conceive its ensemble the chance of Nature's functioning rather than the master product of supreme artistry.

Entrance to the Yosemite by train is from the west, by automobile from east and west both. From whatever direction, the Valley is the first objective, for the hotels are there. It is the Valley, then, which we must see first. Nature's artistic contrivance is apparent even in the entrance. The train-ride from the main line at Merced is a constant up-valley progress, from a hot, treeless plain to the heart of the great, cool forest. Expectation keeps pace. Changing to automobile at El Portal, one quickly enters the park. A few miles of forest and behold—the Gates of the Valley. El Capitan, huge, glistening, rises upon the left, 3,000 feet above the valley floor. At first sight its bulk almost appalls. Opposite upon the right Cathedral Rocks support the Bridal Veil Fall, shimmering, filmy, a fairy thing. Between them, in the distance, lies the unknown.

Progress up the valley makes constantly for climax. Seen presently broadside on, El Capitan bulks double, at least. Opposite, the valley bellies. Cathedral Rocks and the mediæval towers known as Cathedral Spires, are enclosed in a bay, which culminates in the impressive needle known as Sentinel Rock—all richly Gothic. Meantime the broadened valley, another strong contrast in perfect key, delightfully alternates with forest and meadow, and through it the quiet Merced twists and doubles like a glistening snake. And then we come to the Three Brothers.

Already some notion of preconception has possessed the observer. It could not have been chance which set off the filmy Bridal Veil against El Capitan's bulk; which designed the Gothic climax of Sentinel Rock; which wondrously proportioned the consecutive masses of the Three Brothers; which made El Capitan, now looked back upon against a new background, a new and appropriate creation, a thing of brilliance and beauty instead of bulk, mighty of mass, powerful in shape and poise, yet mysteriously delicate and unreal. As we pass on with rapidly increasing excitement to the supreme climax at the Valley's head, where gather together Glacier Point, Yosemite Falls of unbelievable height and graciousness, the Royal Arches, manifestly a carving, the gulf-like entrances of Tenaya and the

From a photograph by J. T. Boysen

EL CAPITAN, SURVIVOR OF THE GLACIERS

Looking eastward up the Yosemite Valley, Half Dome is seen on the right horizon

Merced Canyons, and above all, and pervading all, the distinguished mysterious personality of Half Dome, presiding priest of this Cathedral of Beauty, again there steals over us the uneasy suspicion of supreme design. How could Nature have happened upon the perfect composition, the flawless technique, the divine inspiration of this masterpiece of more than human art? Is it not, in fact, the master temple of the Master Architect?

To appreciate the Valley we must consider certain details. It is eight miles long, and from half a mile to a mile wide. Once prehistoric Lake Yosemite, its floor is as level as a ball field, and except for occasional meadows, grandly forested. The sinuous Merced is forested to its edges in its upper reaches, but lower down occasionally wanders through broad, blooming opens. The rock walls are dark pearl-hued granite, dotted with pines wherever clefts or ledges exist capable of supporting them; even El Capitan carries its pine-tree half way up its smooth precipice. Frequently the walls are sheer; they look so everywhere. The valley's altitude is 4,000 feet. The walls rise from 2,000 to 6,000 feet higher; the average is a little more than 3,000 feet above the valley floor; Sentinel Dome and Mount Watkins somewhat exceed 4,000 feet; Half Dome nearly attains 5,000 feet; Cloud's Rest soars nearly 6,000 feet.

Two large trench-like canyons enter the valley at its head, one on either side of Half Dome. Tenaya Canyon enters from the east in line with the valley, looking as if it were the Valley's upper reach. Merced Canyon enters from the south after curving around the east and south sides of Half Dome. Both are extremely deep. Half Dome's 5,000 feet form one side of each canyon; Mount Watkin's 4,300 feet form the north side of Tenaya Canyon, Glacier Point's 3,200 feet the west side of Merced Canyon. Both canyons are superbly wooded at their outlets, and lead rapidly up to timber-line. Both carry important trails from the Valley floor to the greater park above the rim.

To this setting add the waterfalls and the scene is complete. They are the highest in the world. Each is markedly individualized; no two resemble each other. Yet, with the exception of the Vernal Fall, all have a common note; all are formed of comparatively small streams dropping from great heights; all are wind-blown ribbons ending in clouds of mist. They are so distributed that one or more are visible from most parts of the Valley and its surrounding rim. More than any other feature, they differentiate and distinguish the Yosemite.

The first of the falls encountered, Bridal Veil, is a perfect example of the valley type. A small stream pouring over a perpendicular wall drops six hundred and twenty feet into a volume of mist. The mist, of course, is the bridal veil. How much of the water reaches the bottom as water is a matter of interesting speculation. This and the condensed mists reach the river through a delta of five small brooks. As a spectacle the Bridal Veil Fall is unsurpassed. The deli-

From a photograph by J. T. Boysen

HALF DOME, YOSEMITE'S HOODED MONK

Rising nearly four thousand feet above the valley floor; the view is up Tenaya Canyon to the
High Sierra

cacy of its beauty, even in the high water of early summer, is unequalled by any waterfall I have seen. A rainbow frequently gleams like a colored rosette in the massed chiffon of the bride's train. So pleasing are its proportions that it is difficult to believe the fall nearly four times the height of Niagara.

The Ribbon Fall, directly opposite Bridal Veil, a little west of El Capitan, must be mentioned because for a while in early spring its sixteen hundred foot drop is a spectacle of remarkable grandeur. It is merely the run of a snowfield which disappears in June. Thereafter a dark perpendicular stain on the cliff marks its position. Another minor fall, this from the south rim, is that of Sentinel Creek. It is seen from the road at the right of Sentinel Rock, dropping five hundred feet in one leap of several which aggregate two thousand feet.

Next in progress come Yosemite Falls, loftiest by far in the world, a spectacle of sublimity. These falls divide with Half Dome the honors of the upper Valley. The tremendous plunge of the Upper Fall, and the magnificence of the two falls in apparent near continuation as seen from the principal points of elevation on the valley floor, form a spectacle of extraordinary distinction. They vie with Yosemite's two great rocks, El Capitan and Half Dome, for leadership among the individual scenic features of the continent.

The Upper Fall pours over the rim at a point nearly twenty-six hundred feet above the valley floor. Its sheer drop is fourteen hundred and thirty feet, the equal of nine Niagaras. Two-fifths of a mile south of its foot, the Lower Fall drops three hundred and twenty feet more. From the crest of the Upper Fall to the foot of the Lower Fall lacks a little of half a mile. From the foot of the Lower Fall, after foaming down the talus, Yosemite Creek, seeming a ridiculously small stream to have produced so monstrous a spectacle, slips quietly across a half mile of level valley to lose itself in the Merced.

From the floods of late May when the thunder of falling water fills the valley and windows rattle a mile away, to the October drought when the slender ribbon is little more than mist, the Upper Yosemite Fall is a thing of many moods and infinite beauty. Seen from above and opposite at Glacier Point, sideways and more distantly from the summit of Cloud's Rest, straight on from the valley floor, upwards from the foot of the Lower Fall, upwards again from its own foot, and downwards from the overhanging brink toward which the creek idles carelessly to the very step-off of its fearful leap, the Fall never loses for a moment its power to amaze. It draws and holds the eye as the magnet does the iron.

Looking up from below one is fascinated by the extreme leisureliness of its motion. The water does not seem to fall; it floats; a pebble dropped alongside surely would reach bottom in half the time. Speculating upon this appearance, one guesses that the air retards the water's drop, but this idea is quickly dispelled by the observation that the solid inner body

drops no faster than the outer spray. It is long before the wondering observer perceives that he is the
victim of an illusion; that the water falls normally;
that it appears to descend with less than natural speed
only because of the extreme height of the fall, the eye
naturally applying standards to which it has been
accustomed in viewing falls of ordinary size.

On windy days the Upper Fall swings from the
brink like a pendulum of silver and mist. Back and
forth it lashes like a horse's tail. The gusts lop off
puffy clouds of mist which dissipate in air. Muir tells
of powerful winter gales driving head on against the
cliff, which break the fall in its middle and hold it in
suspense. Once he saw the wind double the fall back
over its own brink. Muir, by the way, once tried to
pass behind the Upper Fall at its foot, but was nearly
crushed.

By contrast with the lofty temperamental Upper
Fall, the Lower Fall appears a smug and steady pigmy.
In such company, for both are always seen together,
it is hard to realize that the Lower Fall is twice the
height of Niagara. Comparing Yosemite's three most
conspicuous features, these gigantic falls seem to appeal even more to the imagination than to the sense
of beauty. El Capitan, on the other hand, suggests
majesty, order, proportion, and power; it has its many
devotees. Half Dome suggests mystery; to many
it symbolizes worship. Of these three, Half Dome
easily is the most popular.

Three more will complete the Valley's list of notable waterfalls. All of these lie up the Merced Canyon. Illilouette, three hundred and seventy feet in height, enters from the west, a frothing fall of great beauty, hard to see. Vernal and Nevada Falls carry the Merced River over steep steps in its rapid progress from the upper levels to the valley floor. The only exception to the valley type, Vernal Fall, which some consider the most beautiful of all, and which certainly is the prettiest, is a curtain of water three hundred and seventeen feet high, and of pleasing breadth. The Nevada Fall, three-fifths of a mile above, a majestic drop of nearly six hundred feet, shoots watery rockets from its brink. It is full-run, powerful, impressive, and highly individualized. With many it is the favorite waterfall of Yosemite.

In sharp contrast with these valley scenes is the view from Glacier Point down into the Merced and Tenaya Canyons, and out over the magical park landscape to the snow-capped mountains of the High Sierra. Two trails lead from the valley up to Glacier Point, and high upon the precipice, three thousand feet above the valley floor, is a picturesque hotel; it is also reached by road. Here one may sit at ease on shady porches and overlook one of the most extended, varied and romantic views in the world of scenery. One may take dinner on this porch and have sunset served with dessert and the afterglow with coffee.

Here again one is haunted by the suggestion of artistic intention, so happy is the composition of this extraordinary picture. The foreground is the dark,

tremendous gulf of Merced Canyon, relieved by the
silver shimmer of Vernal and Nevada Falls. From
this in middle distance rises, in the centre of the canvas, the looming tremendous personality of Half
Dome, here seen in profile strongly suggesting a monk
with outstretched arms blessing the valley at close of
day. Beyond stretches the horizon of famous, snowy,
glacier-shrouded mountains, golden in sunset glow.

III

Every summer many thousands of visitors gather
in Yosemite. Most of them, of course, come tourist-
fashion, to glimpse it all in a day or two or three. A
few thousands come for long enough to taste most of
it, or really to see a little. Fewer, but still increasingly
many, are those who come to live a little with Yosemite;
among these we find the lovers of nature, the poets,
the seers, the dreamers, and the students.

Living is very pleasant in the Yosemite. The
freedom from storm during the long season, the dry
warmth of the days and the coldness of the nights, the
inspiration of the surroundings and the completeness
of the equipment for the comfort of visitors make it
extraordinary among mountain resorts. There is a
hotel in the Valley, and another upon the rim at
Glacier Point. There are three large hotel-camps in
the Valley, where one may have hotel comforts under
canvas at camp prices. Two of these hotel-camps
possess swimming pools, dancing pavilions, tennis

courts electrically lighted for night play, hot and cold-water tubs and showers, and excellent table service. One of the hotel-camps, the largest, provides evening lectures, song services, and a general atmosphere suggestive of Chatauqua. Still a third is for those who prefer quiet retirement and the tradition of old-fashioned camp life.

Above the valley rim, besides the excellent hotel upon Glacier Point, there are at this writing hotel-camps equipped with many hotel comforts, including baths, at such outlying points as Merced Lake and Tenaya Lake; the former centring the mountain climbing and trout fishing of the stupendous region on the southwest slope of the park, and the latter the key to the entire magnificent region of the Tuolumne. These camps are reached by mountain trail, Tenaya Lake Camp also by motor road. The hotel-camp system is planned for wide extension as growing demand warrants. There are also hotels outside park limits on the south and west which connect with the park roads and trails.

The roads, by the way, are fair. Three enter from the west, centring at Yosemite Village in the Valley; one from the south by way of the celebrated Mariposa Grove of giant sequoias; one from El Portal, terminus of the Yosemite Railway; and one from the north, by way of several smaller sequoia groves, connecting directly with the Tioga Road.

Above the valley rim and north of it, the Tioga Road crosses the national park and emerges at Mono

Lake on the east, having crossed the Sierra over Tioga Pass on the park boundary. The Tioga Road, which was built in 1881, on the site of the Mono Trail, to connect a gold mine west of what has since become the national park with roads east of the Sierra, was purchased in 1915 by patriotic lovers of the Yosemite and given to the Government. The mine having soon failed, the road had been impassable for many years. Repaired with government money it has become the principal highway of the park and the key to its future development. The increase in motor travel to the Yosemite from all parts of the country which began the summer following the Great War, has made this gift one of growing importance. It affords a new route across the Sierra.

But hotels and hotel-camps, while accommodating the great majority of visitors, by no means shelter all. Those who camp out under their own canvas are likely to be Yosemite's most appreciative devotees. The camping-out colony lives in riverside groves in the upper reaches of the Valley, the Government assigning locations without charge. Many families make permanent summer homes here, storing equipment between seasons in the village. Others hire equipment complete, from tents to salt-cellars, on the spot. Some who come to the hotels finish the season under hired canvas, and next season come with their own. An increasing number come in cars, which they keep in local garages or park near their canvas homes.

Living is easy and not expensive in these camp

homes. Mid-day temperatures are seasonable, and nights are always cool. As it does not rain, tents are concessions to habit; many prefer sleeping under the trees. Markets in the village supply meats, vegetables, milk, bread, and groceries at prices regulated by Government, and deliver them at your kitchen tent. Shops furnish all other reasonable needs. It is not camping out as commonly conceived; you are living at home on the banks of the Merced, under the morning shadow of Half Dome, and within sight of Yosemite Falls.

From these Valley homes one rides into the High Sierra on horses hired from the government concessioner, tours to the Tuolumne Meadows or the Mariposa Grove by automobile, wanders long summer afternoons in the Valley, climbs the great rocks and domes, picnics by moonlight under the shimmering falls or beneath the shining tower of El Capitan, explores famous fishing waters above the rim, and, on frivolous evenings, dances or looks at motion pictures at the greater hotel-camps.

No wonder that camp homes in the Yosemite are growing in popularity.

IV

The trail traveller finds the trails the best in the country, and as good as the best in the world; they are the models for the national system. Competent guides, horses, supplies, and equipment are easy to hire at regulated prices in the village.

As for the field, there is none nobler or more varied in the world. There are dozens of divides, scores of towering, snow-splashed peaks, hundreds of noble valleys and shining lakes, thousands of cascading streams, great and small, from whose depths fighting trout rise to the cast fly. There are passes to be crossed which carry one through concentric cirques of toothed granite to ridges from which the High Sierra spreads before the eye a frothing sea of snowy peaks.

Such a trip is that through Tuolumne Meadows up Lyell Canyon to its headwaters, over the Sierra at Donohue Pass, and up into the birth chambers of rivers among the summit glaciers of Lyell and McClure —a never-to-be-forgotten journey, which may be continued, if one has time and equipment, down the John Muir Trail to Mount Whitney and the Sequoia National Park. Or one may return to the park by way of Banner Peak and Thousand Island Lake, a wonder spot, and thence north over Parker and Mono Passes; trips like these produce views as magnificent as the land possesses.

Space does not permit even the suggestion of the possibilities to the trail traveller of this wonderland above the rim. It is the summer playground for a nation.

Second in magnificence among the park valleys is Hetch Hetchy, the Yosemite of the north. Both are broad, flowered and forested levels between lofty granite walls. Both are accented by gigantic rock personalities. Kolana Rock, which guards Hetch Hetchy at its western gateway as El Capitan guards Yosemite, must be ranked in the same class. Were there no Yosemite Valley, Hetch Hetchy, though it lacks the distinction which gives Yosemite Valley its world-wide fame, would be much better known than it now is—a statement also true about other features of the national park.

Hetch Hetchy is now being dammed below Kolana Rock to supply water for San Francisco. The dam will be hidden from common observation, and the timber lands to be flooded will be cut so as to avoid the unsightliness usual with artificial reservoirs in forested areas. The reservoir will cover one of the most beautiful bottoms in America. It will destroy forests of luxuriance. It will replace these with a long sinuous lake, from which sheer Yosemite-like granite walls will rise abruptly two or three thousand feet. There will be places where the edges are forested. Down into this lake from the high rim will cascade many roaring streams.

The long fight in California, in the press of the whole country, and finally in Congress, between the advocates of the Hetch Hetchy reservoir and the defenders of the scenic wilderness is one of the stirring episodes in the history of our national parks. At this writing, time enough has not yet passed to heal the wounds of battle, but at least we may look calmly at what remains. One consideration, at least, affords a little comfort. Hetch Hetchy was once, in late prehistoric times, a natural lake of great nobility. The

From a photograph by J. T. Boysen

THE CLIMAX OF YOSEMITE NATIONAL PARK
Mount Lyell and its glacier from Lyell Fork

THE GREATEST WATERWHEEL OF THE TUOLUMNE
It is fifty feet in height and seventy-five feet long; Yosemite National Park

remains of Nature's dam, not far from the site of man's, are plain to the geologist's eye. It is possible that, with care in building the dam and clearing out the trees to be submerged, this restoration of one of Nature's noble features of the past may not work out so inappropriately as once we feared.

The Grand Canyon of the Tuolumne, through which the river descends from the level of the Tuolumne Meadows almost five thousand feet to the Hetch Hetchy Valley, possesses real Yosemite grandeur. Much of this enormous drop occurs within a couple of amazing miles west of the California Falls. Here the river slips down sharply tilted granite slopes at breathless speed, breaking into cascades and plunging over waterfalls at frequent intervals. It is a stupendous spectacle which few but the hardiest mountaineers saw previous to 1918, so steep and difficult was the going. During that season a trail was opened which makes accessible to all one of the most extraordinary examples of plunging water in the world.

The climax of this spectacle is the Waterwheels. Granite obstructions in the bed of the steeply tilted river throw solid arcs of frothing water fifty feet in air. They occur near together, singly and in groups.

V

The fine camping country south of the Yosemite Valley also offers its sensation. At its most southern point, the park accomplishes its forest climax in the

Mariposa Grove. This group of giant sequoias (Sequoia washingtoniana) ranks next, in the number and magnificence of its trees, to the Giant Forest of the Sequoia National Park and the General Grant grove.

The largest tree of the Mariposa Grove is the Grizzly Giant, which has a diameter of twenty-nine feet, a circumference of sixty-four feet, and a height of two hundred and four feet. One may guess its age from three thousand to thirty-two hundred years. It is the third in size and age of living sequoias; General Sherman, the largest and oldest, has a diameter of thirty-six and a half feet, and General Grant a diameter of thirty-five feet, and neither of these, in all probability, has attained the age of four thousand years. General Sherman grows in the Sequoia National Park, seventy miles or more south of Yosemite; General Grant has a little national park of its own a few miles west of Sequoia.

The interested explorer of the Yosemite has so far enjoyed a wonderfully varied sequence of surprises. The incomparable valley with its towering monoliths and extraordinary waterfalls, the High Sierra with its glaciers, serrated cirques and sea of snowy peaks, the Grand Canyon of the Tuolumne with its cascades, rushing river and frothing Waterwheels, are but the headliners of a long catalogue of the unexpected and extraordinary. It only remains, to complete this new tale of the Arabian Nights, to make one's first visit to the sequoias of Mariposa Grove. The first sight of the calm tremendous columns which support the lofty roof of this forest temple provokes a new sensation.   Unconsciously the visitor removes his hat and speaks his praise in whispers.

The sequoias are considered at greater length in the chapter describing the Sequoia National Park, which was created especially to conserve and exhibit more than a million of these most interesting of trees. It will suffice here to say that their enormous stems are purplish red, that their fine, lace-like foliage hangs in splendid heavy plumes, that their enormous limbs crook at right angles, the lowest from a hundred to a hundred and fifty feet above the ground, and that all other trees, even the gigantic sugar pine and Douglas fir, are dwarfed in their presence. Several of the sequoias of the Mariposa grove approach three hundred feet in height.   The road passes through the trunk of one.

VI

The human history of the Yosemite is quickly told.   The country north of the Valley was known from early times by explorers and trappers who used the old Mono Indian Trail, now the Tioga Road, which crossed the divide over Mono Pass.   But, though the trail approached within a very few miles of the north rim of the Yosemite Valley, the valley was not discovered till 1851, when Captain Boling of the Mariposa Battalion, a volunteer organization for the protection of settlers, entered it from the west in pursuit of Indians who had raided mining settlements in the foothills.

These savages were known as the Yosemite or
Grizzly Bear Indians. Tenaya, their chief, met their
pursuers on the uplands and besought them to come
no further. But Captain Boling pushed on through
the heavy snows, and on March 21, entered the valley,
which proved to be the Indians' final stronghold.
Their villages, however, were deserted.

The original inhabitants of the Valley were called
the Ahwahneechees, the Indian name for the Valley
being Ahwahnee, meaning a deep grassy canyon. The
Ahwahneechees, previous to Captain Boling's expedition, had been decimated by war and disease. The
new tribe, the Yosemites, or Grizzly Bears, was made
up of their remainder, with Monos and Piutes added.

Captain Boling's report of the beauty of the valley having been questioned, he returned during the
summer to prove his assertions to a few doubters.
Nevertheless, there were no further visitors until 1853,
when Robert B. Stinson of Mariposa led in a hunting-party. Two years later J. M. Hutchings, who was
engaged in writing up the beauties of California for
the *California Magazine*, brought the first tourists;
the second, a party of sixteen, followed later the same
year.

Pleasure travel to the Yosemite Valley may be
said to have commenced with 1856, the year the first
house was built. This house was enlarged in 1858 by
Hite and Beardsley and used for a hotel. Sullivan
and Cushman secured it for a debt the following year,
and it was operated in turn by Peck, Longhurst, and

Hutchings until 1871. Meantime J. C. Lamon settled in 1860, the first actual resident of the valley, an
honor which he did not share with others for four
years.

The fame of the valley spread over the country
and in 1864 Congress granted to the State of California "the Cleft or Gorge of the Granite Peak of
the Sierra Nevada Mountains" known as the Yosemite Valley, with the understanding that all income
derived from it should be spent for improving the
reservation or building a road to it. The Mariposa
Big Tree Grove was also granted at the same time.
California carefully fulfilled her charge. The Yosemite Valley became world-famous, and in 1890 the
Yosemite National Park was created.

VII

The Yosemite's geological history is much more
thrilling. Everyone who sees it asks, How did Nature
make the Yosemite Valley? Was it split by earth
convulsions or scooped by glacier? Few ask what
part was played by the gentle Merced.

The question of Yosemite's making has busied
geologists from Professor Whitney of the University
of California, who first studied the problem, down to
F. E. Matthes, of the United States Geological Survey,
whose recent exhaustive studies have furnished the
final solution. Professor Whitney maintained that
glaciers never had entered the valley; he did not even

consider water erosion. At one time he held that the valley was simply a cleft or rent in the earth's crust. At another time he imagined it formed by the sudden dropping back of a large block in the course of the convulsions that resulted in the uplift of the Sierra Nevada. Galen Clark, following him, carried on his idea of an origin by force. Instead of the walls being cleft apart, however, he imagined the explosion of close-set domes of molten rock the riving power, but conceived that ice and water erosion finished the job. With Clarence King the theory of glacial origin began its long career. John Muir carried this theory to its extreme.

Since the period of Muir's speculations, the tremendous facts concerning the part played by erosion in the modification of the earth's surface strata have been developed. Beginning with W. H. Turner, a group of Yosemite students under the modern influence worked upon the theory of the stream-cut valley modified by glaciers. The United States Geological Survey then entered the field, and Matthes's minute investigations followed; the manuscript of his monograph has helped me reconstruct the dramatic past.

The fact is that the Yosemite Valley was cut from the solid granite nearly to its present depth by the Merced River; before the glaciers arrived, the river-cut valley was twenty-four hundred feet deep opposite El Capitan, and three thousand feet deep opposite Eagle Peak. The valley was then V-shaped, and the present waterfalls were cascades; those which are now the Yosemite Falls were eighteen hundred feet deep, and those of Sentinel Creek were two thousand feet deep. All this in pre-glacial times.

Later on the glaciers of several successive epochs greatly widened the valley, and measurably deepened it, making it U-shaped. The cascades then became waterfalls.

But none will see the Yosemite Valley and its cavernous tributary canyons without sympathizing a little with the early geologists. It is difficult to imagine a gash so tremendous cut into solid granite by anything short of force. One can think of it gouged by massive glaciers, but to imagine it cut by water is at first inconceivable.

To comprehend it we must first consider two geological facts. The first is that no dawdling modern Merced cut this chasm, but a torrent considerably bigger; and that this roaring river swept at tremendous speed down a sharply tilted bed, which it gouged deeper and deeper by friction of the enormous masses of sand and granite fragments which it carried down from the High Sierra. The second geological fact is that the Merced and Tenaya torrents sand-papered the deepening beds of these canyons day and night for several million years; which, when we remember the mile-deep canyons which the Colorado River and its confluents cut through a thousand or more miles of Utah and Arizona, is not beyond human credence, if not conception.

But, objects the sceptical, the Merced couldn't

keep always tilted; in time it would cut down to a level and slow up; then the sand and gravel it was carrying would settle, and the stream stop its digging. Again, if the stream-cut valley theory is correct, why isn't every Sierra canyon a Yosemite?

Let us look for the answer in the Sierra's history.

The present Sierra Nevada is not the first mountain chain upon its site. The granite which underlay the folds of the first Sierra are still disclosed in the walls of the Yosemite Valley. The granites which underlay the second and modern Sierra are seen in the towering heights of the crest.

Once these mountains overran a large part of our present far west. They formed a level and very broad and high plateau; or, more accurately, they tended to form such a plateau, but never quite succeeded, because its central section kept caving and sinking in some of its parts as fast as it lifted in others. Finally, in the course, perhaps, of some millions of years, the entire central section settled several thousand feet lower than its eastern and western edges; these edges it left standing steep and high. This sunken part is the Great Basin of to-day. The remaining eastern edge is the Wasatch Mountains; the remaining western edge is the Sierra. That is why the Sierra's eastern front rises so precipitously from the deserts of the Great Basin, while its western side slopes gradually toward the Pacific.

But other crust changes accompanied the sinking of the Great Basin. The principal one was the rise, in a series of upward movements, of the remaining crest of the Sierra.   These movements may have corresponded with the sinkings of the Great Basin; both were due to tremendous internal readjustments.   And of course, whenever the Sierra crest lifted, it tilted more sharply the whole granite block of which it was the eastern edge.   These successive tiltings are what kept the Merced and Tenaya channels always so steeply inclined that, for millions of years, the streams remained torrents swift enough to keep on sandpapering their beds.

The first of these tiltings occurred in that far age which geologists call the Cretaceous.   It was inconsiderable, but enough to hasten the speed of the streams and establish general outlines for all time.   About the middle of the Tertiary Period volcanic eruptions changed all things.   Nearly all the valleys except the Yosemite became filled with lava.   Even the crest of the range was buried a thousand feet in one place. This was followed by a rise of the Sierra Crest a couple of thousand feet, and of course a much sharper tilting of the western slopes.   The Merced and Tenaya Rivers must have rushed very fast indeed during the many thousand years that followed.

The most conservative estimate of the duration of the Tertiary Period is four or five million years, and until its close volcanic eruptions continued to fill valleys with lava, and the Great Basin kept settling, and the crest of the Sierra went on rising; and with each lifting of the crest, the tilt of the rivers sharpened and the speed of the torrents hastened. The canyon deepened during this time from seven hundred to a thousand feet. The Yosemite was then a mountain valley whose sloping sides were crossed by cascades.

Then, about the beginning of the Quaternary Period, came the biggest convulsion of all. The crest of the Sierra was hoisted, according to Matthes's calculations, as much as eight thousand feet higher in this one series of movements, and the whole Sierra block was again tilted, this time, of course, enormously.

For thousands of centuries following, the torrents from Lyell's and McClure's melting snows must have descended at a speed which tore boulders from their anchorages, ground rocks into sand, and savagely scraped and scooped the river beds. Armed with sharp hard-cutting tools ripped from the granite cirques of Sierra's crest, these mad rivers must have scratched and hewn deep and fast. And because certain valleys, including the Yosemite, were never filled with lava like the rest, these grew ever deeper with the centuries.

The great crust movement of the Quaternary Period was not the last, by any means, though it was the last of great size. There were many small ones later. Several even have occurred within historic times. On March 26, 1872, a sudden earth movement left an escarpment twenty-five feet high at the foot of the range in Owens Valley. The village of Lone Pine was levelled by the accompanying earthquake. John Muir, who was in the Yosemite Valley at the time, de-

scribes in eloquent phrase the accompanying earthquake which was felt there. A small movement,
doubtless of similar origin, started the San Francisco
fire in 1906.

Conditions created by the great Quaternary tilting deepened the valley from eighteen hundred feet
at its lower end to twenty-four hundred feet at its
upper end. It established what must have been an
unusually interesting and impressive landscape, which
suggested the modern aspect, but required completion
by the glaciers.

Geologically speaking, the glaciers were recent.
There were several ice invasions, produced probably
by the same changes in climate which occasioned the
advances of the continental ice sheet east of the
Rockies. Matthes describes them as similar to the
northern glaciers of the Canadian Rockies of to-day.
For unknown thousands of years the Valley was filled
by a glacier three or four thousand feet thick, and the
surrounding country was covered with tributary ice-
fields. Only Cloud's Rest, Half Dome, Sentinel Dome,
and the crown of El Capitan emerged above this ice.
The glacier greatly widened and considerably deepened
the valley, turned its slopes into perpendiculars, and
changed its side cascades into waterfalls. When it
receded it left Yosemite Valley almost completed.

There followed a long period of conditions not
unlike those of to-day. Frosts chipped and scaled the
granite surfaces, and rains carried away the fragments.
The valley bloomed with forests and wild flowers.

Then came other glaciers and other intervening periods. The last glacier advanced only to the head of Bridal Veil Meadow. When it melted it left a lake which filled the Valley from wall to wall, three hundred feet deep. Finally the lake filled up with soil, brought down by the streams, and made the floor of the present valley.

The centuries since have been a period of decoration and enrichment. Frost and rain have done their perfect work. The incomparable valley is complete.

III

THE PROPOSED ROOSEVELT NATIONAL PARK

INCLUDING THE PRESENT SEQUOIA NATIONAL PARK, WEST CENTRAL CALIFORNIA. AREA, 1,600 SQUARE MILES

I

WHERE the lava billows of the Cascade Mountains end in northern California the granite knobs of the Sierra begin. Sharply differentiated in appearance and nature a few miles further in either direction, here their terminals overlap, and so nearly merge that the southern end of the one and the northern beginning of the other are not easily distinguished by the untrained eye.

But southward the Sierra Nevada, the snowy saw-toothed range of the Spaniards, the Sierra of modern American phrase, rapidly acquires the bulk and towering height, the craggy cirqued summits and the snowy shoulders which have made it celebrated. Gathering grandeur as it sweeps southward close to the western boundary of California, its western slopes slashed deep with canyons, its granite peaks and domes pushing ever higher above the scattering forests of its middle zones, its eastern ramparts dropping in precipices to the desert, it valiantly guards its sunny state against the passage of eastern highways, and forces hard engineering problems upon the builders of trans-

continental railroads. Where it becomes the eastern
boundary of the Yosemite National Park it breaks
into climaxes of magnificence.

From this point on the Sierra broadens and bulks.
It throws out spurs, multiplies paralleling ranges, heaps
peaks and ridges between gulf-like canyons which
carry roaring waters through their forested trenches.
Pushing ever higher above timber-line, it breaks into
large lake-bearing cirques, sometimes cirque within
cirque, walled in silvery granite, hung with garlands
of snow and dripping with shining glaciers. Ninety
miles south of Yosemite it culminates in a close grouping of snow-daubed, glacier-gouged, lightning-splin-
tered peaks, one of which, Mount Whitney, highest
summit in the United States, raises his head just a
little above his gigantic neighbors.

South of Whitney, the Sierra subsides rapidly and
merges into the high plateaus and minor ranges of
southern California.

Seventy-five miles of the crest of this titanic
range at the climax of its magnificence, sixty-five miles
of it north of Whitney and ten miles of it south, constitute the western boundary of an area of sixteen
hundred square miles which Congress is considering
setting apart under the title of the Roosevelt National
Park; a region so particularly characterized by rug-
gedness, power, and unified purpose that it is eminently
fitted to serve as the nation's memorial to Theodore
Roosevelt. Besides its stupendous mountains, it includes the wildest and most exuberant forested can-

yons, and the most luxuriant groves in the United States, for its boundaries will enclose also the present Sequoia National Park, in which a million trunks of the famous Sequoia Washingtoniana cluster around the General Sherman Tree, believed to be the biggest and oldest living thing in all the world.

Wide though its range from bleak crest to warm forest, every part of this region is a necessary part of its whole. Nature's subtle finger has so knitted each succeeding zone into the fabric of its neighbors that it would be a vandal's hand which should arbitrarily cut the picture short of the full completion of its perfect composition. It is one of Nature's masterpieces, through whose extremest contrasts runs the common note of supremacy.

Whether or not, then, Congress insures its perpetuity and unified development. we can consider it scenically only as a whole.

Similar in kind to the Yosemite National Park, Roosevelt is far ruggeder and more masterful. It will be the national park of superlatives. Yet each of these similar areas is a completed unit of striking individuality. Yosemite, taking its note from its incomparable Valley, never will be equalled for sheer beauty; Roosevelt knows no peer for exuberance and grandeur. Yosemite will remain Mecca for the tourist; Roosevelt will draw into its forest of giant trees, and upon its shoulders of chiselled granite, thousands of campers-out and lovers of the high trail.

Joined near the crest of the Sierra by the John

Muir Trail, California's memorial to her own prophet of the out-of-doors, these two national parks, so alike and yet so different, each striking surely its own note of sublimity, are, in a very real sense, parts of one still greater whole; the marriage of beauty and strength.

II

The region is roughly pear-shaped. A straight line drawn from Pine Creek Pass at its northern end to Sheep Mountain on the southern base line measures sixty-eight miles; the park is thirty-six miles wide at its widest, just north of Mount Whitney. Its eastern boundary, the crest of the Sierra, divides many notable peaks. From north to south we pass, as we travel the John Muir Trail, Mount Humphreys, 13,972 feet; Mount Darwin, 13,841 feet; Mount Winchell, 13,749 feet; Split Mountain, 14,051 feet; Striped Mountain, 13,160 feet; Mount Baxter, 13,118 feet; Junction Peak, 13,903 feet; Mount Tyndall, 14,025 feet; and Mount Whitney, 14,501 feet; supporting Whitney on the south is Mount Langley, 14,042 feet; all these connected by splintered peaks, granite ledges, and mountain masses scarcely less in altitude.

Between the bristling crest of this snow-daubed eastern boundary and the park's western boundary, thousands of feet lower where the forests begin, the region roughly divides into parallel zones. That which immediately adjoins the crest upon its west side, a strip ten miles or more in width, is known to its devotees as the High Sierra. It is a country of tremendous jagged peaks, of intermediate pinnacled walls, of enormous cirques holding remnants of once mighty glaciers, of great fields of sun-cupped snow, of turquoise lakes resting in chains upon enormous granite steps; the whole gleaming like chased silver in the noon sun; a magical land of a thousand Matterhorns, whose trails lead from temple to temple, so mighty of size and noble of design that no mind less than the Creator's could ever have conceived them.

The High Sierra has been celebrated for many years in the fast-growing brotherhood of American mountain climbers, east as well as west, many of whom proclaim its marked superiority to all parts of the Swiss Alps except the amazing neighborhood of Mont Blanc. With the multiplication of trails and the building of shelters for the comfort of the inexperienced, the veriest amateur of city business life will find in these mountains of perpetual sunshine a satisfaction which is only for the seasoned mountaineer abroad.

The zone adjoining the High Sierra upon its west is one of far wider range of pleasure. Subsiding rapidly in elevation, it becomes a knobbed and bouldered land which includes timber-line and the thin forests of wind-twisted pines which contend with the granite for foothold. It is crossed westward by many lesser ranges buttressing the High Sierra; from these cross ranges many loftier peaks arise, and between them roar the rivers whose thousands of contributing streams drain the snow-fields and the glaciers of the white heights.

Finally, paralleling the western boundary, is the narrow zone in which this region meets and merges with the greater forests and the meadows beyond the boundary. Here, in the southwestern corner, is the marvellous warm forest in which trees of many kinds attain their maximum of size and proportion, and which encloses a million sequoia trees, including the greatest and oldest embodiments of the principle of life. This extraordinary forest was reserved in 1890 under the title of the Sequoia National Park. At the same time was created the General Grant National Park, a reservation of four square miles of similar forest, virtually a part of it, but separated because of an intervening area of privately owned lands.

Thus does this region run the gamut of supremacy from the High Sierra upon its east, to the Giant Forest upon its west.

Of no less distinction are its waters. Innumerable lakelets of the High Sierra, born of the snows, overflow in tiny streams which combine into roaring, frothing creeks. These in turn, augmented by the drainage of the lofty tumbled divides, combine into powerful little rivers. Four river systems originate in this region.

Far in the north a lake, more than eleven thousand feet high, lying at the western foot of Mount Goddard, begins the South Fork of the San Joaquin River, which drains the park's northern area. Incidentally, it has cut a canyon of romantic beauty, up which the John Muir Trail finds its way into the park.

The northern middle area of the park is drained by the Middle and South Forks of the Kings River, which find their origins in perhaps forty miles of Sierra's crest. The drainage basins of these splendid streams cover nearly half of the park's total area, and include some of the biggest, as well as some of the wildest and most beautiful mountain scenery in the world. Bounded upon their west by an arc of snowy mountains, separated by the gigantic Monarch Divide, flanked by twisted ranges and towering peaks, they cascade westward through meadows of rank grasses and vividly colored wild-flowers, alternating with steep-sided gorges and canyons of sublimity. Dropping thousands of feet within a few miles, they abound in cascades and majestic falls, between which swift rapids alternate with reaches of stiller, but never still, waters which are the homes of cut-throat trout. Each of these rivers has its canyon of distinguished magnificence. The Tehipite Valley of the Middle Fork and the Kings River Canyon of the South Fork are destined to world celebrity.

The southwestern area of the park is drained by five forks of the beautiful Kaweah River. These streams originate on the north in the divide of the South Fork of the Kings River, and on the east in a conspicuously fine range known as the Great Western Divide. They wind through the wooded valleys of the Sequoia National Park. Upon their banks grow the monsters of the American forest.

The southern area is drained by the Kern River,

into which flow the waters of Mount Whitney and his giant neighbors. The Kern Canyon is one of Roosevelt's noblest expressions. Flowing southward between precipitous walls three thousand feet and more in height, flanked upon the east by monsters of the High Sierra, and on the west by the splendid elevations of the Great Western Divide, it is a valley supremely fitted for the highest realization of the region's gifts of enjoyment. From camps beside its trout-haunted waters, it is a matter of no difficulty for those equipped for the trail to reach the summit of Whitney, on the one hand, and the Giant Forest on the other.

Near the southern boundary of the park, Golden Trout Creek enters the Kern. It originates at the very crest of the Sierra, which it follows closely for many miles before swinging westward to its outlet. In this stream is found a trout which appears, when fresh caught, as though carved from gold. Popularly it is known as the golden trout; its scientific name is Salmo Rooseveltii. Originally, no doubt, the color evolved from the peculiar golden hues of the rocks through which its waters flow. The golden trout has been transplanted into other Sierra streams, in some of which, notably the open upper waters of the Middle Fork of the Kings, it has thrived and maintained its vivid hue. In sheltered waters it has apparently disappeared, a fact which may merely mean that its color has changed with environment.

III

There are many gateways, two by road, the rest by trail. For years to come, as in the past, the great majority of visitors will enter through the Giant Forest of the Sequoia National Park and through the General Grant National Park. The traveller by rail will find motor stages at Visalia for the run into the Giant Forest, and at Fresno for the General Grant National Park. The motorist will find good roads into both from California's elaborate highway system. In both the traveller will find excellent hotel camps, and, if his purpose is to live awhile under his private canvas, public camp grounds convenient to stores and equipped with water supply and even electric lights. Under the gigantic pines, firs, and ancient sequoias of these extraordinary forests, increasing thousands spend summer weeks and months.

From these centres the lovers of the sublime take saddle-horses and pack-trains, or, if they are hikers, burros to carry their equipment, and follow the trails to Kern Canyon, or the summit of Whitney, or the Kings River Canyon, or the Tehipite Valley, or the John Muir Trail upon the Sierra's crest. Many are the trip combinations, the choice of which depends upon the time and the strenuousness of the traveller. Camping-out on trail in Roosevelt is an experience which demands repetition. Sure of clear weather, the traveller does not bother with tents, but snuggles at night in a sleeping-bag under a roof of spreading pine.

But it is possible to equip for the trail elsewhere. The principal point upon the north is the Yosemite National Park, where one may provide himself with horses and supplies for a journey of any desired duration. Starting in the Yosemite Valley, and leaving the park near the carved cirques of Mount Lyell, the traveller will find the intervening miles of the John Muir Trail a panorama of magnificence. Thousand Island Lake, reflecting the glorious pyramid of Banner Peak, the Devil's Postpile, a group of basaltic columns, far finer than Ireland's celebrated Giant's Causeway, the Mono Valley, with its ancient volcano split down through the middle so that all may see its vent and spreading crater, are merely the more striking features of a progress of spectacles to the north entrance of Roosevelt Park; this is at the junction of the South Fork of the San Joaquin River and Piute Creek. The principal eastern gateway is Kearsarge Pass, on the crest of the Sierra a few miles north of Mount Whitney. The trail ascends from Independence, where one also may comfortably outfit.

These four are, at this writing, the principal entrance gates, each opening from points at which parties may be sure of securing horses, equipment, and guides. But several other trails enter from the east, south, southwest, and west sides. All of these in time will become, with development, well travelled trails into the heart of the great wilderness.

IV

Any description of the glories of the John Muir Trail from its entrance into the park to its climax upon the summit of Mount Whitney far passes the limits of a chapter.   In time it will inspire a literature.

Approaching from Yosemite through the canyon of the San Joaquin, the traveller swings around the north side of Mount Goddard, crosses gorgeous Muir Pass, and enters the fringe of cirques and lakes which borders the western edge of Sierra's crest from end to end. Through this he winds his way southward, skirting lakes, crossing snowfields, encircling templed cirques, plunging into canyons, climbing divides, rounding gigantic peaks, surprising views of sublimity, mounting ever higher until he stands upon the shoulders of Mount Whitney.   Dismounting here, he scrambles up the few hundred feet of stiff climb which places him on the summit, from which he looks out north, west, and south over the most diversified high mountain landscape in America, and eastward over the Sierra foothills to Death Valley, lowest land in the United States.

No thrilling Alpine feat is the ascent of our loftiest summit.   But those who want to measure human strength and skill in terms of perpendicular granite may find among Whitney's neighbors peaks which will present harder problems than those offered abroad, peaks which themselves well may become as celebrated in future years.

The John Muir Trail is destined to a fame and a use perhaps many times as great as those men thought who conceived it as a memorial to a lover of the trail, and of all that that implies. It will play a distinguished part in the education of the nation in the love of mountains. It will win artists to a phase of the sublime in America which they have overlooked. It will bring students to the class-rooms where Nature displays her most tremendous exhibits.

Nevertheless, Roosevelt's lower levels will draw many times as many devotees as will the High Sierra; and these visitors will stay longer. It is the valleys and the canyons which will prove the greatest lure, for here one may camp leisurely and in entire comfort, and thence make what trips he chooses into the regions of the peaks and the cirques.

There are literally thousands of canyons and of many kinds. Besides the Kern Canyon there are two which must rank with Yosemite. In the summer of 1916 I travelled the length of the park, as far as the Giant Forest, with a party led by Director Stephen T. Mather, of the National Park Service, then Assistant to the Secretary of the Interior, and was powerfully impressed with the scenic qualities of the Tehipite Valley, and the Kings River Canyon, at that time little known.

Time will not dim my memory of Tehipite Dome, the august valley and the leaping, singing river which it overlooks. Well short of the Yosemite Valley in the kind of beauty that plunges the observer into silence, the Tehipite Valley far excels it in bigness, power, and majesty. Lookout Point on the north rim, a couple of miles south of the Dome, gave us our first sensation. Three thousand feet above the river, it offered by far the grandest valley view I have looked upon, for the rim view into Yosemite by comparison is not so grand as it is beautiful.

The canyon revealed itself to the east as far as Mount Woodworth, its lofty diversified walls lifting precipitously from the heavy forests of the floor and sides, and yielding to still greater heights above. Enormous cliffs abutted, Yosemitelike, at intervals. South of us, directly across the canyon, rose the strenuous heights of the Monarch Divide, Mount Harrington, towering a thousand feet higher above the valley floor than Clouds Rest above the Yosemite. Down the slopes of the Monarch Divide, seemingly from its turreted summits, cascaded many frothing streams. The Eagle Peaks, Blue Canyon Falls, Silver Spur, the Gorge of Despair, Lost Canyon—these were some of the romantic and appropriate titles we found on the Geological Survey map.

And, close at hand, opposite Mount Harrington and just across Crown Creek Canyon, rose mighty Tehipite. We stood level with its rounded glistening dome. The Tehipite Dome is a true Yosemite feature. It compares in height and prominence with El Capitan. In fact, it stands higher above the valley floor and occupies a similar position at the valley's western gate. It is not so massive as El Capitan, and therefore not so impressive; but it is superb. It is better compared with Half Dome, though again perhaps not so impressive. But it has its own august personality, as notably so as either of these world-famed rocks; and, if it stood in the Yosemite, would share with them the incomparable valley's highest honors.

Descending to the floor, the whole aspect of the valley changed. Looking up, Tehipite Dome, now outlined against the sky, and the neighboring abrupt castellated walls, towered more hugely than ever. We did not need the contour map to know that some of these heights exceeded Yosemite's. The sky-line was fantastically carved into spires and domes, a counterpart in gigantic miniature of the Great Sierra of which it was the valley climax. The Yosemite measure of sublimity, perhaps, lacked, but in its place was a more rugged grandeur, a certain suggestion of vastness and power that I have not seen elsewhere.

This impression was strengthened by the floor itself, which contains no suggestion whatever of Yosemite's exquisiteness. Instead, it offers rugged spaciousness. In place of Yosemite's peaceful woods and meadows, here were tangled giant-studded thickets and mountainous masses of enormous broken talus. Instead of the quiet winding Merced, here was a surging, smashing, frothing, cascading, roaring torrent, several times its volume, which filled the valley with its turbulence.

Once step foot on the valley floor and all thought of comparison with Yosemite vanishes forever. This

TEHIPITE DOME, GUARDIAN ROCK OF THE TEHIPITE VALLEY

It rises abruptly more than three thousand feet; proposed Roosevelt National Park

is a different thing altogether, but a thing in its own way no less superlative. The keynote of the Tehipite Valley is wild exuberance. It thrills where Yosemite enervates. Yet its temperature is quite as mild.

The Middle Fork contains more trout than any other stream I have fished. We found them in pools and riffles everywhere; no water was too white to get a rise. In the long, greenish-white borders of fast rapids they floated continually into view. In five minutes' watching I could count a dozen or more such appearances within a few feet of water. They ran from eight to fourteen inches. No doubt larger ones lay below. So I got great fun by picking my particular trout and casting specially for him. Stop your fly's motion and the pursuing fish instantly stops, backs, swims round the lure in a tour of examination, and disappears. Start it moving and he instantly reappears from the white depth, where, no doubt, he has been cautiously watching. A pause and a swift start often tempted to a strike.

These rainbows of the torrents are hard fighters. And many of them, if ungently handled, availed of swift currents to thresh themselves free.

You must fish a river to appreciate it. Standing on its edges, leaping from rock to rock, slipping waist deep at times, wading recklessly to reach some pool or eddy of special promise, searching the rapids, peering under the alders, testing the pools; that's the way to make friends with a river. You study its moods and its ways as those of a mettlesome horse.

And after a while its spirit seeps through and finds yours. Its personality unveils. A sweet friendliness unites you, a sense of mutual understanding. There follows the completest detachment that I know. Years and the worries disappear. You and the river dream away the unnoted hours.

Passing on from the Tehipite Valley to the Kings River Canyon, the approach to Granite Pass was nothing short of magnificent. We crossed a superb cirque studded with lakelets; we could see the pass ahead of us on a fine snow-crowned bench. We ascended the bench and found ourselves, not in the pass, but in the entrance to still another cirque, also lake-studded, a loftier, nobler cirque encircling the one below. Ahead of us upon another lofty bench surely was the pass. Those inspiring snow-daubed heights whose serrated edges cut sharply into the sky certainly marked the supreme summit. Our winding trail up steep, rocky ascents pointed true; an hour's toil would carry us over. But the hour passed and the crossing of the shelf disclosed, not the glowing valley of the South Fork across the pass, but still a vaster, nobler cirque above, sublime in Arctic glory!

How the vast glaciers that cut these titanic carvings must have swirled among these huge concentric walls, pouring over this shelf and that, piling together around these uplifting granite peaks, concentrating combined effort upon this unyielding mass and that, and, beaten back, pouring down the tortuous main channel with rendings and tearings unimaginable!

EAST VIDETTE FROM A FOREST OF FOXTAIL PINES

This is one of the great granite peaks of the proposed Roosevelt National Park

Granite Pass is astonishing! We saw no less than four of these vast concentric cirques, through three of which we passed. And the Geological Survey map discloses a tributary basin adjoining which enclosed a group of large volcanic lakes, and doubtless other vast cirque-like chambers.

We took photographs, but knew them vain.

A long, dusty descent of Copper Creek brought us, near day's end, into the exquisite valley of the South Fork of the Kings River, the Kings River Canyon.

Still another Yosemite!

It is not so easy to differentiate the two canyons of the Kings. They are similar and yet very different. Perhaps the difference lies chiefly in degree. Both lie east and west, with enormous rocky bluffs rising on either side of rivers of quite extraordinary beauty. Both present carved and castellated walls of exceptional boldness of design. Both are heavily and magnificently wooded, the forests reaching up sharp slopes on either side. Both possess to a marked degree the quality that lifts them above the average of even the Sierra's glacial valleys.

But the outlines here seem to be softer, the valley floor broader, the river less turbulent. If the keynote of the Tehipite Valley is wild exuberance, that of the Kings River Canyon is wild beauty. The one excites, the other lulls. The one shares with Yosemite the distinction of extraordinary outline, the other shares with Yosemite the distinction of extraordinary charm.

There are few nobler spots than the junction of
Copper Creek with the Kings. The Grand Sentinel
is seldom surpassed. It fails of the personality of
El Capitan, Half Dome, and Tehipite, but it only
just fails. If they did not exist, it would become the
most celebrated rock in the Sierra, at least. The view
up the canyon from this spot has few equals. The
view down the canyon is not often excelled. When
the day of the Kings River Canyon dawns, it will
dawn brilliantly.

V

The western slopes of the Pacific ranges, from
the Canadian border southward to the desert, carry
the most luxuriant forest in the United States. The
immense stands of yellow pine and Douglas fir of the
far north merge into the sugar pines and giant sequoias
of the south in practically an unbroken belt which, on
Sierra's slopes, lies on the middle levels between the
low productive plains of the west and the towering
heights of the east. The Sequoia National Park and
its little neighbor, the General Grant National Park,
enclose areas of remarkable fertility in which trees,
shrubs, and wild flowers reach their greatest development. The million sequoia trees which grow here
are a very small part, numerically, of this amazing
forest.

These slopes are rich with the soil of thousands of
years of accumulations. They are warmed in summer
by mild Pacific winds heated in their passage across

the lowlands, and blanketed in winter by many feet of soft snow. They are damp with countless springs and streams sheltered under heavy canopies of foliage. In altitude they range from two thousand feet at the bottom of Kaweah's canyon, as it emerges from the park, to eight thousand feet in the east, with mountains rising three or four thousand feet higher. It is a tumbled land of ridges and canyons, but its slopes are easy and its outline gracious. Oases of luscious meadows dot the forests.

This is the Court of King Sequoia. Here assemble in everlasting attendance millions of his nobles, a statelier gathering than ever bowed the knee before human potentate. Erect, majestic, clothed in togas of perpetual green, their heads bared to the heavens, stand rank upon rank, mile upon mile, the noblest personalities of the earth.

Chief among the courtiers of the king is the sugar-pine, towering here his full two hundred feet, straight as a ruler, his stem at times eight feet in thickness, scarcely tapering to the heavy limbs of his high crown. Largest and most magnificent of the Pacific pines, reaching sometimes six hundred years of age, the greater trunks clear themselves of branches a hundred feet from the ground, and the bark develops long dark plates of armor. So marked is his distinguished personality that, once seen, he never can be mistaken for another.

Next in rank and scarcely less in majesty is the massive white fir, rising at times even to two hundred feet, his sometimes six-foot trunk conspicuously rough, dark brown in color, deeply furrowed with ashen gray. His pale yellow-green crown is mysteriously tinged with white. His limit of age is three hundred and fifty years.

Last of the ranking trio is the western yellow pine, a warrior clad in plates of russet armor. A hundred and sixty feet in natural height, here he sometimes towers even with his fellow knights. He guards the outer precincts of the court, his cap of yellow-green, his branching arms resting upon his sides.

These are the great nobles, but with them are millions of lesser courtiers, the incense cedar from whose buttressed, tapering trunks spring countless branches tipped with fan-like plumes; many lesser conifers; the splendid Pacific birches in picturesque pose; the oaks of many kinds far different from their eastern cousins. And among the feet of these courtiers of higher degree crowd millions upon millions of flowering shrubs, massing often in solid phalanxes, disputing passage with the deer.

All mingle together, great and small. The conifers, in the king's honor, flaunt from stem and greater branch long fluttering ribbons of pale green moss. Thousands of squirrels chatter in the branches. Millions of birds make music. It is a gala day.

Enter the King.

The King of Trees is of royal lineage. The patient searchers in the rocks of old have traced his ancestry unknown millions of years, back to the forests of the Cretaceous Period. His was Viking stock from arctic zones where trees can live no more.

To-day he links all human history. The identical tree around which gather thousands of human courtiers every year emerged, a seedling, while Nebuchadnezzar besieged Jerusalem. No man knows how old his predecessors were when finally they sank into death— mighty fall! But John Muir counted four thousand rings in the trunk of one fallen giant, who must have lived while Pharaoh still held captive the Children of Israel.

The General Sherman Tree of the Giant Forest, the oldest living thing to-day, so far as I have been able to ascertain, probably has seen thirty-six hundred years. It is evident to the unlearned observer that, while mature, he is long short of the turn of life. A thousand years from now he still may be the earth's biggest and oldest living thing; how much beyond that none may venture to predict.

Picture, now, the Giant Forest, largest of the several sequoia groves in the Sequoia National Park. You have entered, say, in the dusk of the night before, and after breakfast wander planless among the trees. On every side rise the huge pines and firs, their dark columns springing from the tangled brush to support the cathedral roof above. Here an enormous purplish-red column draws and holds your astonished eye. It is a gigantic thing in comparison with its monster neighbors; it glows among their dull columns; it is clean and spotless amid their moss-hung trunks; branchless, it disappears among their upper foliage, hinting at steeple heights above. Yet your guide tells you that this tree is small; that its diameter is less than twenty feet; that in age it is a youngster of only two thousand years! Wait, he tells you, till you see the General Sherman Tree's thirty-six and a half feet of diameter; wait till you see the hundreds, yes thousands, which surpass this infant!

But you heed him not, for you see another back among those sugar pines! Yes, and there's another. And there on the left are two or three in a clump! Back in the dim cathedral aisles are reddish glows which must mean still others. Your heart is beating with a strange emotion. You look up at the enormous limbs bent at right angles, at the canopy of feathery foliage hanging in ten thousand huge plumes. You cry aloud for the sheer joy of this great thing, and plunge into the forest's heart.

The Giant Forest contains several thousand sequoia trees of large size, and many young trees. You see these small ones on every hand, erect, sharply pointed, giving in every line a vivid impression of quivering, bounding life. Later on, as they emerge above the roof of the forest, for some of them are more than three hundred feet high, they lose their sharp ambitious tops; they become gracefully rounded. Springing from seed less than a quarter of an inch in diameter, they tend, like their cousins the redwoods, to grow in groups, and these groups tend to grow in

From a photograph by S. H. Willard

BULL FROG LAKE, PROPOSED ROOSEVELT NATIONAL PARK

Along the crest of the Sierra extends a region of lofty cirques and innumerable glacier-fed lakelets

UNDER A GIANT SEQUOIA

From right to left: Benjamin Ide Wheeler, William Loeb, Jr., Nicholas Murray Butler, John Muir, Surgeon-General Rixey, U. S. N., Theodore Roosevelt, then President, George C. Pardee, and William H. Moody

groves. But there are scattering individuals in every grove, and many small isolated groves in the Sierra. The Giant Forest is the largest grove of greatest trees. The General Grant Grove, in a small national park of its own, near by, is the second grove in size and importance; its central figure is the General Grant Tree, second in size and age to the General Sherman Tree.

The dimensions of the greatest trees are astonishing. Glance at this table:

NAME	HEIGHT FEET	DIAMETER FEET
GIANT FOREST GROVE		
General Sherman	279.9	36.5
Abraham Lincoln	270	31
William McKinley	291	28
MUIR GROVE		
Dalton	292	27
GARFIELD GROVE		
California	260	30
GENERAL GRANT GROVE		
General Grant	264	35
George Washington	255	29

The Theodore Roosevelt Tree, which has not been measured at this writing, is one of the noblest of all, perfect in form and color, abounding in the glory of young maturity.

To help realization at home of the majesty of the General Sherman Tree, mark its base diameter, thirty-six and a half feet, plainly against the side of some building, preferably a church with a steeple and neighboring trees; then measure two hundred and eighty feet, its height, upon the ground at right angles to the church; then stand on that spot and, facing the church, imagine the trunk rising, tapering slightly, against the building's side and the sky above it; then slowly lift your eyes until you are looking up into the sky at an angle of forty-five degrees, this to fix its height were it growing in front of the church.

Imagine its lowest branches, each far thicker than the trunks of eastern elms and oaks, pushing horizontally out at a height above ground of a hundred and fifty feet, which is higher than the tops of most of the full-grown trees of our eastern forests. Imagine these limbs bent horizontally at right angles, like huge elbows, as though holding its green mantle close about its form. Imagine the upper branches nearly bare, shattered perhaps by lightning. And imagine its crown of foliage, dark yellowish-green, hanging in enormous graceful plumes.

This is the King of Trees.

THE HEART OF THE ROCKIES

I

THE Sierra Nevada Mountains of California and the Cascade Range of California, Oregon, and Washington have each three national parks which fully represent their kind and quality. The great central system of the United States, the Rocky Mountains, which also possess three national parks, are represented in kind by only one, for Yellowstone is an exceptional volcanic interlude, and Glacier is the chance upheaval of shales and limestones from a period antedating the granite Rockies by many millions of years; neither in any sense exhibits the nature and scenic quality of the backbone of our continent.

This is one of the reasons for the extraordinary distinction of the reservation appropriately called the Rocky Mountain National Park, namely that it is the only true example of the continental mountain system in the catalogue of our national parks. It is well, therefore, to lay the foundations for a sound comprehension of its differentiating features.

The Rocky Mountains, which began to rise at the close of the Cretaceous Period at a rate so slow that geologists think they are making a pace to-day as

rapid as their maximum, extend from the plateau of
New Mexico northwesterly until they merge into the
mountains of eastern Alaska. In the United States
physiographers consider them in two groups, the
Northern Rockies and the Southern Rockies, the point
of division being the elevated Wyoming Basin. There
are numerous ranges, known, like the Wasatch Mountains, by different names, which nevertheless are consistent parts of the Rocky Mountain System.

The Rockies attain their most imposing mass and
magnificence in their southern group, culminating in
Colorado. So stupendous is this heaping together of
granitic masses that in Colorado alone are found forty-
two of the fifty-five named peaks in the United States
which attain the altitude of fourteen thousand feet.
Of the others, twelve are in the Sierra of California,
and one, Mount Rainier, in Washington. Mount El-
bert, in Colorado, our second highest peak, rises within
eighty-two feet of the height of California's Mount
Whitney, our first in rank; Colorado's Mount Massive
attains an altitude only four feet less than Washington's Mount Rainier, which ranks third. In point of
mass, one seventh of Colorado rises above ten thousand feet of altitude. The state contains three hundred and fifty peaks above eleven thousand feet of
altitude, two hundred and twenty peaks above twelve
thousand feet, and a hundred and fifty peaks above
thirteen thousand feet; besides the forty-two named
peaks which exceed fourteen thousand feet, there are
at least three others which are unnamed.

Geologists call the Rockies young, by which they mean anything, say, from five to twenty million years. They are more or less contemporary with the Sierra. Like the Sierra, the mountains we see to-day are not the first; several times their ranges have uplifted upon wrecks of former ranges, which had yielded to the assaults of frost and rain. Before they first appeared, parts of the Eastern Appalachians had paralleled our eastern sea coast for many million years. The Age of Mammals had well dawned before they became a feature in a landscape which previously had been a mid-continental sea.

II

The Front Range, carrying the continental divide, is a gnarled and jagged rampart of snow-splashed granite facing the eastern plains, from which its grim summits may be seen for many miles. Standing out before it like captains in front of gray ranks at parade rise three conspicuous mountains, Longs Peak, fifty miles northwest of Denver, Mount Evans, west of Denver, and Pikes Peak, seventy miles to the south. Longs Peak is directly connected with the continental divide by a series of jagged cliffs. Mount Evans is farther away. Pikes Peak stands sentinel-like seventy-five miles east of the range, a gigantic monadnock, remainder and reminder of a former range long ages worn away.

Though many massive mountains of greater altitude lie farther west, the Front Range for many reasons is representative of the Rockies' noblest. To represent them fully, the national park should include the three sentinel peaks and their neighborhoods, and it is earnestly hoped that the day will come when Congress will recognize this need. At this writing only the section of greatest variety and magnificence, the nearly four hundred square miles of which Longs Peak is the climax, has been thus entitled. In fact, even this was unfortunately curtailed in the making, the straight southern boundary having been arbitrarily drawn through the range at a point of sublimity, throwing out of the park the St. Vrain Glaciers which form one of the region's wildest and noblest spectacles, and Arapaho Peak and its glaciers which in several respects constitute a climax in Rocky Mountain scenery.

Thus carelessly cropped, despoiled of the completeness which Nature meant it to possess, nevertheless the Rocky Mountain National Park is a reservation of distinguished charm and beauty. It straddles the continental divide, which bisects it lengthwise, north and south. The western slopes rise gently to the divide; at the divide, the eastern front drops in a precipice several thousand feet deep, out of which frosts, rains, glaciers and streams have gouged gigantic gulfs and granite-bound vales and canyons, whose intervening cliffs are battlemented walls and monoliths.

As if these features were not enough to differentiate this national park from any other, Nature has provided still another element of popularity and dis-

From a photograph by Wiswall Brothers

ESTES PARK PLATEAU, LOOKING EAST

Showing the village and the foothills, which are remnants of a former great range, now almost washed away by erosion; Rocky Mountain National Park

From a photograph by Wiswall Brothers

FRONT RANGE OF THE ROCKIES FROM BIERSTADT LAKE

From right to left: Flattop Mountain, Tyndall Glacier, Hallett Peak, Otis Peak, Andrews Glacier

tinction. East of this splendid rampart spreads a broad area of rolling plateau, carpeted with wild flowers, edged and dotted with luxuriant groves of pine, spruce, fir, and aspen, and diversified with hills and craggy mountains, carved rock walls, long forest-grown moraines and picturesque ravines; a stream-watered, lake-dotted summer and winter pleasure paradise of great size, bounded on the north and west by snow-spattered monsters, and on the east and south by craggy wooded foothills, only less in size, and no less in beauty than the leviathans of the main range. Here is summer living room enough for several hundred thousand sojourners from whose comfortable camps and hotels the wild heart of the Rockies may be visited afoot or on horseback between early breakfast and late supper at home.

This plateau has been known to summer visitors for many years under the titles of several settlements; Moraine Park, Horseshoe Park, and Longs Peak, each had its hotels long before the national park was created; Estes Park and Allen's Park on the east side, and Grand Lake on the west side lie just outside the park boundaries, purposely excluded because of their considerable areas of privately owned land. Estes Park, the principal village and the distributing centre of all incoming routes from the east, is the Eastern Gateway; Grand Lake is the Western Gateway.

And still there is another distinction, one which will probably always hold for Rocky Mountain its present great lead in popularity. That is its position nearer to the middle of the country than other great national parks, and its accessibility from large centres of population. Denver, which claims with some justice the title of Gateway to the National Parks, meaning of course the eastern gateway to the western parks, is within thirty hours by rail from Chicago and St. Louis, through one or other of which most travellers from the east find it convenient to reach the west. It is similarly conveniently located for touring motorists, with whom all the national parks are becoming ever more popular. From Denver several railroads lead to east-side towns, from which the park is reached by motor stages through the foothills, and a motor stage line runs directly from Denver to Estes Park, paralleling the range. The west side is reached through Granby.

III

Entry to the park by any route is dramatic. If the visitor comes the all-motor way through Ward he picks up the range at Arapaho Peak, and follows it closely for miles. If he comes by any of the rail routes, his motor stage emerges from the foothills upon a sudden spectacle of magnificence—the snowy range, its highest summits crowned with cloud, looming upon the horizon across the peaceful plateau. By any route the appearance of the range begins a panorama of ever-changing beauty and inspiration, whose progress will outlive many a summer's stay.

Having settled himself in one of the hotels or

camps of the east-side plateau, the visitor faces the choice between two practical ways of enjoying himself. He may, as the majority seem to prefer, spend his weeks in the simple recreations familiar in our eastern hill and country resorts; he may motor a little, walk a little, fish a little in the Big Thompson and its tributaries, read and botanize a little in the meadows and groves, golf a little on the excellent courses, climb a little on the lesser mountains, and dance or play bridge in hotel parlors at night. Or else he may avail himself of the extraordinary opportunity which Nature offers him in the mountains which spring from his comfortable plateau, the opportunity of entering into Nature's very workshop and of studying, with her for his teacher, the inner secrets and the mighty examples of creation.

In all our national parks I have wondered at the contentment of the multitude with the less when the greater, and such a greater, was there for the taking. But I ceased to criticize the so-called popular point of view when I realized that its principal cause was ignorance of the wealth within grasp rather than deliberate choice of the more commonplace; instead, I write this book, hoping that it may help the cause of the greater pleasure. Especially is the Rocky Mountain National Park the land of opportunity because of its accessibility, and of the ease with which its inmost sanctuaries may be entered, examined, and appreciated. The story is disclosed at every step. In fact the revelation begins in the foothills on the way in from the railroad, for the red iron-stained cliffs seen upon their eastern edges are remainders of former Rocky Mountains which disappeared by erosion millions of years ago. The foothills themselves are remnants of mountains which once were much loftier than now, and the picturesque canyon of the Big Thompson, through which it may have been your good fortune to enter the park, is the stream-cut outlet of a lake or group of lakes which once covered much of the national park plateau.

Summer life on the plateau is as effective as a tonic. The altitude varies from seven to nine thousand feet; Rocky Mountain's valley bottoms are higher than the summits of many peaks of celebrity elsewhere. On every hand stretch miles of tumbled meadows and craggy cliffs. Many are the excellent roads, upon which cluster, at intervals of miles, groups of hotels and camps. Here one may choose his own fashion of living, for these hostelries range from the most formal and luxurious hotel to the simplest collection of tents or log cabins around a central log dining structure. Some of these camps are picturesque, the growth of years from the original log hut. Some are equipped with modern comforts; others are as primitive as their beginnings. All the larger resorts have stables of riding horses, for riding is the fashion even with those who do not venture into the mountains.

Or, one may camp out in the good old-fashioned way, and fry his own morning bacon over his fire of sticks.

Wherever one lives, however one lives, in this broad tableland, he is under the spell of the range. The call of the mountains is ever present. Riding, walking, motoring, fishing, golfing, sitting under the trees with a book, continually he lifts his eyes to their calm heights. Unconsciously he throws them the first morning glance. Instinctively he gazes long upon their gleaming moon-lit summits before turning in at night. In time they possess his spirit. They calm him, exalt him, ennoble him. Unconsciously he comes to know them in all their myriad moods. Cold and stern before sunrise, brilliant and vivid in mid-morning, soft and restful toward evening, gorgeously colored at sunset, angry, at times terrifying, in storm, their fascination never weakens, their beauty changes but it does not lessen.

Mountains of the height of these live in constant communion with the sky. Mummy Mountain in the north and Longs Peak in the south continually gather handfuls of fleecy cloud. A dozen times a day a mist appears in the blue, as if entangled while passing the towering summit. A few moments later it is a tiny cloud; then, while you watch, it thickens and spreads and hides the peak. Ten minutes later, per-haps, it dissipates as rapidly as it gathered, leaving the granite photographed against the blue. Or it may broaden and settle till it covers a vast acreage of sky and drops a brief shower in near-by valleys, while meadows half a mile away are steeped in sunshine. Then, in a twinkling, all is clear again. Sometimes, when the clearing comes, the summit is white with snow. And sometimes, standing upon a high peak in a blaze of sunshine from a cleared sky, one may look down for a few moments upon the top of one of these settled clouds, knowing that it is sprinkling the hidden valley.

The charm of the mountains from below may satisfy many, but sooner or later temptation is sure to beset. The desire comes to see close up those monsters of mystery. Many, including most women, ignorant of rewards, refuse to venture because they fear hardship. "I can never climb mountains in this rarefied air," pleads one, and in most cases this is true; it is important that persons unused to the higher altitudes be temperate and discreet. But the lungs and muscles of a well-trained mountain horse are always obtainable, and the least practice will teach the unaccustomed rider that all he has to do is to sit his saddle limply and leave everything else to the horse. It is my proud boast that I can climb any mountain, no matter how high and difficult, up which my horse can carry me.

And so, at last and inevitably, we ascend into the mountains.

IV

The mountains within the park fall naturally in two groupings. The Front Range cuts the southern boundary midway and runs north to Longs Peak, where it swings westerly and carries the continental divide out of the park at its northwestern corner.

The Mummy Range occupies the park's entire north end. The two are joined by a ridge 11,500 feet in altitude, over which the Fall River Road is building to connect the east and the west sides of the park.

The lesser of these two, the Mummy Range, is a mountain group of distinguished beauty. Its climax is an arc of gray monsters, Ypsilon Mountain, 13,507 feet, Mount Fairchild, 13,502 feet, Hagues Peak, 13,562 feet, and Mount Dunraven, 12,326 feet; these gather around Mummy Mountain with its 13,413 feet. A noble company, indeed, herded in close comradeship, the centre of many square miles of summits scarcely less. Ypsilon's big Greek letter, outlined in perpetual snow, is one of the famous landmarks of the northern end. Hagues Peak supports Hallett Glacier, the most interesting in the park. Dunraven, aloof and of slenderer outline, offers marked contrast to the enormous sprawling bulk of Mummy, always portentous, often capped with clouds. The range is split by many fine canyons and dotted with glacial lakes, an undeveloped wilderness designed by kindly nature for summer exploration.

But it is the Front Range, the snowy pinnacled rampart, which commands profoundest attention.

From Specimen Mountain in the far northwest, a spill of lava, now the haunt of mountain sheep, the continental divide southward piles climax upon climax. Following it at an elevation well exceeding twelve thousand feet, the hardy, venturesome climber looks westward down a slope of bald granite, thickly strewn with boulders; eastward he gazes into a succession of gigantic gorges dropping upon the east, forest grown, lake-set canyons deep in mid-foreground, the great plateau spreading to its foothills far beyond the canyons, with now and then a sun glint from some irrigation pond beyond the foothills on the misty plains of eastern Colorado. Past the monolith of Terra Tomah Peak, with its fine glacial gorge of many lakes, past the Sprague Glacier, largest of the several shrunken fields of moving ice which still remain, he finds, from the summit of Flattop Mountain, a broad spectacle of real sublimity.

But there is a greater viewpoint close at hand. Crossing the Flattop Trail which here ascends from the settlements below on its way to the west side, and skirting the top of the Tyndall Glacier, a scramble of four hundred feet lands him on the summit of Hallett Peak, 12,725 feet in altitude. Here indeed is reward. Below him lies the sheer abyss of the Tyndall Gorge, Dream Lake, a drop of turquoise in its depths; beyond it a moraine reaches out upon the plateau— six miles in length, a mile and more in width, nearly a thousand feet in height, holding Bierstadt Lake upon its level forested crown, an eloquent reminder of that ancient time when enormous glaciers ripped the granite from these gorges to heap it in long winding hills upon the plains below. Turning southerly, the Wild Gardens further spread before his gaze, a tumble of granite masses rising from lake-dotted, richly forested bottoms. The entrance to Loch Vale, gem canyon of

the Rockies, lies in the valley foreground. Adjoining
it, the entrance to Glacier Gorge, showing one of its
several lakes, rests in peaceful contrast with its impressive eastern wall, a long, winding, sharp-edged
buttress pushing southward and upward to support
the northern shoulder of the monster, Longs Peak,
whose squared summit, from here for all the world
like a chef's cap, outlines sharply against the sky.
Hallett Peak welcomes the climber to the Heart of
the Rockies at perhaps their most gorgeous point.

South of Hallett difficult going will disclose new
viewpoints of supreme wildness. Otis Peak, nearly
as high as Hallett, looks down upon the Andrews Glacier, and displays the length of Loch Vale, at whose
head towers Taylor Peak, a giant exceeding thirteen
thousand feet.

I have not sketched this tour of the continental
divide as a suggestion for travel, for there are no trails,
and none but the mountaineer, experienced in pioneer-
ing, could accomplish it with pleasure and success, but
as a convenient mode of picturing the glories of the
continental divide. Some day a trail, even perhaps a
road, for one is practicable, should make it fully accessible to the greater public. Meantime Flattop Trail
invites valley dwellers of all degrees, afoot and horseback, up to a point on the divide from which Hallett's
summit and its stupendous view is no great conquest.

The gorges of the Wild Gardens are most enjoyed
from below. Trails of no difficulty lead from the
settlements to Fern and Odessa Lakes in a canyon un-

surpassed; to Bear Lake at the outlet of the Tyndall Gorge; to Loch Vale, whose flower-carpeted terraces and cirque lakelets, Sky Pond and the Lake of Glass, are encircled with mighty canyon walls; and to Glacier Gorge, which leads to the foot of Longs Peak's western precipice. These are spots, each a day's round trip from convenient over-night hotels, which deserve all the fame that will be theirs when the people come to know them, for as yet only a few hundreds a summer of Rocky Mountain's hundred thousand take the trouble to visit them.

To better understand the charm of these gray monsters, and the valleys and chasms between their knees, we must pause a moment to picture what architects call the planting, for trees and shrubs and flowers play as important a part in the informal architectural scheme of the Front Range as they do in the formality of a palace. It will be recalled that the zones of vegetation from the equator to the frozen ice fields of the far north find their counterparts in altitude. The foothills bordering the Rocky Mountain National Park lie in the austral zone of our middle and eastern states; its splendid east-side plateau and inter-mountain valleys represent the luxuriance of the Canadian zone; its mountains pass rapidly up in a few thousand feet through the Hudsonian zone, including timberline at about 11,500 feet; and its highest summits carry only the mosses, lichens, stunted grasses, and tiny alpine flowerets of the Arctic Zone.

Thus one may walk waist deep through the mar-

vellous wild flower meadows of Loch Vale, bordered
by luxuriant forests of majestic Engelmann spruce,
pines, firs, junipers, and many deciduous shrubs, and
look upward at the gradations of all vegetation to the
arctic seas.

Especially interesting is the revelation when one
takes it in order, climbing into the range. The Fall
River Road displays it, but not dramatically; the
forest approach is too long, the climb into the Hudsonian Zone too short, and not typical. The same is
true of the trail up beautiful Forest Canyon. The
reverse is true of the Ute Trail, which brings one too
quickly to the stupendous arctic summit of Trail
Ridge. The Flattop Trail is in many respects the most
satisfying, particularly if one takes the time to make
the summit of Hallett Peak, and hunts for arctic
flowerets on the way. But one may also accomplish
the purpose in Loch Vale by climbing all the way to
Sky Pond, at the very foot of steep little Taylor Glacier, or by ascending Glacier Gorge to its head, or by
climbing the Twin Sisters, or Longs Peak as far as
Boulder Field, or up the St. Vrain valley to the top of
Meadow Mountain, or Mount Copeland.

All of these ascents are made by fair trails, and all
display the fascinating spectacle of timber-line, which
in Rocky Mountain National Park, I believe, attains
its most satisfying popular expression; by which I
mean that here the panorama of the everlasting struggle between the ambitious climbing forests and the
winter gales of the summits seems to be condensed

and summarized, to borrow a figure from the text-books, as I have not happened to find it elsewhere. Following up some sheltered forested ravine to its head, we swing out upon the wind-swept slopes leading straight to the summit. Snow patches increase in size and number as the conifers thin and shrink. Presently the trees bend eastward, permanently mis-shaped by the icy winter blasts. Presently they curve in semi-circles, or rise bravely in the lee of some great rock, to bend at right angles from its top. Here and there are full-grown trees growing prostrate, like a rug, upon the ground.

Close to the summit trees shrink to the size of shrubs, but some of these have heavy trunks a few feet high, and doubtless have attained their fulness of development. Gradually they thin and disappear, giving place to wiry, powerful, deciduous shrubs, and these in turn to growths still smaller. There are forests of willows just above Rocky Mountain's timber-line, two or three inches tall, and many acres in extent.

From the Front Range, well in the south of the park, a spur of toothed granite peaks springs two miles eastward to the monarch of the park, Longs Peak. It is this position in advance of the range, as much as the advantage of its 14,255 feet of altitude, which enables this famous mountain to become the climax of every east-side view.

Longs Peak has a remarkable personality. It is an architectural creation, a solid granite temple, strongly buttressed upon four sides. From every point of view it is profoundly different, but always consistent and recognizable. Seen from the east, it is supported on either side by mountains of majesty. Joined with it on the north, Mount Lady Washington rises 13,269 feet, the cleft between their summits being the way of the trail to Longs Peak summit. Merging with it in mass upon the south, Mount Meeker rises 13,911 feet. Once the three were one monster mountain. Frosts and rains carried off the crust strata, bared the granite core, and chipped it into three summits, while a glacier of large size gouged out of its middle the abyss which divides the mountains, and carved the precipice, which drops twenty-four hundred feet from Longs Peak summit to Chasm Lake. The Chasm, which is easily reached by trail from the hotels at the mountain's foot, is one of the wildest places in America. It may be explored in a day.

Mountain climbing is becoming the fashion in Rocky Mountain National Park among those who never climbed before, and it will not be many years before its inmost recesses are penetrated by innumerable trampers and campers. The "stunt" of the park is the ascent of Longs Peak. This is no particular matter for the experienced, for the trail is well worn, and the ascent may be made on horseback to the boulder field, less than two thousand feet from the summit; but to the inexperienced it appears an undertaking of first magnitude. From the boulder field the trail carries out upon a long sharp slant which drops into the precipice of Glacier Gorge, and ascends the box-like summit cap by a shelf trail which sometimes has terrors for the unaccustomed. Several hundred persons make the ascent each summer without accident, including many women and a few children. The one risk is that accidental snow obscure the trail; but Longs Peak is not often ascended without a guide.

The view from the summit of the entire national park, of the splendid range south which should be in the park but is not, of the foothills and pond-spotted plains in the east, of Denver and her mountain background, and of the Medicine Bow and other ranges west of the park, is one of the country's great spectacles. Longs Peak is sometimes climbed at night for the sunrise.

The six miles of range between Longs Peak and the southern boundary of the park show five towering snow-spotted mountains of noble beauty, Mount Alice, Tanima Peak, Mahana Peak, Ouzel Peak, and Mount Copeland. Tributary to the Wild Basin, which corresponds, south of Longs Peak, to the Wild Gardens north of it, are gorges of loveliness the waters of whose exquisite lakes swell St. Vrain Creek.

The Wild Basin is one of Rocky Mountain's lands of the future. The entire west side is another, for, except for the lively settlement at Grand Lake, its peaks and canyons, meadows, lakes, and valleys are seldom visited. It is natural that the east side, with its broader plateaus and showier range, should have the first development, but no accessible country of the splendid beauty of the west side can long remain

From a photograph by Wiswall Brothers

SUMMIT OF LONGS PEAK, ROCKY MOUNTAIN NATIONAL PARK

Twenty-four hundred feet from water to peak, a mighty chasm carved by an ancient glacier

neglected. Its unique feature is the broad and beautiful valley of the North Fork of the Grand River, here starting for its great adventure in the Grand Canyon of the Colorado.

V

The Rockies are a masterpiece of erosion. When forces below the surface began to push them high in air, their granite cores were covered thousands of feet deep with the sediments of the great sea of whose bottom once they were a part. The higher they rose the more insistently frosts and rains concentrated upon their uplifting summits; in time all sedimentary rocks were washed away, and the granite beneath exposed.

Then the frosts and rains, and later the glaciers, attacked the granite, and carved it into the jagged forms of to-day. The glaciers moulded the gorges which the streams had cut. The glaciers have passed, but still the work goes on. Slowly the mountains rise, and slowly, but not so slowly, the frosts chisel and the rains carry away. If conditions remain as now, history will again repeat itself, and the gorgeous peaks of to-day will decline, a million years or more from now, into the low rounded summits of our eastern Appalachians, and later into the flat, soil-hidden granites of Canada.

These processes may be seen in practical example. Ascend the precipitous east side by the Flattop Trail, for instance, and notice particularly the broad, rolling level of the continental divide. For many miles it is nothing but a lofty, bare, undulating plain, interspersed with summits, but easy to travel except for its accumulation of immense loose boulders. This plain slopes gently toward the west, and presently breaks, as on the east, into cliffs and canyons. It is a stage in the reduction by erosion of mountains which, except for erosion, might have risen many thousands of feet higher. Geologists call it a peneplain, which means nearly-a-plain; it is from fragmentary remains of peneplains that they trace ranges long ages washed away. History may, in some dim future age, repeat still another wonder, for upon the flattened wreck of the Front Range may rise, by some earth movement, a new and even nobler range.

But what about the precipitous eastern front?

That masterpiece was begun by water, accomplished by ice, and finished by water. In the beginning, streams determined the direction of the valleys and carved these valleys deep. Then came, in very recent times, as geologists measure earth's history, the Great Ice Age. As a result of falling temperature, the mountains became covered, except their higher summits and the continental divide, with glaciers. These came in at least two invasions, and remained many hundreds of thousands of years. When changing climate melted them away, the Rocky Mountain National Park remained not greatly different from what it is to-day. Frosts and rains have softened and beautified it since.

These glaciers, first forming in the beds of streams

From a photograph by Willis T. Lee

THE ANDREWS GLACIER HANGS FROM THE CONTINENTAL DIVIDE

A glacier in the Rocky Mountain National Park which can be studied by visitors

From a photograph by H. T. Cowling

A ROCKY MOUNTAIN CIRQUE CARVED FROM SOLID GRANITE

Iceberg Lake was cut eighteen hundred feet deep by an ancient glacier

the high curved hill which springs from the northeastern shoulder of Longs Peak, and encircles the eastern foot of Mount Meeker.

These and other moraines are fascinating features of any visit to Rocky Mountain National Park. The motor roads disclose them, the trails travel them. In combination with the gulfs, the shelved canyons and the scarred and serrated peaks and walls, these moraines offer the visitor a thrilling mystery story of the past, the unravelling of whose threads and the reconstruction of whose plot and climax will add zest and interest to a summer's outing, and bring him, incidentally, in close communion with nature in a thousand happy moods.

VI

The limitations of a chapter permit no mention of the gigantic prehistoric monsters of land, sea, and air which once haunted the site of this noble park, nor description of its more intimate beauties, nor detail of its mountaineering joys; for all of which and much other invaluable information I refer those interested to publications of the National Park Service, Department of the Interior, by Doctor Willis T. Lee and Major Roger W. Toll. But something must be told of its early history.

In 1819 the exploring expedition which President Madison sent west under Colonel S. H. Long, while camping at the mouth of La Poudre River, was greatly impressed by the magnificence of a lofty, square-topped mountain. They approached it no nearer, but named it Longs Peak, in honor of their leader. Parkman records seeing it in 1845.

The pioneers, of course, knew the country. Deer, elk, and sheep were probably hunted there in the forties and fifties. Joel Estes, the first settler, built a cabin in the foothills in 1860, hence the title of Estes Park. James Nugent, afterward widely celebrated as "Rocky Mountain Jim," arrived in 1868. Others followed slowly.

William N. Byers, founder of the *Rocky Mountain News*, made the first attempt to climb Longs Peak in 1864. He did not succeed then, but four years later, with a party which included Major J. W. Powell, who made the first exploration of the Grand Canyon the following year, he made the summit. In 1871 the Reverend E. J. Lamb, the first regular guide on Longs Peak, made the first descent by the east precipice, a dangerous feat.

The Earl of Dunraven visited Estes Park in 1871, attracted by the big game hunting, and bought land. He projected an immense preserve, and induced men to file claims which he planned to acquire after they had secured possession; but the claims were disallowed. Albert Bierstadt visited Dunraven in 1874, and painted canvases which are famous in American art.

It was Dunraven, also, who built the first hotel. Tourists began to arrive in 1865. In 1874 the first stage line was established, coming in from Longmont. Telephone connection was made in 1906.

Under the name of Estes Park, the region prospered. Fifty thousand people were estimated to have visited it in 1914. It was not, however, till the national park was created, in 1915, that the mountains assumed considerable importance except as an agreeable and inspiring background to the broad plateau.

V

McKINLEY, GIANT OF GIANTS

MOUNT McKINLEY NATIONAL PARK, ALASKA. AREA,
ABOUT 2,200 SQUARE MILES

THE monster mountain of this continent, "the
majestic, snow-crowned American monarch," as
General Greeley called it, was made a national park in
1917. Mount McKinley rises 20,300 feet above tide-
water, and 17,000 feet above the eyes of the beholder
standing on the plateau at its base. Scenically, it is
the highest mountain in the world, for those summits
of the Andes and Himalayas which are loftier as measured from sea level, can be viewed closely only from
valleys whose altitudes range from 10,000 to 15,000
feet. Its enormous bulk is shrouded in perpetual
snow two-thirds down from its summit, and the foothills and broad plains upon its north and west are
populated with mountain sheep and caribou in unprecedented numbers.

To appreciate Mount McKinley's place among
national parks, one must know what it means in the
anatomy of the continent. The western margin of
North America is bordered by a broad mountainous
belt known as the Pacific System, which extends from
Mexico northwesterly into and through Alaska, to the
very end of the Aleutian Islands, and includes such
celebrated ranges as the Sierra Nevada, the Cascade,

and the St. Elias. In Alaska, at the head of Cook Inlet, it swings a sharp curve to the southwest and becomes Alaska's mountain axis. This sharp curve, for all the world like a monstrous granite hinge connecting the northwesterly and southwesterly limbs of the System, is the gigantic Alaska Range, which is higher and broader than the Sierra Nevada, and of greater relief and extent than the Alps. Near the centre of this range, its climax in position, height, bulk, and majesty, stands Mount McKinley. Its glistening peak can be seen on clear days in most directions for two hundred miles.

For many years Mount St. Elias, with its eighteen thousand feet of altitude, was considered North America's loftiest summit. That was because it stands in that part of Alaska which was first developed. The Klondike region, far northward, was well on the way to development before McKinley became officially recognized as the mountain climax of the continent. But that does not mean that it remained unknown. The natives of the Cook Inlet country on the east knew it as Doleika, and tell you that it is the rock which a god threw at his eloping wife. They say it was once a volcano, which is not the fact. The Aleutes on the south called it Traleika, the big mountain. The natives of the Kuskokwim country on the west knew it as Denalai, the god, father of the great range. The Russians who established the first permanent white settlement in Alaska on Kodiak Island knew it as Bulshia Gora, the great mountain. Captain Cook, who in 1778 explored the inlet which since has borne his name, does not mention it, but Vancouver in 1794 unquestionably meant it in his reference to "distant stupendous mountains."

After the United States acquired Alaska, in 1867, there is little mention of it for some years. But Frank Densmore, an explorer of 1889, entered the Kuskokwim region, and took such glowing accounts of its magnificence back to the Yukon that for years it was known through the settlements as Densmore's Mountain. In 1885 Lieutenant Henry C. Allen, U. S. A., made a sketch of the range from his skin boat on the Tanana River, a hundred and fifty miles away, which is the earliest known picture of McKinley.

Meantime the neighborhood was invaded by prospectors from both sides. The Cook Inlet gold fields were exploited in 1894. Two years later W. A. Dickey and his partner, Monks, two young Princeton graduates, exploring north from their workings, recognized the mountain's commanding proportions and named it Mount McKinley, by which it rapidly became known, and was entered on the early maps. With crude instruments improvised on the spot, Dickey estimated the mountain's height as twenty thousand feet—a real achievement. When Belmore Browne, who climbed the great peak in 1912, asked Dickey why he chose the name, Dickey told him that he was so disgusted with the free-silver arguments of men travelling with him that he named the mountain after the most ardent gold-standard man he knew.

The War Department sent several parties to the region during the next few years to explore, and the United States Geological Survey, beginning in 1898 with the Eldridge-Muldrow party, has had topographical and geological parties in the region almost continuously since. In 1915 the Government began the railroad from Seward to Fairbanks. Its course lies from Cook Inlet up the Susitna River to the headwaters of the Nenana River, where it crosses the range. This will make access to the region easy and comfortable. It was to safeguard the enormous game herds from the hordes of hunters which the railroad was expected to bring rather than to conserve an alpine region scenically unequalled that Congress set aside twenty-two hundred square miles under the name of the Mount McKinley National Park.

From the white sides of McKinley and his giant neighbors descend glaciers of enormous bulk and great length. Their waters drain on the east and south, through the Susitna River and its tributaries, into the Pacific; and on the north and west, through tributaries of the Yukon and Kuskokwim, into Bering Sea.

The south side of McKinley is forbidding in the extreme, but its north and west fronts pass abruptly into a plateau of gravels, sands, and silts twenty-five hundred to three thousand feet in altitude, whose gentle valleys lead the traveller up to the very sides of the granite monster, and whose mosses and grasses pasture the caribou.

The national park boundaries enclose immense

areas of this plateau. The contours of its rounded
rolling elevations mark the courses of innumerable
streams, and occasionally abut upon great sweeping
glaciers. Low as it is, the plateau is generally above
timber-line. The day will come when roads will wind
through its valleys, and hotels and camps will nestle
in its sheltered hollows; while the great herds of caribou, more than one of which has been estimated at
fifteen hundred animals, will pasture like sheep within
close range of the camera. For the wild animals of
McKinley National Park, having never been hunted,
were fearless of the explorers, and now will never learn
to fear man. The same is true in lesser measure of
the more timid mountain sheep which frequent the
foot-hills in numbers not known elsewhere. Charles
Sheldon counted more than five hundred in one
ordinary day's foot journey through the valleys.

The magic of summer life on this sunlit plateau,
with its limitless distances, its rushing streams, its
enormous crawling glaciers, its waving grasses, its
sweeping gentle valleys, its myriad friendly animals,
and, back of all and commanding all, its never-for-
gotten and ever-controlling presence, the shining Range
and Master Mountain, powerfully grip imagination
and memory. One never can look long away from the
mountain, whose delicate rose tint differentiates it
from other great mountains. Here is ever present an
intimate sense of the infinite, which is reminiscent of
that pang which sometimes one may get by gazing
long into the starry zenith. From many points of

view McKinley looks its giant size. As the climber ascends the basal ridges there are places where its height and bulk appall.

Along the northern edge of the park lies the Kantishna mining district. In 1906 there was a wild stampede to this region. Diamond City, Bearpaw City, Glacier City, McKinley City, Roosevelt, and other rude mining settlements came into rapid existence. Results did not adequately reward the thousands who flocked to the new field, and the "cities" were abandoned. A hundred or two miners remain, scattered thinly over a large area, which is forested here and there with scrubby growths, and, in localities, is remarkably productive of cultivated fruits and vegetables.

Few know and few will know Mount McKinley. It is too monstrous for any but the hardiest to discover its ice-protected secrets. The South Peak, which is the summit, has been climbed twice, once by the Parker-Browne party in 1912, after two previous unsuccessful expeditions, and once, the year following, by the party of Archdeacon Hudson Stuck, who gratified an ambition which had arisen out of his many years of strenuous missionary work among the Alaskan Indians. From the records of these two parties we gather nearly all that is known of the mountain. The North Peak, which is several hundred feet lower, was climbed by Anderson and Taylor of the Tom Lloyd party, in 1913.

From each of these peaks an enormous buttressing ridge sweeps northward until it merges into the foothills and the great plain. These ridges are roughly parallel, and carry between them the Denali Glacier, to adopt Belmore Browne's suggested name, and its forks and tributaries. Up this glacier is the difficult passage to the summit. Tremendous as it is, the greatest perhaps of the north side, the Denali Glacier by no means compares with the giants which flow from the southern front.

In 1903 Judge James Wickersham, afterward Delegate to Congress from Alaska, made the first attempt to climb McKinley; it failed through his underestimation of the extensive equipment necessary. In 1906 Doctor Frederick A. Cook, who meantime also had made an unsuccessful attempt from the north side, led an expedition from the south which included Professor Herschel Parker of Columbia University, and Mr. Belmore Browne, artist, explorer, and big game hunter. Ascending the Yentna River, it reached a point upon the Tokositna Glacier beyond which progress was impossible, and returned to Cook Inlet and disbanded. Parker returned to New York, and Cook proposed that Browne should lay in a needed supply of game while he, with a packer named Barrill, should make what he described as a rapid reconnaissance preparatory to a further attempt upon the summit the following year. Browne wanted to accompany him, but was overpersuaded. Cook and Barrill then ascended the Susitna, struck into the country due south of McKinley, and returned to Tyonik with the announcement that they had reached the summit.

Cook exhibited a photograph of Barrill standing upon a crag, which he said was the summit. A long and painful controversy followed upon Cook's return east with this claim.

In all probability the object of the Parker-Browne expedition of 1910 was as much to follow Cook's course and check his claim as to reach the summit. The first object was attained, and Herman L. Tucker, a national forester, was photographed standing on the identical crag upon which Cook had photographed Barrill four years before. This crag was found miles south of McKinley, with other peaks higher than its own intervening. From here the party advanced up a glacier of enormous size to the very foot of the upper reaches of the mountain's south side, but was stopped by gigantic snow walls, which defeated every attempt to cross. "At the slightest touch of the sun," writes Browne, "the great cliffs literally *smoke* with avalanches."

The Parker-Browne expedition undertaken in 1912 for purposes of exploration, also approached from the south, but, following the Susitna River farther up, crossed the Alaska Range with dog trains to the north side at a hitherto unexplored point. Just before crossing the divide it entered what five years later became the Mount McKinley National Park, and, against an April blizzard, descended into a land of many gorgeous glaciers. "We were now," writes Belmore Browne, "in a wilderness paradise. The mountains had a wild, picturesque look, due to their bare rock summits, and big game was abundant. We were wild with enthusiasm over the beauty of it all, and every few minutes as we jogged along some one would gaze fondly at the surrounding mountains and ejaculate: 'This is sure a white man's country.'"

Of these "happy hunting grounds," as Browne chapters the park country in his book, Stephen R. Capps of the United States Geological Survey says in his report:

"Probably no part of America is so well supplied with wild game, unprotected by reserves, as the area on the north slope of the Alaska Range, west of the Nanana River. This region has been so little visited by white men that the game herds have, until recent years, been little molested by hunters. The white mountain sheep are particularly abundant in the main Alaska Range, and in the more rugged foot-hills. Caribou are plentiful throughout the entire area, and were seen in bands numbering many hundred individuals. Moose are numerous in the lowlands, and range over all the area in which timber occurs. Black bears may be seen in or near timbered lands, and grizzly bears range from the rugged mountains to the lowlands. Rabbits and ptarmigan are at times remarkably numerous."

Parker and Browne camped along the Muldrow Glacier, now a magnificent central feature of the park. Then they made for McKinley summit. Striking the Denali Glacier, they ascended it with a dog train to an altitude of eleven thousand feet, where they made a base camp and went on afoot, packing provisions and camp outfit on their backs. At one place they ascended an incoming glacier over ice cascades, four thousand feet high. From their last camp they cut steps in the ice for more than three thousand feet of final ascent, and attained the top on July 1 in the face of a blizzard. On the northeastern end of the level summit, and only five minutes' walk from the little hillock which forms the supreme summit, the blizzard completely blinded them. It was impossible to go on, and to wait meant rapid death by freezing; with extreme difficulty they returned to their camp. Two days later they made a second attempt, but were again enveloped in an ice storm that rendered progress impossible. Exhaustion of supplies forbade another try, and saved their lives, for a few days later a violent earthquake shook McKinley to its summit. Later on Mr. Browne identified this earthquake as concurrent with the terrific explosive eruption which blew off the top of Mount Katmai, on the south coast of Alaska.

The following spring the Stuck-Karstens party made the summit upon that rarest of occasions with Mount McKinley, a perfect day. Archdeacon Stuck describes the "actual summit" as "a little crater-like snow basin, sixty or sixty-five feet long, and twenty to twenty-five feet wide, with a hay-cock of snow at either end—the south one a little higher than the north." Ignoring official and recognized nomenclature, and calling McKinley and Foraker by their Kuskokwim Indian names, he writes of Mount Foraker: "Denali's

Wife does not appear at all save from the actual summit of Denali, for she is completely hidden by his South Peak, until the moment when his South Peak is surmounted. And never was nobler sight displayed to man than that great isolated mountain spread out completely, with all its spurs and ridges, its cliffs and its glaciers, lofty and mighty, and yet far beneath us."

"Above us," he writes a few pages later, "the sky took on a blue so deep that none of us had ever gazed upon a midday sky like it before. It was deep, rich, lustrous, transparent blue, as dark as Prussian blue, but intensely blue; a hue so strange, so increasingly impressive, that to one at least it 'seemed like special news of God,' as a new poet sings. We first noticed the darkening tint of the upper sky in the Grand Basin, and it deepened as we rose. Tyndall observed and discussed this phenomenon in the Alps, but it seems scarcely to have been mentioned since."

A couple of months before the Parker-Browne party started for the top, there was an ascent of the lower North Peak which, for sheer daring and endurance must rank high in the history of adventure. Four prospectors and miners from the Kantishna region organized by Tom Lloyd, took advantage of the hard ice of May, and an idle dog team, to make for the summit. Their motive seems to have been little more than to plant a pole where it could be seen by telescope, as they thought, from Fairbanks; that was why they chose the North Peak. They used no ropes, alpenstocks, or scientific equipment of any sort, and

From a photograph by G. B. Gordon

MOUNT McKINLEY, LOOMING ABOVE THE GREAT ALASKAN RANGE

From a photograph by LaVoy

ARCHDEACON STUCK'S PARTY HALF-WAY UP THE MOUNTAIN

THE SUMMIT OF MOUNT McKINLEY

carried only one camera, the chance possession of McGonagall.

They made their last camp at an altitude of eleven thousand feet. Here Lloyd remained, while Anderson, Taylor, and McGonagall attempted the summit in one day's supreme effort. Near the top McGonagall was overcome by mountain sickness. Anderson and Taylor went on and planted their pole near the North summit, where the Stuck-Karstens party saw it a year later in their ascent of the South Peak.

So extraordinary a feat of strength and endurance will hardly be accomplished again unless, perhaps, by hardy miners of the arctic wilderness. "The North Pole's nothing to fellows like us," one of them said later on; "once strike gold there, and we'll build a town on it in a month."

The published records of the Parker-Browne and Stuck-Karstens expeditions emphasize the laborious nature of the climbing. The very isolation which gives McKinley its spectacular elevation multiplies the difficulties of ascent by lowering the snow line thousands of feet below the snow line of the Himalayas and Andes with their loftier surrounding valleys. Travel on the glaciers was trying in the extreme, for much of the way had to be sounded for hidden crevasses, and, after the selection of each new camping place, the extensive outfit must be returned for and sledded or carried up. Frequent barriers, often of great height, had to be surmounted by tortuous and exhausting detours over icy cliffs and soft snow. And always special care must be taken against avalanches; the roar of avalanches for much of the latter journey was almost continuous.

Toward the end, the thermometer was rarely above zero, and at night far below; but the heat and glare of the sun was stifling and blinding during much of the day; often they perspired profusely under their crushing burdens, with the thermometer nearly at zero. Snow fell daily, and often several times a day.

It is probable that no other of the world's mountain giants presents climbing conditions so strenuous. Farming is successfully carried on in the Himalayas far above McKinley's level of perpetual snow, and Tucker reports having climbed a twenty-thousand-foot peak in the Andes with less exertion than it cost the Parker-Browne party, of which he had been a member, to mount the first forty-five hundred feet of McKinley.

While McKinley will be climbed again and again in the future, the feat will scarcely be one of the popular amusements of the national park.

Yet Mount McKinley is the northern landmark of an immense unexplored mountain region south of the national park, which very far surpasses the Alps in every feature that has made the Alps world-famous. Of this region A. H. Brooks, Chief of the Alaska Division of the United States Geological Survey, writes:

"Here lies a rugged highland area far greater in extent than all of Switzerland, a virgin field for explorers and mountaineers. He who would master unattained summits, explore unknown rivers, or traverse untrodden glaciers in a region whose scenic beauties are hardly equalled, has not to seek them in South America or Central Asia, for generations will pass before the possibilities of the Alaskan Range are exhausted. But this is not Switzerland, with its hotels, railways, trained guides, and well-worn paths. It will appeal only to him who prefers to strike out for himself, who can break his own trail through trackless wilds, can throw the diamond hitch, and will take the chances of life and limb so dear to the heart of the true explorer."

The hotels will come in time to the Mount McKinley National Park, and perhaps they will come also to the Alaskan Alps. Perhaps it is not straining the credulity of an age like ours to suggest that McKinley's commanding summit may be attained some day by aeroplane, with many of the joys and none of the distressing hardships endured by the weary climber. When this time comes, if it does come, there will be added merely another extraordinary experience to the very many unique and pleasurable experiences of a visit to the Mount McKinley National Park.

LAFAYETTE AND THE EAST

LAFAYETTE NATIONAL PARK, MAINE.   AREA, 10,000 ACRES

IT has been the policy of Congress to create national parks only from public lands, the title to which costs nothing to acquire. It may be many years before the nation awakes to the fact that areas distinguished for supreme scenery, historical association, or extraordinary scientific significance are worth conserving even if conservation involves their purchase. The answer to the oft-asked question why the national parks are all in the west is that the east passed into private possession before the national park idea assumed importance in the national consciousness.

The existence of the two national parks east of the Rocky Mountains merely emphasizes the fact. The Hot Springs of Arkansas were set apart in 1832 while the Ozark Mountains were still a wilderness. The Lafayette National Park, in Maine, is made up of many small parcels of privately owned land which a group of public-spirited citizens, because of the impossibility of securing national appropriations, patiently acquired during a series of laborious years, and presented, in 1916, to the people of the United States.

While refusing to purchase land for national parks, Congress nevertheless is buying large areas of eastern mountain land for national forest, the purpose being not only to conserve water sources, which national parks would accomplish quite as thoroughly, but particularly to control lumbering operations in accord with principles which will insure the lumber supply of the future. Here and there in this reserve are limited areas of distinguished national park quality, but whether they will be set aside as national parks is a question for the people and the future to decide. Certainly the mountain topography and the rich deciduous forests of the eastern United States should be represented in the national parks system by several fine examples.

The Lafayette National Park differs from all other members of the national parks system in several important respects. It is in the far east; it combines seashore and mountain; it is clothed with a rich and varied growth of deciduous trees and eastern conifers; it is intimately associated with the very early history of America. Besides which, it is a region of noble beauty, subtle charm and fascinating variety.

The Appalachian Mountain uplift, which, roughly speaking, embraces all the ranges constituting the eastern rib of the continent, may be considered to include also the very ancient peneplains of New England. These tumbled hills and shallow valleys, accented here and there by ranges and monadnocks, by which the geologist means solitary peaks, are all that the frosts and rains of very many millions of years and the glaciers of more recent geologic times have left of what once must have been a towering mountain region crested in snow. The wrinkling of the earth's surface which produced this range occurred during the Devonian period when fishes were the predominant inhabitants of the earth, many millions of years before birds or even reptiles appeared. Its rise was accompanied by volcanic disturbances, whose evidences are abundant on islands between the mouth of the Penobscot and Mount Desert Island, though not within the park. The mind cannot conceive the lapse of time which has reduced this range, at an erosional speed no greater than to-day's, to its present level. During this process the coast line was also slowly sinking, changing valleys into estuaries and land-encircled bays. The coast of Maine is an eloquent chapter in the continent's ancient history, and the Lafayette National Park is one of the most dramatic paragraphs in the chapter.

Where the Penobscot River reaches the sea, and for forty miles east, the sinking continental shore has deeply indented the coast line with a network of broad, twisting bays, enclosing many islands. The largest and finest of these is Mount Desert Island, for many years celebrated for its romantic beauty. Upon its northeast shore, facing Frenchman's Bay, is the resort town of Bar Harbor; other resorts dot its shores on every side. The island has a large summer population drawn from all parts of the country. Besides its hotels, there are many fine summer homes.

The feature which especially distinguishes Mount

IN LAFAYETTE NATIONAL PARK

Echo Lake in the foreground, Sommes Harbor beyond Acadia

SEA CAVES IN THE GRANITE

Thus does the ocean everlastingly undermine the foundations of the mountains. Photograph
taken at low tide; Lafayette National Park

Desert Island from other islands, in fact from the entire Atlantic coast, is a group of granitic mountains which rise abruptly from the sea. They were once towering monsters, perhaps only one, unquestionably the loftiest for many miles around. They are the sole remainders upon the present coast line of a great former range. They are composed almost wholly of granite, worn down by the ages, but massive enough still to resist the agencies which wiped away their comrades. They rise a thousand feet or more, grim, rounded, cleft with winding valleys and deep passes, divided in places by estuaries of the sea, holding in their hollows many charming lakes.

Their abrupt flanks gnawed by the beating sea, their valleys grown with splendid forests and brightened by wild flowers, their slopes and domes sprinkled with conifers which struggle for foothold in the cracks which the elements are widening and deepening in their granite surface, for years they have been the resort of thousands of climbers, students of nature and seekers of the beautiful; the views of sea, estuary, island, plain, lake, and mountain from the heights have no counterpart elsewhere.

All this mountain wilderness, free as it was to the public, was in private ownership. Some of it was held by persons who had not seen it for years. Some of it was locked up in estates. The time came when owners began to plan fine summer homes high on the mountain slopes. A few, however, believed that the region should belong to the whole people, and out of this belief grew the movement, led by George B. Dorr and Charles W. Eliot, to acquire title and present it to the nation which would not buy it. They organized a holding association, to which they gave their own properties; for years afterward Mr. Dorr devoted most of his time to persuading others to contribute their holdings, and to raising subscriptions for the purchase of plots which were tied up in estates. In 1916 the association presented five thousand acres to the Government, and President Wilson created it by proclamation the Sieur de Monts National Monument. The gift has been greatly increased since. In 1918 Congress made appropriations for its upkeep and development. In February, 1919, Congress changed its name and status; it then became the Lafayette National Park.

The impulse to name the new national park after the French general who came to our aid in time of need arose, of course, out of the war-time warmth of feeling for our ally, France. The region had been identified with early French exploration; the original monument had been named in commemoration of this historical association. The first European settlement in America north of the latitude of the Gulf of Mexico was here. Henry of Navarre had sent two famous adventurers to the new world, de Monts and Champlain. The first colony established by de Monts was at the mouth of the St. Croix River, which forms the eastern boundary of Maine, and the first land within the present United States which was reached by Champlain was Mount Desert Island. This was in 1604. It was Champlain who gave the island its present name, after the mountains which rise so prominently from its rock-bound shore. To him, however, the name had a different significance than it first suggests to us. L'Isle des Monts Deserts meant to him the Island of the Lonely Mountains, and lonely indeed they must have seemed above the flat shore line. Thus named, the place became a landmark for future voyagers; among others Winthrop records seeing the mountains on his way to the Massachusetts colony in 1630. He anchored opposite and fished for two hours, catching "sixty-seven great cod," one of which was "a yard around."

"By a curious train of circumstances," writes George B. Dorr, "the titles by which these mountains to the eastward of Somes Sound are held go back to the early ownership of Mount Desert Island by the Crown of France. For it was granted by Louis XIV, grandson of Henry IV, to Antoine de la Mothe Cadillac, an officer of noble family from southwestern France, then serving in Acadia, who afterward became successively the founder of Detroit and Governor of Louisiana—the Mississippi Valley. Cadillac lost it later, through English occupation of the region, ownership passing, first to the Province, then to the Commonwealth of Massachusetts. But presently the Commonwealth gave back to his granddaughter— Madame de Gregoire—and her husband, French refugees, the Island's eastern half, moved thereto by the part that France had taken in the recent War of Independence and by letters they had brought from Lafayette. And they came down and lived there."

And so it naturally followed that, under stress of war enthusiasm, this reservation with its French associations should commemorate not only the old Province of Acadia, which the French yielded to England only after half a century of war, and England later on to us after another war, but the great war also in which France, England, and the United States all joined as allies in the cause of the world's freedom. In accord with this idea, the highest mountain looking upon the sea has been named the Flying Squadron, in honor of the service of the air, born of an American invention, and carried to perfection by the three allies in common.

The park may be entered from any of the surrounding resorts, but the main gateway is Bar Harbor, which is reached by train, automobile, and steamboat. No resort may be reached more comfortably, and hotel accommodations are ample.

The mountains rise within a mile of the town. They extend westward for twelve miles, lying in two groups, separated by a fine salt-water fiord known as Somes Sound. The park's boundary is exceedingly irregular, with deep indentations of private property. It is enclosed, along the shore, by an excellent automobile road; roads also cross it on both sides of Somes Sound.

There are ten mountains in the eastern group; the three fronting Bar Harbor have been renamed, for historic reasons, Cadillac Mountain, the Flying Squadron, and Champlain Mountain. For the same reason mountains upon Somes Sound have been re-named Acadia Mountain, St. Sauveur Mountain, and Norumbega Mountain, the last an Indian name; similar changes commemorating the early English occupation also have been made in the nomenclature of the western group. Tablets and memorials are also projected in emphasis of the historical associations of the place.

Both mountain groups are dotted with lakes; those of the western group are the largest of the island.

The pleasures, then, of the Lafayette National Park cover a wide range of human desire. Sea bathing, boating, yachting, salt-water and fresh-water fishing, tramping, exploring the wilderness, hunting the view spots—these are the summer occupations of many visitors, the diversions of many others. The more thoughtful will find its historical associations fascinating, its geological record one of the richest in the continent, its forests well equipped schools for tree study, their branches a museum of bird life.

To climb these low mountains, wandering by the hour in their hollows and upon their sea-horizoned shoulders, is, for one interested in nature, to get very close indeed to the secrets of her wonderful east. One may stand upon Cadillac's rounded summit and let imagination realize for him the day when this was a glaciered peak in a mighty range which forged southward from the far north, shoulder upon shoulder, peak upon peak, pushing ever higher as it approached the sea, and extending far beyond the present ocean horizon; for these mountains of Mount Desert are by no means the terminal of the original mighty range; the slow subsidence of the coast has wholly submerged several, perhaps many, that once rose south of them. The valley which now carries the St. Croix River drained this once towering range's eastern slopes; the valley of the Penobscot drained its western slopes.

The rocks beneath his feet disclose not only this vision of the geologic past; besides that, in their slow decay, in the chiselling of the trickling waters, in the cleavage of masses by winter's ice, in the peeling of the surface by alternate freezing and melting, in the dissolution and disintegration everywhere by the chemicals imprisoned in air and water, all of which he sees beneath his feet, they disclose to him the processes by which Nature has wrought this splendid ruin. And if, captivated by this vision, he studies intimately the page of history written in these rocks, he will find it full of fascinating detail.

The region also offers an absorbing introduction to the study of our eastern flora. The exposed bogs and headlands support several hundred species of plants typical of the arctic, sub-arctic, and Hudsonian zones, together with practically all of the common plants of the Canadian zone, and many of the southern coasts. So with the trees. Essentially coastal, it is the land of conifers, the southern limit of some which are common in the great regions of the north, yet ex-

FRENCHMAN'S BAY FROM THE EAST CLIFF OF CHAMPLAIN MOUNTAIN
Lafayette National Park

hibiting in nearly full variety the species for many
miles south; yet it is also, in its sheltered valleys, remarkably representative of the deciduous growths of
the entire Appalachian region.

The bird life is full and varied. The food supply
attracts migratory birds, and aquatic birds find here
the conditions which make for increase. Deer are
returning in some numbers from the mainland.

In brief, the Lafayette National Park, small
though it is, is one of the most important members of
the national parks system. For the pleasure seeker
no other provides so wide and varied an opportunity.
To the student, no other offers a more readable or more
distinctive volume; it is the only national museum of
the fascinating geology of the east, and I can think
of no other place in the east where classes can find so
varied and so significant an exhibit. To the artist,
the poet, and the dreamer it presents vistas of ocean,
inlet, fiord, shore, wave-lashed promontory, bog,
meadow, forest, and mountain—an answer to every
mood.

If this nation, as now appears, must long lack national parks representative of the range of its splendid
east, let us be thankful that this one small park is so
complete and so distinguished.

THE VOLCANIC NATIONAL PARKS

ON THE VOLCANO IN SCENERY

THE volcanic national parks are Lassen Volcanic, Crater Lake, Mount Rainier, Yellowstone, and Hawaii. Though several of them exhibit extremely high mountains, their scenic ensemble differs in almost all respects from that of the granite parks. The landscape tends to broad elevated surfaces and rolling hills, from which rise sharp towering cones or massive mountains whose irregular bulging knobs were formed by outbreaks of lava upon the sides of original central vents.

The Cascade Mountains in Washington, Oregon, and northern California are one of the best examples of such a landscape; from its low swelling summits rise at intervals the powerful master cones of Shasta, Rainier, Adams, Hood, Baker, and others. Fujiyama, the celebrated mountain of Japan, may be cited as a familiar example of the basic mountain form, the single-cone volcanic peak. Vesuvius is a familiar example of simple complication, the double-cone volcano, while Mauna Loa in Hawaii, including Kilauea of the pit of fire, a neighbor volcano which it has almost engulfed in its swollen bulk, well illustrates the volcano built up by outpourings of lava from vents broken through its sides. Flat and rolling Yellowstone with its geyser fields, is one of the best possible examples of a dead and much eroded volcanic region.

The scenic detail of the volcanic landscape is interesting and different from any other. Centuries and the elements create from lava a soil of great fertility. No forests and wild flowers excel those growing on the lavas of the Cascades, and the fertility of the Hawaiian Islands, which are entirely volcanic, is world-famous. Streams cut deep and often highly colored canyons in these broad lava lands, and wind and rain, while eroding valleys, often leave ornately modelled edifices of harder rock, and tall thin needles pointing to the zenith.

In the near neighborhood of the volcanoes, as well as on their sloping sides, are found lava formations of many strange and wonderful kinds. Hot springs and bubbling paint pots abound; and in the Yellowstone National Park, geysers. Fields of fantastic, twisted shapes, masses suggesting heaps of tumbled ropes, upstanding spatter cones, caves arched with lava roofs, are a very few of the very many phenomena which the climber of a volcano encounters on his way. And at the top, broad, bowl-shaped craters, whose walls are sometimes many hundred feet deep, enclose, if the crater has long been dormant, sandy floors, from which, perhaps, small cinder cones arise. If the crater still is active, the adventurer's experiences are limited only by his daring.

The entire region, in short, strikingly differs from any other of scenic kind.

Of the several processes of world-making, all of which are progressing to-day at normal speed, none is so thrilling as volcanism, because no other concentrates action into terms of human grasp. Lassen

Peak's eruption of a thousand cubic yards of lava in a few hours thrills us more than the Mississippi's erosion of an average foot of her vast valley in a hundred thousand years; yet the latter is enormously the greater. The explosion of Mount Katmai, the rise and fall of Kilauea's boiling lava, the playing of Yellowstone's monster geysers, the spectacle of Mazama's lake-filled crater, the steaming of the Cascade's myriad bubbling springs, all make strong appeal to the imagination. They carry home the realization of mysterious, overwhelming power.

Lava is molten rock of excessively high temperature, which suddenly becomes released from the fearful pressures of earth's interior. Hurled from volcanic vents, or gushing from cracks in the earth's skin, it spreads rapidly over large neighborhoods, filling valleys and raising bulky rounded masses.

Often it is soft and frothy, like pumice. Even in its frequent glass forms, obsidian, for example, it easily disintegrates. There are as many kinds of lava as there are kinds of rock from which it is formed.

Volcanic scenery is by no means confined to what we call the volcanic national parks. Volcanoes were frequent in many parts of the continent. We meet their remnants unexpectedly among the granites of the Rockies and the Sierra, and the sedimentary rocks of the west and the southwest. Several of our national parks besides those prevailingly volcanic, and several of our most distinguished national monuments, exhibit interesting volcanic interludes.

VII

LASSEN PEAK AND MOUNT KATMAI

THE ONE A NATIONAL PARK IN NORTHERN CALIFORNIA,
THE OTHER A NATIONAL MONUMENT IN ALASKA

BECAUSE most of the conspicuous volcanic eruptions of our day have occurred in warmer climes
nearer the equator, we usually think of volcanoes as
tropical, or semi-tropical, phenomena. Vesuvius is in
the Mediterranean, Pelee in the Caribbean, Mauna
Loa and Kilauea on the Hawaiian Islands. Of course
there is Lassen Peak in California—the exception, as
we say, which proves the rule.

As a fact, many of the world's greatest volcanoes
are very far indeed from the tropics. Volcanoes result
from the movement of earth masses seeking equilib-
rium underneath earth's crust, but near enough to the
surface to enable molten rock under terrific pressure
to work upward from isolated pockets and break
through. Volcanoes occur in all latitudes. Even
Iceland has its great volcano. It is true that the volcano map shows them congregating thickly in a broad
band, of which the equator is the centre, but it also
shows them bordering the Pacific Coast from Pata-
gonia to Alaska, crossing the ocean through the Aleutian Islands, and extending far down the Asian coast.
It also shows many inland volcanoes, isolated and in
series. The distribution is exceedingly wide.

Volcanoes usually occur in belts which may or may not coincide with lines of weakening in the earth's crust below.   Hence the series of flaming torches of prehistoric days which, their fires now extinguished and their sides swathed in ice, have become in our day the row of spectacular peaks extending from northern California to Puget Sound.   Hence also the long range of threatening summits which skirts Alaska's southern shore, to-day the world's most active volcanic belt. Here it was that Katmai's summit was lost in the mighty explosion of June, 1912, one of enormous violence, which followed tremendous eruptions elsewhere along the same coast, and is expected to be followed by others, perhaps of even greater immensity and power.

These two volcanic belts contain each an active volcano which Congress has made the centre of a national reservation.   Lassen Peak, some wise men believe, is the last exhibit of activity in the dying volcanism of the Cascade Mountains.   Mount Katmai is the latest and greatest exhibit in a volcanic belt which is believed to be young and growing.

THE BUILDING OF THE CASCADES

Millions of years ago, in the period which geologists call Tertiary, the pressure under that part of the crust of the earth which now is Washington, Oregon, and northern California, became too powerful for solid rock to withstand.   Long lines of hills appeared parallel to the sea, and gradually rose hundreds, and perhaps thousands, of feet. These cracked, and from the long summit-fissures issued hot lava, which spread over enormous areas and, cooling, laid the foundations for the coming Cascade Mountains.

When the gaping fissures eased the pressure from beneath, they filled with ash and lava except at certain vent holes, around which grew the volcanoes which, when their usefulness as chimneys passed, became those cones of ice and snow which now are the glory of our northwest.

There may have been at one time many hundreds of these volcanoes, big and little. Most of them doubtless quickly perished under the growing slopes of their larger neighbors, and, as they became choked with ash, the lava which had been finding vent through them sought other doors of escape, and found them in the larger volcanoes. Thus, by natural selection, there survived at last that knightly company of monsters now uniformed in ice, which includes, from north to south, such celebrities as Mount Baker, Mount Rainier, Mount Adams, Mount St. Helens, Mount Hood, vanished Mount Mazama, Mount Shasta, and living Lassen Peak.

Whether or not several of these vast beacons lit Pacific's nights at one time can never be known with certainty, but probability makes the claim. Whether or not in their decline the canoes of prehistoric men found harbor by guidance of their pillars of fire by night, and their pillars of smoke by day is less probable but possible. One at least of the giant band,

Lassen Peak, is semi-active to-day. At least two others, Mount Rainier and Mount Baker, offer evidences of internal heat beneath their mail of ice. And early settlers in the northwest report Indian traditions of the awful cataclysm in which Mount Rainier lost two thousand feet of cone.

LASSEN PEAK NATIONAL PARK

Lassen Peak, the last of the Cascades in active eruption, rises between the northern end of the Sierra Nevada Mountains, of which it is locally but wrongly considered a part, and the Klamath Mountains, a spur of the Cascades. Actually it is the southern terminus of the Cascades.

Though quiet for more than two hundred years, the region long has enjoyed scientific and popular interest because it possesses hot springs, mud volcanoes and other minor volcanic phenomena, and particularly because its cones, which are easily climbed and studied, have remained very nearly perfect. Besides Lassen Peak, whose altitude is 10,437 feet, there are others of large size and great interest close by. Prospect Peak attains the altitude of 9,200 feet; Harkness Peak 9,000 feet; and Cinder Cone, a specimen of unusual beauty, 6,907 feet.

Because it seemed desirable to conserve the best two of these examples of recent volcanism, President Taft in 1906 created the Lassen Peak and the Cinder Cone National Monuments. Doubtless there would have been no change in the status of these reservations had not Lassen Peak broken its long sleep in the spring of 1914 with a series of eruptions covering a period of nineteen months. This centred attention upon the region, and in August, 1916, Congress created the Lassen Volcanic National Park, a reservation of a hundred and twenty-four square miles, which included both national monuments, other notable cones of the neighborhood, and practically all the hot springs and other lesser phenomena. Four months after the creation of the national park Lassen Peak ceased activity with its two hundred and twelfth eruption. It is not expected to resume. For some years, however, scientists will continue to class it as semi-active.

These eruptions, none of which produced any considerable lava flow, are regarded as probably the dying gasps of the volcanic energy of the Cascades. They began in May, 1914, with sharp explosions of steam and smoke from the summit crater. The news aroused wide-spread interest throughout the United States; it was the first volcanic eruption within the national boundaries. During the following summer there were thirty-eight slight similar eruptions, some of which scattered ashes in the neighborhood. The spectacle was one of magnificence because of the heavy columns of smoke. Eruptions increased in frequency with winter, fifty-six occurring during the balance of the year.

About the end of March, 1915, according to Doctor J. S. Diller of the United States Geological Survey,

From a photograph by J. S. Diller

LASSEN PEAK SEEN FROM THE SOUTHWEST

On the left is the material last erupted from the slope of the peak. It is called Chaos

From a photograph by J. S. Diller

LASSEN PEAK CLOSE UP

Showing the northeast slope as seen from Chaos

new lava had filled the crater and overflowed the west slope a thousand feet. On May 22 following occurred the greatest eruption of the series. A mushroom-shaped cloud of smoke burst four miles upward in air. The spectacle, one of grandeur, was plainly visible even from the Sacramento Valley. "At night," writes Doctor Diller, "flashes of light from the mountain summit, flying rocket-like bodies and cloud-glows over the crater reflecting the light from incandescent lavas below, were seen by many observers from various points of view, and appear to indicate that much of the material erupted was sufficiently hot to be luminous."

Another interesting phenomenon was the blast of superheated gas which swept down Lost Creek and Hot Creek Valleys. For ten miles it withered and destroyed every living thing in its path. Large trees were uprooted. Forests were scorched to a cinder. Snow-fields were instantly turned to water and flooded the lower valleys with rushing tides.

Later examination showed that this explosion had opened a new fissure, and that the old and new craters, now joined in one, were filled with a lava lid. Following this, the eruptions steadily declined in violence till their close the following December.

As a national park, though undeveloped and un-equipped as yet, Lassen has many charms besides its volcanic phenomena. Its western and southern slopes are thickly forested and possess fine lakes and streams. Several thousand persons, largely motorists, have visited it yearly of late. There are hot springs at Drakesbad, just within the southern border, which have local popularity as baths. The trout-fishing in lake and stream is excellent, and shooting is encouraged in the extensive national forest which surrounds the park, but not in the park itself, which is sanctuary. In spite of the hunting, deer are still found.

The greatest pleasure, however, will be found in exploring the volcanoes, from whose summits views are obtainable of many miles of this tumbled and splendidly forested part of California and of the dry plains of the Great Basin on its east.

The Katmai National Monument

We turn from the dying flutter of California's last remaining active volcano to the excessive violence of a volcano in the extremely active Alaskan coast range. The Mount Katmai National Monument will have few visitors because it is inaccessible by anything less than an exploring-party. We know it principally from the reports of four expeditions by the National Geographic Society. Informed by these reports, President Wilson created it a national monument in 1918.

A remarkable volcanic belt begins in southern Alaska at the head of Cook Inlet, and follows the coast in a broad southwesterly curve fifteen hundred miles long through the Alaskan Peninsula to the end of the Aleutian Islands, nearly enclosing Behring Sea. It is very ancient. Its mainland segment contains a dozen peaks, which are classed as active or latent, and its island segment many other volcanoes. St. Augustine's eruption in 1883 was one of extreme violence. Kugak was active in 1889. Veniaminof's eruption in 1892 ranked with St. Augustine's. Redoubt erupted in 1902, and Katmai, with excessive violence, in June, 1912. The entire belt is alive with volcanic excitement. Pavlof, at the peninsula's end, has been steaming for years, and several others are under expectant scientific observation. Katmai may be outdone at any time.

Katmai is a peak of 6,970 feet altitude, on treacherous Shelikof Strait, opposite Kodiak Island. It rises from an inhospitable shore far from steamer routes or other recognized lines of travel. Until it announced itself with a roar which was heard at Juneau, seven hundred and fifty miles away, its very existence was probably unknown except to a few prospectors, fishermen, geographers, and geologists. Earthquakes followed the blast, then followed night of smoke and dust. Darkness lasted sixty hours at Kodiak, a hundred miles away. Dust fell as far as Ketchikan, nine hundred miles away. Fumes were borne on the wind as far as Vancouver Island, fifteen hundred miles away. Weather Bureau reports noted haziness as far away as Virginia during succeeding weeks, and the extraordinary haziness in Europe during the following summer is noted by Doctor C. S. Abbott, Director of the Astrophysical Observatory of the Smithsonian Institution, in connection with this eruption.

Nevertheless, Katmai's is by no means the greatest volcanic eruption. Katmai's output of ash was about five cubic miles. Several eruptions have greatly exceeded that in bulk, notably that of Tomboro, in the island of Sumbawa, near Java, in 1815, when more than twenty-eight cubic miles of ash were flung to the winds. Comparison with many great eruptions whose output was principally lava is of course impossible.

The scene of this explosion is the national monument of to-day. The hollowed shell of Katmai's summit is a spectacle of wonderment and grandeur. Robert F. Griggs, who headed the expeditions which explored it, states that the area of the crater is 8.4 square miles, measured along the highest point of the rim. The abyss is 2.6 miles long, 7.6 miles in circumference, and 4.2 square miles in area. A lake has formed within it which is 1.4 miles long and ninetenths of a mile wide. Its depth is unknown. The precipice from the lake to the highest point of the rim measures thirty-seven hundred feet.

The most interesting exhibit of the Katmai National Monument, however, is a group of neighboring valleys just across the western divide, the principal one of which Mr. Griggs, with picturesque inaccuracy, named the "Valley of Ten Thousand Smokes"; for, from its floor and sides and the floors and sides of smaller tributary valleys, superheated steam issues in thousands of hissing columns. It is an appalling spectacle. The temperatures of this steam are extremely high; Griggs reports one instance of 432 degrees Centigrade, which would equal 948 degrees Fahrenheit; in some vents he found a higher temperature at the surface than a few feet down its throat. The very ground is hot.

This phenomenal valley is not to be fully explained offhand; as Griggs says, there are many problems to work out. The steam vents appear to be very recent. They did not exist when Spurr crossed the valley in 1898, and Martin heard nothing of them when he was in the near neighborhood in 1903 and 1904. The same volcanic impulse which found its main relief in the explosive eruption of near-by Katmai in 1912 no doubt cracked the deep-lying rocks beneath this group of valleys, exposing super-heated rocks to subterranean waters which forthwith turned to steam and forced these vents for escape. Griggs reports that volcanic gases mingle freely with the steam.

The waters may have one or more of several sources; perhaps they come from deep springs originating in surface snows and rains; perhaps they seep in from the sea. Whatever their origin the region especially interests us as a probably early stage of phenomena whose later stages find conspicuous examples in several of our national parks. Some day, with the cooling of the region, this may become the valley of ten thousand hot springs.

But it is useful and within scientific probability to carry this conception much further. The comparison between Katmai's steaming valleys and the geyser basin of Yellowstone is especially instructive because Yellowstone's basins doubtless once were what Katmai's steaming valleys are now. The "Valley of Ten Thousand Smokes" may well be a coming geyser-field of enormous size. The explanation is simple. Bunsen's geyser theory, now generally accepted, presupposes a column of water filling the geyser vent above a deep rocky superheated chamber, in which entering water is being rapidly turned into steam. When this steam becomes plentiful enough and sufficiently compressed to overcome the weight of the water in the vent, it suddenly expands and hurls the water out. That is what makes the geyser play.

Now one difference between the Yellowstone geyser-fields and Katmai's steaming valleys is just a difference in temperature. The entire depth of earth under these valleys is heated far above boiling-point, so that it is not possible for water to remain in the vents; it turns to steam as fast as it collects and rushes out at the top in continuous flow. But when enough thousands of centuries elapse for the rocks between the surface and the deep internal pockets to cool, the water will remain in many vents as water until, at regular intervals, enough steam gathers below to hurl it out. Then these valleys will become basins of geysers and hot springs like Yellowstone's.

VIII

MOUNT RAINIER, ICY OCTOPUS

I

MOUNT RAINIER, the loftiest volcano within the boundaries of the United States, one of our greatest mountains, and certainly our most imposing mountain, rises from western central Washington to an altitude of 14,408 feet above mean tide in Puget Sound. It is forty-two miles in direct line from the centre of Tacoma, and fifty-seven miles from Seattle, from both of which its glistening peak is often a prominent spectacle. With favoring atmospheric conditions it can be seen a hundred and fifty miles away.

North and south of Rainier, the Cascade Mountains bear other snow-capped volcanic peaks. Baker rises 10,703 feet; Adams, 12,307 feet; St. Helens, 9,697 feet; Hood, 11,225 feet, and Shasta, 14,162 feet. But Rainier surpasses them all in height, bulk, and majesty. Once it stood 16,000 feet, as is indicated by the slopes leading up to its broken and flattened top. The supposition is that nearly two thousand feet of its apex were carried away in one or more explosive eruptions long before history, but possibly not before man; there are Indian traditions of a cataclysm. There were slight eruptions in 1843, 1854, 1858, and 1870, and from the two craters at its summit issue many jets of steam which comfort the chilled climber.

This immense sleeping cone is blanketed in ice. Twenty-eight well-defined glaciers flow down its sides, several of which are nearly six miles long. Imagining ourselves looking down from an airplane at a great height, we can think of seeing it as an enormous frozen octopus sprawling upon the grass, for its curving arms of ice, reaching out in all directions, penetrate one of the finest forests even of our northwest. The contrast between these cold glaciers and the luxuriantly wild-flowered and forest-edged meadows which border them as snugly as so many rippling summer rivers affords one of the most delightful features of the Mount Rainier National Park. Paradise Inn, for example, stands in a meadow of wild flowers between Rainier's icy front on the one side and the snowy Tatoosh Range on the other, with the Nisqually Glacier fifteen minutes' walk away!

The casual tourist who has looked at the Snowy Range of the Rockies from the distant comfort of Estes Park, or the High Sierra from the dining-porch of the Glacier Point Hotel, receives an invigorating shock of astonishment at beholding Mount Rainier even at a distance. Its isolation gives it enormous scenic advantage. Mount Whitney of the Sierra, our loftiest summit, which overtops it ninety-three feet, is merely the climax in a tempestuous ocean of snowy neighbors which are only less lofty; Rainier towers nearly eight thousand feet above its surrounding mountains. It springs so powerfully into the air that one involuntarily looks for signs of life and action. But no smoke rises from its broken top. It is still and helpless, shackled in bonds of ice. Will it remain bound? Or will it, with due warning, destroy in a day the elaborate system of glaciers which countless centuries have built, and leave a new and different, and perhaps, after years of glacial recovery, even a more gloriously beautiful Mount Rainier than now?

The extraordinary individuality of the American national parks, their difference, each from every other, is nowhere more marked than here. Single-peaked glacial systems of the size of Rainier's, of course, are found wherever mountains of great size rise in close masses far above the line of perpetual snow. The Alaskan Range and the Himalayas may possess many. But if there is anywhere another mountain of approximate height and magnitude, carrying an approximate glacier system, which rises eight thousand feet higher than its neighbors out of a parkland of lakes, forests, and wild-flower gardens, which Nature seems to have made especially for pleasuring, and the heart of which is reached in four hours from a large city situated upon transatlantic railway-lines, I have not heard of it.

Seen a hundred miles away, or from the streets of Seattle and Tacoma, or from the motor-road approaching the park, or from the park itself, or from any of the many interglacier valleys, one never gets used to the spectacle of Rainier. The shock of surprise, the instant sense of impossibility, ever repeats itself. The mountain assumes a thousand aspects which change with the hours, with the position of the beholder, and with atmospheric conditions. Sometimes it is fairy-like, sometimes threatening, always majestic. One is not surprised at the Indian's fear. Often Rainier withdraws his presence altogether behind the horizon mists; even a few miles away no hint betrays his existence. And very often, shrouded in snow-storm or cloud, he is lost to those at his foot.

Mysterious and compelling is this ghostly mountain to us who see it for the first time, unable to look long away while it remains in view. It is the same, old Washingtonians tell me, with those who have kept watching it every day of visibility for many years. And so it was to Captain George Vancouver when, first of white men, he looked upon it from the bridge of the *Discovery* on May 8, 1792.

"The weather was serene and pleasant," he wrote under that date, "and the country continued to exhibit, between us and the eastern snowy range, the same luxuriant appearance. At its eastern extremity, mount Baker bore by compass N. 22 E.; the round snowy mountain, now forming its southern extremity, and which, after my friend Rear Admiral Rainier, I distinguished by the name of MOUNT RAINIER, bore N. (S.) 42 E."

Thus Mount Rainier was discovered and named at the same time, presumably on the same day.

SOUTHEAST SLOPE OF MOUNT RAINIER

The winding glacier is the Cowlitz.   Gibraltar is the rock on the right near the summit

Eighteen days later, having followed "the inlet," meaning Puget Sound, to his point of nearest approach to the mountain, Vancouver wrote:

"We found the inlet to terminate here in an extensive circular compact bay whose waters washed the base of mount Rainier, though its elevated summit was yet at a very considerable distance from the shore, with which it was connected by several ridges of hills rising towards it with gradual ascent and much regularity. The forest trees and the several shades of verdure that covered the hills gradually decreased in point of beauty until they became invisible; when the perpetual clothing of snow commenced which seemed to form a horizontal line from north to south along this range of rugged mountains, from whose summit mount Rainier rose conspicuously, and seemed as much elevated above them as they were above the level of the sea; the whole producing a most grand, picturesque effect."

Vancouver made no attempt to reach the mountain. Dreamer of great dreams though he was, how like a madhouse nightmare would have seemed to him a true prophecy of mighty engines whose like no human mind had then conceived, running upon roads of steel and asphalt at speeds which no human mind had then imagined, whirling thousands upon thousands of pleasure-seekers from the shores of that very inlet to the glistening mountain's flowered sides!

Just one century after the discovery, the Geological Society of America started the movement to make

Mount Rainier a national park. Within a year the American Association for the Advancement of Science, the National Geographic Society, the Appalachian Mountain Club, and the Sierra Club joined in the memorialization of Congress. Six years later, in 1899, the park was created.

II

The principal entrance to the park is up the Nisqually River at the south. Here entered the pioneer, James Longmire, many years ago, and the roads established by him and his fellows determined the direction of the first national-park development. Longmire Springs, for many years the nearest resort to the great mountain, lies just within the southern boundary. Beyond it the road follows the Nisqually and Paradise valleys, under glorious groves of pine, cedar, and hemlock, along ravines of striking beauty, past waterfalls and the snout of the Nisqually Glacier, finally to inimitable Paradise Park, its inn, its hotel camp, and its public camping-grounds. Other centres of wilderness life have been since established, and the marvellous north side of the park will be opened by the construction of a northwesterly highway up the valley of the Carbon River; already a fine trail entirely around the mountain connects these various points of development.

But the southern entrance and Paradise Park will remain for many years the principal centre of exploration and pleasuring. Here begins the popular trail to the summit. Here begin the trails to many of the finest view-points, the best-known falls, the most accessible of the many exquisite interglacier gardens. Here the Nisqually Glacier is reached in a few minutes' walk at a point particularly adapted for ice-climbing, and the comfortable viewing of ice-falls, crevasses, caves, and other glacier phenomena grandly exhibited in fullest beauty. It is a spot which can have in the nature of things few equals elsewhere in scenic variety and grandeur. On one side is the vast glistening mountain; on the other side the high serrated Tatoosh Range spattered with perpetual snow; in middle distance, details of long winding glaciers seamed with crevasses; in the foreground gorgeous rolling meadows of wild flowers dotted and bordered with equally luxuriant and richly varied forest groves; from close-by elevations, a gorgeous tumbled wilderness of hills, canyons, rivers, lakes, and falls backgrounded by the Cascades and accented by distant snowy peaks; the whole pervaded by the ever-present mountain, always the same yet grandly different, from different points of view, in the detail of its glaciered sides.

The variety of pleasuring is similarly very large. One can ride horseback round the mountain in a leisurely week, or spend a month or more exploring the greater wilderness of the park. One can tramp the trails on long trips, camping by the way, or vary a vacation with numerous short tramps. Or one can loaf away the days in dreamy content, with now and then a walk, and now and then a ride. Or one can

explore glaciers and climb minor mountains; the
Tatoosh Range alone will furnish the stiffest as well
as the most delightful climbing, with wonderful rewards upon the jagged summits; while short climbs to
points upon near-by snow-fields will afford coasting
without sleds, an exciting sport, especially appreciated
when one is young. In July, before the valley snows
melt away, there is tobogganing and skiing within a
short walk of the Inn.

The leisurely tour afoot around the mountain,
with pack-train following the trail, is an experience
never to be forgotten. One passes the snouts of a
score of glaciers, each producing its river, and sees the
mountain from every angle, besides having a continuous panorama of the surrounding country, including
Mount Adams, Mount St. Helens, Mount Baker,
Tacoma, Seattle, Mount Olympus, the Pacific Ocean,
and the Cascades from the Columbia to the interna-
tional line. Shorter excursions to other beautiful park-
lands offer a wide variety of pleasure. Indian Henry's
Hunting Ground, Van Trump Park, Summerland, and
others provide charm and beauty as well as fascinating
changes in the aspect of the great mountain.

Of course the ascent of the mountain is the ultimate objective of the climber, but few, comparatively,
will attempt it. It is a feat in endurance which not
many are physically fit to undertake, while to the un-
fit there are no rewards. There is comparatively little
rock-climbing, but what there is will try wind and mus-
cle. Most of the way is tramping up long snow-covered

MOUNT ST. HELENS SEEN FROM MOUNT RAINIER PARK

MOUNT ADAMS SEEN FROM MOUNT RAINIER PARK

and ice-covered slopes, with little rest from the start at midnight to the return, if all goes well, before the following sundown. Face and hands are painted to protect against sunburn, and colored glasses avert snow-blindness. Success is so largely a matter of physical condition that many ambitious tourists are advised to practise awhile on the Tatoosh Range before attempting the trip.

"Do you see Pinnacle Peak up there?" they ask you. "If you can make that you can make Rainier. Better try it first."

And many who try Pinnacle Peak do not make it.

As with every very lofty mountain the view from the summit depends upon the conditions of the moment. Often Rainier's summit is lost in mists and clouds, and there is no view. Very often on the clearest day clouds continually gather and dissipate; one is lucky in the particular time he is on top. Frequently there are partial views. Occasionally every condition favors, and then indeed the reward is great. S. F. Emmons, who made the second ascent, and after whom one of Rainier's greatest glaciers was named, stood on the summit upon one of those fortunate moments. The entire mountain in all its inspiring detail lay at his feet, a wonder spectacle of first magnitude.

"Looking to the more distant country," he wrote, "the whole stretch of Puget Sound, seeming like a pretty little lake embowered in green, could be seen in the northwest, beyond which the Olympic Mountains extend out into the Pacific Ocean. The Cascade

Mountains, lying dwarfed at our feet, could be traced northward into British Columbia and southward into Oregon, while above them, at comparatively regular intervals, rose the ghostlike forms of our companion volcanoes. To the eastward the eye ranged over hundreds of miles, over chain on chain of mountain ridges which gradually disappeared in the dim blue distance."

Notwithstanding the rigors of the ascent parties leave Paradise Inn for the summit every suitable day. Hundreds make the ascent each summer. To the experienced mountain-climber it presents no special difficulties. To the inexperienced it is an extraordinary adventure. Certainly no one knows his Mount Rainier who has not measured its gigantic proportions in units of his own endurance.

The first successful ascent was made by General Hazard Stevens and P. B. Van Trump, both residents of Washington, on August 17, 1870. Starting from James Longmire's with Mr. Longmire himself as guide up the Nisqually Valley, they spent several days in finding the Indian Sluiskin, who should take them to the summit. With him, then, assuming Longmire's place, Stevens and Van Trump started on their great adventure. It proved more of an adventure than they anticipated, for not far below the picturesque falls which they named after Sluiskin, the Indian stopped and begged them to go no farther. From that compilation of scholarly worth, by Professor Edmond S. Meany, President of the Mountaineers, entitled

"Mount Rainier, a Record of Exploration," I quote General Stevens's translation of Sluiskin's protest:

"Listen to me, my good friends," said Sluiskin, "I must talk with you.

"Your plan to climb Takhoma is all foolishness. No one can do it and live. A mighty chief dwells upon the summit in a lake of fire. He brooks no intruders.

"Many years ago my grandfather, the greatest and bravest chief of all the Yakima, climbed nearly to the summit. There he caught sight of the fiery lake and the infernal demon coming to destroy him, and fled down the mountain, glad to escape with his life. Where he failed, no other Indian ever dared make the attempt.

"At first the way is easy, the task seems light. The broad snow-fields over which I have often hunted the mountain-goat offer an inviting path. But above them you will have to climb over steep rocks over-hanging deep gorges, where a misstep would hurl you far down—down to certain death. You must creep over steep snow-banks and cross deep crevasses where a mountain-goat would hardly keep his footing. You must climb along steep cliffs where rocks are continu-ally falling to crush you or knock you off into the bot-tomless depths.

"And if you should escape these perils and reach the great snowy dome, then a bitterly cold and furious tempest will sweep you off into space like a withered leaf. But if by some miracle you should survive all these perils, the mighty demon of Takhoma will surely kill you and throw you into the fiery lake.

"Don't you go. You make my heart sick when you talk of climbing Takhoma. You will perish if you try to climb Takhoma. You will perish and your people will blame me.

"Don't go! Don't go! If you go I will wait here two days and then go to Olympia and tell your people that you perished on Takhoma. Give me a paper to them to let them know that I am not to blame for your death. My talk is ended."

Except for the demon and his lake of fire, Sluiskin's portent of hardship proved to be a literal, even a modest, prophecy. At five o'clock in the evening, after eleven hours of struggle with precipices and glaciers, exhausted, chilled, and without food, they faced a night of zero gales upon the summit. The discovery of comforting steam-jets in a neighboring crater, the reality perhaps of Sluiskin's lake of fire, made the night livable, though one of suffering. It was afternoon of the following day before they reached camp and found an astonished Sluiskin, then, in fact, on the point of leaving to report their unfortunate destruction.

Stevens and Van Trump were doubly pioneers, for their way up the mountain is, in general direction at least, the popular way to-day, greatly bettered since, however, by the short cuts and easier detours which have followed upon experience.

III

Our four volcanic national parks exemplify four states of volcanic history. Lassen Peak is semiactive; Mount Rainier is dormant; Yellowstone is dead, and Crater Lake marks the spot through which a volcano collapsed and disappeared. Rainier's usefulness as a volcanic example, however, is lost in its supreme usefulness as a glacial exhibit. The student of glaciers who begins here with the glacier in action, and then studies the effects of glaciers upon igneous rocks among the cirques of the Sierra, and upon sedimentary rocks in the Glacier National Park, will study the masters; which, by the way, is a tip for universities contemplating summer field-classes.

Upon the truncated top of Mount Rainier, nearly three miles in diameter, rise two small cinder cones which form, at the junction of their craters, the mountain's rounded snow-covered summit. It is known as Columbia Crest. As this only rises four hundred feet above the older containing crater, it is not always identified from below as the highest point. Two commanding rocky elevations of the old rim, Point Success on its southwest side, 14,150 feet, and Liberty Cap on its northwest side, 14,112 feet, appear to be, from the mountain's foot, its points of greatest altitude.

Rainier's top, though covered with snow and ice, except in spots bared by internal heat, is not the source of its glaciers, although its extensive ice-fields flow into and feed several of them. The glaciers themselves, even those continuous with the summit ice, really originate about four thousand feet below the top in cirques or pockets which are principally fed with the tremendous snows of winter, and the wind sweepings and avalanches from the summit. The Pacific winds are charged heavily with moisture which descends upon Rainier in snows of great depth. Even Paradise Park is snowed under from twelve to thirty feet. There is a photograph of a ranger cabin in February which shows only a slight snow-mound with a hole in its top which locates the hidden chimney. F. E. Matthes, the geologist, tells of a snow level of fifty feet depth in Indian Henry's Hunting Ground, one of Rainier's most beautiful parks, in which the wind had sunk a crater-like hollow from the bottom of which emerged a chimney. These snows replenish the glaciers, which have a combined surface of forty-five square miles, along their entire length, in addition to making enormous accumulations in the cirques.

Beginning then in its cirque, as a river often begins in its lake, the glacier flows downward, river-like, along a course of least resistance. Here it pours over a precipice in broken falls to flatten out in perfect texture in the even stretch below. Here it plunges down rapids, breaking into crevasses as the river in corresponding phase breaks into ripples. Here it rises smoothly over rocks upon its bottom. Here it strikes against a wall of rock and turns sharply. The parallel

SLUISKIN RIDGE AND COLUMBIA CREST

From a photograph copyright by A. H. Barnes

MOUNT RAINIER SEEN FROM TACOMA

between the glacier and the river is striking and consistent, notwithstanding that the geologist for technical reasons will quarrel with you if you picturesquely
call your glacier a river of ice. Any elevated view-
point will disclose several or many of these mighty
streams flowing in snake-like curves down the moun-
tainside, the greater streams swollen here and there
by tributaries as rivers are swollen by entering creeks.
And all eventually reach a point, determined by temperature and therefore not constant, where the river
of ice becomes the river of water.

Beginning white and pure, the glacier gradually
clothes itself in rock and dirt.   Gathering as it moves
narrow edges of matter filched from the shores, later
on it heaps these up upon its lower banks.   They are
lateral moraines. Two merging glaciers unite the
material carried on their joined edges and form a
medial moraine, a ribbon broadening and thickening
as it descends; a glacier made up of several tributaries
carries as many medial moraines. It also carries
much unorganized matter fallen from the cliffs or
scraped from the bottom. Approaching the snout, all
these accumulations merge into one moraine; and so
soiled has the ice now become that it is difficult to tell
which is ice and which is rock.   At its snout is an ice-
cave far inside of which the resultant river originates.

But the glacier has one very important function
which the river does not share. Far up at its beginnings it freezes to the back wall of its cirque, and,

moving forward, pulls out, or plucks out, as the geologists have it, masses of rock which it carries away in its current. The resulting cavities in the back of the cirque fill with ice, which in its turn freezes fast and plucks out more rock. And presently the back wall of the cirque, undermined, falls on the ice and also is carried away. There is left a precipice, often sheerly perpendicular; and, as the process repeats itself, this precipice moves backward. At the beginning of this process, it must be understood, the glacier lies upon a tilted surface far more elevated than now when you see it in its old age, sunk deep in its self-dug trench; and, while it is plucking backward and breaking off an ever-increasing precipice above it, it is plucking downward, too. If the rock is even in structure, this downward cutting may be very nearly perpendicular, but if the rock lies in strata of varying hardness, shelves form where the harder strata are encountered because it takes longer to cut them through; in this way are formed the long series of steps which we often see in empty glacial cirques.

By this process of backward and downward plucking, the Carbon Glacier bit its way into the north side of the great volcano until it invaded the very foundations of the summit and created the Willis Wall which drops avalanches thirty-six hundred feet to the glacier below. Willis Wall is nearly perpendicular because the lava rock at this point was homogeneous. But in the alternating shale and limestone strata of Glacier National Park, on the other hand, the glaciers of old

MOUNT RAINIER AND PARADISE INN IN SUMMER

WINTER PLEASURES AT PARADISE INN, MOUNT RAINIER

dug cirques of many shelves. The monster ice-streams which dug Glacier's mighty valleys have vanished, but often tiny remainders are still seen upon the cirques' topmost shelves.

So we see that the glacier acquires its cargo of rock not only by scraping its sides and plucking it from the bottom of its cirque and valley, but by quarrying backward till undermined material drops upon it; all of this in fulfilment of Nature's purpose of wearing down the highlands for the upbuilding of the hollows.

This is not the place for a detailed description of Mount Rainier's twenty-eight glaciers. A glance at the map will tell something of the story. Extending northeasterly from the summit will be seen the greatest unbroken glacial mass. Here are the Emmons and the Winthrop Glaciers, much the largest of all. This is the quarter farthest from the sun, upon which its rays strike at the flattest angle. The melting then is least here. But still a more potent reason for their larger mass is found in their position on the lee quarter of the peak, the prevailing winds whirling in the snow from both sides.

The greater diversification of the other sides of the mountain with extruding cliffs, cleavers, and enormous rock masses tends strongly to scenic variety and grandeur. Some of the rock cleavers which divide glaciers stand several thousand feet in height, veritable fences. Some of the cliffs would be mountains of no mean size elsewhere, and around their sides pour mighty glacial currents, cascading to the depths below where again they may meet and even merge.

The Nisqually Glacier naturally is the most celebrated, not because of scenic superiority, but because it is the neighbor and the playground of the visiting thousands. Its perfect and wonderful beauty are not in excess of many others; and it is much smaller than many. The Cowlitz Glacier near by exceeds it in size, and is one of the stateliest; it springs from a cirque below Gibraltar, a massive near-summit rock, whose well-deserved celebrity is due in some part to its nearness to the travelled summit trail. The point I am making is not in depreciation of any of the celebrated sights from the southern side, but in emphasis of the fact that a hundred other sights would be as celebrated, or more celebrated, were they as well known. The Mount Rainier National Park at this writing is replete with splendors which are yet to be discovered by the greater travelling public.

The great north side, for instance, with its mighty walls, its magnificently scenic glaciers, its lakes, canyons, and enormous areas of flowered and forested pleasure-grounds, is destined to wide development; it is a national park in itself. Already roads enter to camps at the foot of great glaciers. The west side, also, with its four spectacular glaciers which pass under the names of Mowich and Tahoma, attains sublimity; it remains also for future occupation.

Many of the minor phenomena, while common also to other areas of snow and ice, have fascination for the visitor. Snow-cups are always objects of interest and beauty. Instead of reducing a snow surface evenly, the warm sun sometimes melts it in patterned cups set close together like the squares of a checker-board. These deepen gradually till they suggest a gigantic honeycomb, whose cells are sometimes several feet deep. In one of these, one summer day in the Sierra, I saw a stumbling horse deposit his rider, a high official of one of our Western railroads; and there he sat helpless, hands and feet emerging from the top, until we recovered enough from laughter to help him out.

Pink snow always arouses lively interest. A microscopic plant, Protococcus nivalis, growing in occasional patches beneath the surface of old snow gradually emerges with a pink glow which sometimes covers acres. On the tongue its flavor suggests watermelon. No doubt many other microscopic plants thrive in the snow-fields and glaciers which remain invisible for lack of color. Insects also inhabit these glaciers. There are several Thysanura, which suggest the sand-fleas of our seashores, but are seldom noticed because of their small size. More noticeable are the Mesenchytræus, a slender brown worm, which attains the length of an inch. They may be seen in great numbers on the lower glaciers in the summer, but on warm days retreat well under the surface.

IV

The extraordinary forest luxuriance at the base of Mount Rainier is due to moisture and climate. The same heavy snowfalls which feed the glaciers store up water-supplies for forest and meadow. The winters at the base of the mountain are mild.

The lower valleys are covered with a dense growth of fir, hemlock, and cedar. Pushing skyward in competition for the sunlight, trees attain great heights. Protected from winter's severity by the thickness of the growth, and from fire by the dampness of the soil, great age is assured, which means thick and heavy trunks. The Douglas fir, easily the most important timber-tree of western America, here reaches its two hundred feet in massive forests, while occasional individuals grow two hundred and fifty to two hundred and seventy feet with a diameter of eight feet. The bark at the base of these monsters is sometimes ten inches thick. The western hemlock also reaches equal heights in competition for the light, with diameters of five feet or more. Red cedar, white pines of several varieties, several firs, and a variety of hemlocks complete the list of conifers. Deciduous trees are few and not important. Broad-leaved maples, cottonwoods, and alders are the principal species.

Higher up the mountain-slopes the forests thin and lessen in size, while increasing in picturesqueness. The Douglas fir and other monsters of the lower levels disappear, their places taken by other species. At an altitude of four thousand feet the Englemann spruce and other mountain-trees begin to appear, not in the massed ranks of the lower levels, but in groves bordering the flowered opens.

The extreme limit of tree growth on Mount Rainier is about seven thousand feet of altitude, above which one finds only occasional distorted, wind-tortured mountain-hemlocks. There is no well-defined timber-line, as on other lofty mountains. Avalanches and snow-slides keep the upper levels swept and bare.

The wild-flower catalogue is too long to enumerate here. John Muir expresses the belief that no other subalpine floral gardens excel Rainier's in profusion and gorgeousness. The region differs little from other Pacific regions of similar altitude in variety of species; in luxuriance it is unsurpassed.

V

According to Theodore Winthrop who visited the northwest in 1853 and published a book entitled "The Canoe and the Saddle," which had wide vogue at the time and is consulted to-day, Mount Rainier had its Indian Rip Van Winkle. The story was told him in great detail by Hamitchou, "a frowsy ancient of the Squallyamish." The hero was a wise and wily fisherman and hunter. Also, as his passion was gain, he became an excellent business man. He always had salmon and berries when food became scarce and prices high. Gradually he amassed large savings in hiaqua, the little perforated shell which was the most valued form of wampum, the Indian's money. The richer he got the stronger his passion grew for hiaqua, and, when a spirit told him in a dream of vast hoards at the summit of Rainier, he determined to climb the mountain. The spirit was Tamanoüs, which, Winthrop explains, is the vague Indian personification of the supernatural.

So he threaded the forests and climbed the mountain's glistening side. At the summit he looked over the rim into a large basin in the bottom of which was a black lake surrounded by purple rock. At the lake's eastern end stood three monuments. The first was as tall as a man and had a head carved like a salmon; the second was the image of a camas-bulb; the two represented the great necessities of Indian life. The third was a stone elk's head with the antlers in velvet. At the foot of this monument he dug a hole.

Suddenly a noise behind him caused him to turn. An otter clambered over the edge of the lake and struck the snow with its tail. Eleven others followed. Each was twice as big as any otter he had ever seen; their chief was four times as big. The eleven sat themselves in a circle around him; the leader climbed upon the stone elk-head.

At first the treasure-seeker was abashed, but he had come to find hiaqua and he went on digging. At every thirteenth stroke the leader of the otters tapped the stone elk with his tail, and the eleven followers tapped the snow with their tails. Once they all gathered closer and whacked the digger good and hard with their tails, but, though astonished and badly bruised, he went on working. Presently he broke his elkhorn pick, but the biggest otter seized another in his teeth and handed it to him.

Finally his pick struck a flat rock with a hollow sound, and the otters all drew near and gazed into the hole, breathing excitedly. He lifted the rock and under it found a cavity filled to the brim with pure-white hiaqua, every shell large, unbroken and beautiful. All were hung neatly on strings.

Never was treasure-quest so successful! The otters, recognizing him as the favorite of Tamanoüs, retired to a distance and gazed upon him respectfully.

"But the miser," writes the narrator, "never dreamed of gratitude, never thought to hang a string from the buried treasure about the salmon and kamas tamanoüs stones, and two strings around the elk's head; no, all must be his own, all he could carry now, and the rest for the future."

Greedily he loaded himself with the booty and laboriously climbed to the rim of the bowl prepared for the descent of the mountain. The otters, puffing in concert, plunged again into the lake, which at once disappeared under a black cloud.

Straightway a terrible storm arose through which the voice of Tamanoüs screamed tauntingly. Blackness closed around him. The din was horrible. Terrified, he threw back into the bowl behind him five strings of hiaqua to propitiate Tamanoüs, and there followed a momentary lull, during which he started homeward. But immediately the storm burst again with roarings like ten thousand bears.

Nothing could be done but to throw back more hiaqua. Following each sacrifice came another lull, followed in turn by more terrible outbreaks. And so, string by string, he parted with all his gains. Then he sank to the ground insensible.

When he awoke he lay under an arbutus-tree in a meadow of camas. He was shockingly stiff and every movement pained him. But he managed to gather and smoke some dry arbutus-leaves and eat a few camas-bulbs. He was astonished to find his hair very long and matted, and himself bent and feeble. "Tamanoüs," he muttered. Nevertheless, he was calm and happy. Strangely, he did not regret his lost strings of hiaqua. Fear was gone and his heart was filled with love.

Slowly and painfully he made his way home. Everything was strangely altered. Ancient trees grew where shrubs had grown four days before. Cedars under whose shade he used to sleep lay rotting on the ground. Where his lodge had stood now he saw a new and handsome lodge, and presently out of it came a very old decrepit squaw who, nevertheless, through her wrinkles, had a look that seemed strangely familiar to him. Her shoulders were hung thick with hiaqua strings. She bent over a pot of boiling salmon and crooned:

"My old man has gone, gone, gone.
My old man to Tacoma has gone.
To hunt the elk he went long ago.
When will he come down, down, down
To salmon pot and me?"

"He has come down," quavered the returned traveller, at last recognizing his wife.

He asked no questions. Charging it all to the wrath of Tamanoüs, he accepted fate as he found it. After all, it was a happy fate enough in the end, for the old man became the Great Medicine-Man of his tribe, by whom he was greatly revered.

The name of this Rip Van Winkle of Mount Rainier is not mentioned in Mr. Winthrop's narrative.

IX

CRATER LAKE'S BOWL OF INDIGO

Crater Lake National Park, Southwestern Oregon.
Area, 249 Square Miles

CRATER LAKE is in southwestern Oregon
among the Cascade Mountains, and is reached
by an automobile ride of several hours from Medford.
The government information circular calls it "the
deepest and bluest lake in the world." Advertising
circulars praise it in choicest professional phrase.
Its beauty is described as exceeding that of any other
lake in all the world. Never was blue so wonderful
as the blue of these waters; never were waters so deep
as its two thousand feet.

Lured by this eloquence the traveller goes to Crater
Lake and finds it all as promised—in fact, far better
than promised, for the best intended adjectives, even
when winged by the energetic pen of the most talented
ad writer, cannot begin to convey the glowing, changing, mysterious loveliness of this lake of unbelievable
beauty. In fact, the tourist, with expectation at fever-
heat by the time he steps from the auto-stage upon
the crater rim, is silenced as much by astonishment
as by admiration.

Before him lies a crater of pale pearly lava several
miles in diameter. A thousand feet below its rim is a
lake whose farthest blues vie in delicacy with the

horizon lavas, and deepen as they approach till at his feet they turn to almost black. There is nothing with which to compare the near-by blue looked sharply down upon from Crater's rim. The deepest indigo is nearest its intensity, but at certain angles falls far short.

Nor is it only the color which affects him so strongly; its kind is something new, startling, and altogether lovely. Its surface, so magically framed and tinted, is broken by fleeting silver wind-streaks here and there; otherwise, it has the vast stillness which we associate with the Grand Canyon and the sky at night. The lava walls are pearly, faintly blue afar off, graying and daubed with many colors nearer by. Pinks, purples, brick-reds, sulphurs, orange-yellows and many intermediates streak and splash the foreground gray. And often pine-green forests fringe the rim, and funnel down sharply tilted canyons to the water's edge; and sometimes shrubs of livelier green find foothold on the gentler slopes, and, spreading, paint bright patches. Over all, shutting down and around it like a giant bowl, is a sky of Californian blue overhead softening to the pearl of the horizon. A wonder spectacle indeed!

And then our tourist, recovering from his trance, walks upon the rim and descends the trail to the water's edge to join a launch-party around the lake. Here he finds a new and different experience which is quite as sensational as that of his original discovery. Seen close by from the lake's surface these tinted lava cliffs are carved as grotesquely as a Japanese ivory. Precipices rise at times two thousand feet, sheer as a wall. Elsewhere gentle slopes of powdery lava, moss-tinted, connect rim and water with a ruler line. And between these two extremes are found every fashion and kind and degree of lava wall, many of them pre-cipitous, most of them rugged, all of them contorted and carved in the most fantastic manner that imagina-tion can picture. Caves open their dark doors at water's edge. Towered rocks emerge from submerged reefs. A mimic volcano rises from the water near one side. Perpetual snow fills sheltered crevices in the southern rim.

And all this wonder is reflected, upside down, in the still mirror through which the launch ploughs its rapid way. But looking backward where the inverted picture is broken and tossed by the waves from the launch's prow, he looks upon a kaleidoscope of color which he will remember all his life; for, to the gorgeous disarray of the broken image of the cliffs is added the magic tint of this deep-dyed water, every wavelet of which, at its crest, seems touched for the fraction of a second with a flash of indigo; the whole dancing, spar-kling, shimmering in a glory which words cannot convey; and on the other side, and far astern, the subsiding waves calming back to normal in a flare of robin's-egg blue.

Our tourist returns to the rim-side hotel to the ceremony of sunset on Crater Lake, for which the lake abandons all traditions and clothes itself in gold and crimson. And in the morning after looking, before sunrise, upon a Crater Lake of hard-polished steel from which a falling rock would surely bounce and bound away as if on ice, he breakfasts and leaves without another look lest repetition dull his priceless memory of an emotional experience which, all in all, can never come again the same.

It is as impossible to describe Crater Lake as it is to paint it. Its outlines may be photographed, but the photograph does not tell the story. Its colors may be reproduced, but the reproduction is not Crater Lake. More than any other spot I know, except the Grand Canyon from its rim, Crater Lake seems to convey a glory which is not of line or mass or color or composition, but which seems to be of the spirit. No doubt this vivid impression which the stilled observer seems to acquire with his mortal eye, is born somehow of his own emotion. Somehow he finds himself in communion with the Infinite. Perhaps it is this quality which seems so mysterious that made the Klamath Indians fear and shun Crater Lake, just as the Indians of the great plateau feared and shunned the Grand Canyon. It is this intangible, seemingly spiritual quality which makes the lake impossible either to paint or to describe.

So different is this spectacle from anything else upon the continent that the first question asked usually is how it came to be. The answer discloses one of the most dramatic incidents in the history of the earth.

In the evolution of the Cascades, many have been the misadventures of volcanoes. Some have been buried alive in ash and lava, and merged into conquering rivals. Some have been buried in ice which now, organized as glaciers, is wearing down their sides. Some have died of starvation and passed into the hills. Some have been blown to atoms. Only one in America, so far as known, has returned into the seething gulf which gave it birth. That was Mount Mazama.

The processes of creation are too deliberate for human comprehension. The Mississippi takes five thousand years to lower one inch its valley's surface. The making of Glacier National Park required many—perhaps hundreds—of millions of years. It seems probable that the cataclysm in which Mount Mazama disappeared was exceptional; death may have come suddenly, even as expressed in human terms.

What happened seems to have been this. Some foundation underpinning gave way in the molten gulf below, and the vast mountain sank and disappeared within itself. Imagine the spectacle who can! Mount Mazama left a clean-cut rim surrounding the hole through which it slipped and vanished. But there was a surging back. The eruptive forces, rebounding, pushed the shapeless mass again up the vast chimney. They found it too heavy a load. Deep within the ash-choked vent burst three small craters, and that was all. Two of these probably were short-lived, the third lasted a little longer. And, centuries later, spring water seeped through, creating Crater Lake.

Crater Lake is set in the summit of the Cascade Range, about sixty-five miles north of the California boundary. The road from the railway-station at Medford leads eighty miles eastward up the picturesque volcanic valley of the Rogue River. The country is magnificently forested. The mountains at this point

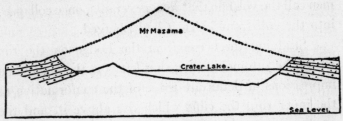

Mt Mazama

Crater Lake.

Sea Level.

CROSS-SECTION OF CRATER LAKE SHOWING PROBABLE OUTLINE OF MOUNT MAZAMA

are broad, gently rolling plateaus from which suddenly rise many volcanic cones, which, seen from elevated opens, are picturesque in the extreme. Each of these cones is the top of a volcano from whose summit has streamed the prehistoric floods of lava which have filled the intervening valleys, raising and levelling the country.

Entering the park, a high, broad, forested elevation is quickly encountered which looks at a glance exactly what it is, the base which once supported a towering cone. At its summit, this swelling base is found to be the outside supporting wall of a roughly circular lake, about five miles in diameter, the inside wall of which is steeply inclined to the water's surface a thousand feet below. The strong contrast between the outer and inner walls tells a plainly read story.

The outer walls, all around, slope gently upward at an angle of about fifteen degrees; naturally, if carried on, they would converge in a peaked summit higher than that of Shasta. The inner walls converge downward at a steep angle, suggesting a funnel of enormous depth. It was through this funnel that Mount Mazama, as men call the volcano that man never saw, once collapsed into the gulf from which it had emerged.

Studying the scene from the Lodge on the rim where the automobile-stage has left you, the most vivid impressions of detail are those of the conformation of the inner rim, the cliffs which rise above it, and the small volcano which emerges from the blue waters of the lake.

The marvellous inner slope of the rim is not a continuous cliff, but a highly diversified succession of strata. Examination shows the layers of volcanic conglomerate and lava of which, like layers of brick and stone, the great structure was built. The downward dip of these strata away from the lake is everywhere discernible. The volcano's early story thus lies plain to eyes trained to read it. The most interesting of these strata is the lava flow which forms twelve thousand feet of the total precipice of Llao Rock, a prominence of conspicuous beauty.

Many of these cliffs are magnificently bold. The loftiest is Glacier Peak, which rises almost two thousand feet above the water's surface. But Dutton Cliff is a close rival, and Vidæ Cliff, Garfield Peak, Llao Rock, and the Watchman fall close behind. Offsetting

From a photograph copyright by Scenic America Company

DUTTON CLIFF AND THE PHANTOM SHIP, CRATER LAKE

From a photograph copyright by Scenic America Company

SUNSET FROM GARFIELD PEAK, CRATER LAKE NATIONAL PARK

these are breaks where the rim drops within six hundred feet of the water. The statement of a wall height of a thousand feet expresses the general impression, though as an average it is probably well short of the fact.

At the foot of all the walls, at water's edge, lie slopes of talus, the rocky fragments which erosion has

CROSS-SECTION OF CRATER LAKE

broken loose and dropped into the abyss. Nowhere is there a beach. The talus shallows the water for a few hundred feet, and descending streams build small deltas. These shallows edge the intense blue of the depths with exquisite lighter tints which tend to green. But this edging is very narrow.

The next most striking object after the gigantic carven cliffs is Wizard Island. This complete volcano in miniature, notwithstanding that it is forest-clothed and rises from water, carries the traveller's mind instantly to the thirteen similar cones which rise within the enormous desert crater of dead Haleakala, in the Hawaii National Park. Wizard Island's crater may easily be seen in the tip of its cone. Its two fellow volcanoes are invisible four hundred feet under water.

Scanning the blue surface, one's eye is caught by an interesting sail-like rock rising from the waters on the far right close to the foot of Dutton Cliff. This is the Phantom Ship. Seen two miles away in certain lights the illusion is excellent. The masts seem to tilt rakishly and the sails shine in the sun. There are times when the Phantom Ship suddenly disappears, and times again when it as suddenly appears where nothing was before. Hence its name and mysterious repute. But there is nothing really mysterious about this ghostly behavior, which occurs only when the heated atmosphere lends itself readily to mirage.

Days and weeks of rare pleasure may be had in the exploration of these amazing walls, a pleasure greatly to be enhanced by discovering and studying the many plain evidences of Mazama's slow upbuilding and sudden extinction. The excellent automobile road around the rim affords easy approach afoot as well as by automobile and bicycle. Its passage is enlivened by many inspiring views of the outlying Cascades with their great forests of yellow pine and their lesser volcanic cones, some of which, within and without the park boundaries, hung upon the flanks of Mount Mazama while it was belching flame and ash, while others, easing the checked pressure following the great catastrophe, were formed anew or enlarged from older vents.

From this road any part of the fantastic rim may be reached and explored, often to the water's edge, by adventurous climbers. What more enjoyable day's outing, for instance, than the exploration of the splendid pile of pentagonal basaltic columns suspended halfway in the rim at one point of picturesque beauty? What more inspiring than the climbing of Dutton

Cliff, or, for experienced climbers, of many of the striking lava spires? The only drawback to these days of happy wandering along this sculptured and painted rim is the necessity of carrying drinking-water from the Lodge.

Then there are days of pleasure on the water. Wizard Island may be thoroughly explored, with luncheon under its trees by the lakeside. The Phantom Ship's gnarled lavas may be examined and climbed. Everywhere the steep rocky shore invites more intimate acquaintance; its caves may be entered, some afoot, at least one afloat. The lake is well stocked with rainbow trout, some of them descendants of the youngsters which Will G. Steel laboriously carried across country from Gordon's Ranch, forty-nine miles away, in 1888. They are caught with the fly from shore and boat. A pound trout in Crater Lake is a small trout. Occasionally a monster of eight or ten pounds is carried up the trail to the Lodge.

During all these days and weeks of pleasure and study, the vision of ancient Mount Mazama and its terrible end grows more and more in the enlightened imagination. There is much in the conformation of the base to justify a rather definite picture of this lost brother of Hood, Shasta, St. Helens, and Rainier. At the climax of his career, Mazama probably rose sixteen thousand feet above the sea, which means ten thousand feet above the level of the present lake. We are justified too in imagining his end a cataclysm. Volcanic upbuildings are often spasmodic and slow, a series of impulses separated by centuries of quiescence, but their climaxes often are sudden and excessively violent. It seems more probable that Mazama collapsed during violent eruption. Perhaps like a stroke of lightning at the moment of triumph, death came at the supreme climax of his career.

Certainly no mausoleum was ever conceived for human hero which may be compared for a moment with this glorified grave of dead Mazama!

The human history of Crater Lake has its interest. The Indians feared it. John W. Hillman was the first white man to see it. Early in 1853 a party of Californian miners ascended the Rogue River to rediscover a lost gold-mine of fabulous richness. The expedition was secret, but several Oregonians who suspected its object and meant to be in at the finding, quickly organized and followed. Hillman was of this party. The Californians soon learned of the pursuit.

"Then," wrote Hillman half a century later, "it was a game of hide and seek until rations on both sides got low. The Californians would push through the brush, scatter, double backward on their trail, and then camp in the most inaccessible places to be found, and it sometimes puzzled us to locate and camp near enough to watch them."

Eventually the rivals united. A combination search-party was chosen which included Hillman, and this party, while it found no gold-mine, found Crater Lake.

"While riding up a long sloping mountain," Hill-

PHANTOM SHIP FROM GARFIELD PEAK

APPLEGATE CLIFF, CRATER LAKE

man continued, "we suddenly came in sight of water and were very much surprised as we did not expect to see any lakes. We did not know but what we had come in sight and close to Klamath Lake, and not until my mule stopped within a few feet of the rim of Crater Lake did I look down, and if I had been riding a blind mule I firmly believe I would have ridden over the edge to death and destruction. . . .

"The finding of Crater Lake," he concludes, "was an accident, as we were not looking for lakes; but the fact of my being the first upon its banks was due to the fact that I was riding the best saddle mule in southern Oregon, the property of Jimmy Dobson, a miner and packer with headquarters at Jacksonville, who had furnished me the mule in consideration of a claim to be taken in his name should we be successful. Stranger to me than our discovery was the fact that after our return I could get no acknowledgment from any Indian, buck or squaw, old or young, that any such lake existed; each and every one denied any knowledge of it, or ignored the subject completely."

The next development in Crater's history introduces Will G. Steel, widely known as "the Father of Crater Lake National Park," a pioneer of the highest type, a gold-seeker in the coast ranges and the Klondike, a school-teacher for many years, and a public-spirited enthusiast. In 1869, a farmer's boy in Kansas, he read a newspaper account of an Oregon lake with precipice sides five thousand feet deep. Moving to Oregon in 1871, he kept making inquiries for seven years before he verified the fact of the lake's existence, and it was two years later before he found a man who had seen it. This man's description decided him to visit it, then an undertaking of some difficulty.

He got there in 1885. Standing on the rim he suggested to Professor Joseph Le Conte that an effort be made to induce the national government to save it from defacement and private exploitation. Returning home they prepared a petition to President Cleveland, who promptly withdrew ten townships from settlement pending a bill before Congress to create a national park. Congress refused to pass the bill on the ground that Oregon should protect her own lake. Then Steel began an effort, or rather an unbroken succession of efforts, to interest Congress. For seventeen years he agitated the project at home, where he made speeches winter and summer all over the State, and at Washington, which he deluged with letters and circulars. Finally the bill was passed. Crater Lake became a national park on May 22, 1902.

Mr. Steel's work was not finished. He now began just as vigorous a campaign to have the lake properly stocked with trout. It required years but succeeded. Then he began a campaign for funds to build a road to the lake. This was a stubborn struggle which carried him to Washington for a winter, but it finally succeeded.

During most of this time Mr. Steel was a country school-teacher without other personal income than his salary. He spent many of his summers talking Crater-Lake projects to audiences in every part of the State, depending upon his many friends for entertainment and for "lifts" from town to town. He was superintendent of the park from 1913 to the winter of 1920, when he became United States commissioner for the park.

The attitude of the Indians toward Crater Lake remains to be told. Steel is authority for the statement that previous to 1886 no modern Indian had looked upon its waters. Legends inherited from their ancestors made them greatly fear it. I quote O. C. Applegate's "Klamath Legend of La-o," from *Steel Points* for January, 1907:

"According to the mythology of the Klamath and Modoc Indians, the chief spirit who occupied the mystic land of Gaywas, or Crater Lake, was La-o. Under his control were many lesser spirits who appeared to be able to change their forms at will. Many of these were monsters of various kinds, among them the giant crawfish (or dragon) who could, if he chose, reach up his mighty arms even to the tops of the cliffs and drag down to the cold depths of Crater Lake any too venturesome tourist of the primal days.

"The spirits or beings who were under the control of La-o assumed the forms of many animals of the present day when they chose to go abroad on dry land, and this was no less true of the other fabulous inhabitants of Klamath land who were dominated by other chief spirits, and who occupied separate localities; all these forms, however, were largely or solely subject to the will of Komookumps, the great spirit.

"Now on the north side of Mount Jackson, or La-o Yaina (La-o's Mountain), the eastern escarpment of which is known as La-o Rock, is a smooth field sloping a little toward the north which was a common playground for the fabled inhabitants of Gaywas and neighboring communities.

"Skell was a mighty spirit whose realm was the Klamath Marsh country, his capital being near the Yamsay River on the eastern side of the marsh. He had many subjects who took the form of birds and beasts when abroad on the land, as the antelope, the bald eagle, the bliwas or golden eagle, among them many of the most sagacious and active of all the beings then upon the earth.

"A fierce war occurred between Skell and La-o and their followers, which raged for a long time. Finally Skell was stricken down in his own land of Yamsay and his heart was torn from his body and was carried in triumph to La-o Yaina. Then a great gala day was declared and even the followers of Skell were allowed to take part in the games on Mount Jackson, and the heart of Skell was tossed from hand to hand in the great ball game in which all participated.

"If the heart of Skell could be borne away so that it could be restored to his body he would live again, and so with a secret understanding among themselves the followers of Skell watched for the opportunity to bear it away. Eventually, when it reached the hands of Antelope, he sped away to the eastward like the wind. When nearly exhausted, he passed it on to Eagle, and he in turn to Bliwas, and so on, and although La-o's followers pursued with their utmost speed, they failed to overtake the swift bearers of the precious heart. At last they heard the far-away voice of the dove, another of Skell's people, and then they gave up the useless pursuit.

"Skell's heart was restored and he lived again, but the war was not over and finally La-o was himself overpowered and slain and his bleeding body was borne to the La-o Yaina, on the very verge of the great cliff, and a false message was conveyed to La-o's monsters in the lake that Skell had been killed instead of La-o, and, when a quarter of the body was thrown over, La-o's monsters devoured it thinking it a part of Skell's body. Each quarter was thrown over in turn with the same result, but when the head was thrown into the lake the monsters recognized it as the head of their master and would not touch it, and so it remains to-day, an island in the lake, to all people now known as Wizard Island."

In 1885, at Fort Klamath, Steel obtained from Allen David, the white-headed chief of the Klamath Indians, the story of how the Indians returned to Crater Lake. It was "long before the white man appeared to drive the native out." Several Klamaths while hunting were shocked to find themselves on the lake rim, but, gazing upon its beauty, suddenly it was revealed to them that this was the home of the Great

Spirit. They silently left and camped far away. But one brave under the spell of the lake returned, looked again, built his camp-fire and slept. The next night he returned again, and still again. Each night strange voices which charmed him rose from the lake; mysterious noises filled the air. Moons waxed and waned. One day he climbed down to the water's edge, where he saw creatures "like in all respects to Klamath Indians" inhabiting the waters. Again and again he descended, bathed, and soon began to feel mysteriously strong, "stronger than any Indian of his tribe because of his many visits to the waters."

Others perceiving his growing power ventured also to visit the lake, and, upon bathing in its waters also received strength.

"On one occasion," said David solemnly, "the brave who first visited the lake killed a monster, or fish, and was at once set upon by untold numbers of excited Llaos (for such they were called), who carried him to the top of the cliffs, cut his throat with a stone knife, then tore his body into small pieces which were thrown down to the waters far beneath and devoured by angry Llaos."

In 1886 two Klamaths accompanied Captain Clarence E. Dutton's Geological Survey party to Crater Lake and descended to the water's edge. The news of the successful adventure spread among the Indians, and others came to look upon the forbidden spot. That was the beginning of the end of the superstition. Steel says that two hundred Klamaths camped upon the rim in 1896, while he was there with the Mazamas.

The lake was variously named by its early visitors. The Hillman party which discovered it named it Deep Blue Lake on the spot. Later it was known as Lake Mystery, Lake Majesty, and Hole in the Ground. A party from Jacksonville named it Crater Lake on August 4, 1869.

X

YELLOWSTONE, A VOLCANIC INTERLUDE

THE YELLOWSTONE NATIONAL PARK, WYOMING, NORTH-
WESTERN WYOMING. AREA, 3,348 SQUARE MILES

I

JOHN COULTER'S story of hot springs at the
upper waters of the Yellowstone River was laughed
at by the public of 1810. Jim Bridger's account of the
geysers in the thirties made his national reputation
as a liar. Warren Angus Ferris's description of the
Upper Geyser Basin was received in 1842 in unbeliev-
ing silence. Later explorers who sought the Yellowstone to test the truth of these tales thought it wholesome to keep their findings to themselves, as magazines and newspapers refused to publish their accounts
and lecturers were stoned in the streets as impostors.
It required the authority of the semiofficial Washburn-
Langford expedition of 1869 to establish credence.

The original appeal of the Yellowstone, that to
wonder, remains its most popular appeal to-day,
though science has dissipated mystery these many
years. Many visitors, I am persuaded, enjoy the
wonder of it more even than the spectacle. I have
heard people refuse to listen to the explanation of
geyser action lest it lessen their pleasure in Old Faithful. I confess to moods in which I want to see the blue

flames and smell the brimstone which Jim Bridger described so eloquently. There are places where it is not hard to imagine both.

For many years the uncanny wonders of a dying volcanic region absorbed the public mind to the exclusion of all else in the Yellowstone neighborhood, which Congress, principally in consequence of these wonders, made a national park in 1872. Yet all the time it possessed two other elements of distinction which a later period regards as equal to the volcanic phenomena; elements, in fact, of such distinction that either one alone, without the geysers, would have warranted the reservation of so striking a region for a national park. One of these is the valley of the Yellowstone River with its spectacular waterfalls and its colorful canyon. The other is its population of wild animals which, in 1872, probably was as large and may have been larger than to-day's. Yet little was heard of the Grand Canyon of the Yellowstone in those days, although Moran's celebrated painting, now in the Capitol at Washington, helped influence Congress to make it a national park; and so little did the wild animals figure in the calculations of the period that they were not even protected in the national park until 1894, when hunting had reduced the buffalo to twenty-five animals.

Even in these days of enlightenment and appreciation the great majority of people think of the Yellowstone only as an area enclosing geysers. There are tourists so possessed with this idea that they barely

glance at the canyon in passing. I have heard tourists
refuse to walk to Inspiration Point because they had
already looked over the rim at a convenient and un-
impressive place. Imagine coming two thousand miles
to balk at two miles and a half to the only spectacle
of its kind in the world and one of the world's great
spectacles at that! As for the animals, few indeed
see any but the occasional bears that feed at the hotel
dumps in the evening.

The Yellowstone National Park lies in the recesses
of the Rocky Mountains in northwestern Wyoming.
It slightly overlaps Montana on the north and northwest, and Idaho on the southwest. It is rectangular,
with an entrance about the middle of each side. It is
the largest of the national parks, enclosing 3,348 square
miles. It occupies a high plain girt with mountains.
The Absarokas bound it on the east, their crest in-
vading the park at Mount Chittenden. The Gallatin
Range pushes into the northwestern corner from the
north. The continental divide crosses the southwestern corner over the lofty Madison Plateau and the
ridge south of Yellowstone Lake. Altitudes are generally high. The plains range from six to eight thousand feet; the mountains rise occasionally to ten
thousand feet. South of the park the Pitchstone
Plateau merges into the foot-hills of the Teton Mountains, which, thirty miles south of the southern boundary, rise precipitously seven thousand feet above the
general level of the country.

Though occupying the heart of the Rocky Mountains, the region is not of them. In no sense is it typical. The Rockies are essentially granite which was forced molten from the depths when, at the creation of this vast central mountain system, lateral pressures lifted the earth's skin high above sea-level, folded it, and finally eroded it along the crest of the folds. In this granite system the Yellowstone is a volcanic interlude, and of much later date. It belongs in a general way to the impulse of volcanic agitation which lighted vast beacons over three hundred thousand square miles of our northwest. The Cascade Mountains belong in this grouping. Four national parks of to-day were then in the making, Mount Rainier in Washington, Crater Lake in Oregon, Lassen Volcanic in California, and the Yellowstone in Wyoming. Subterranean heat, remaining from those days of volcanic activity, to-day boils the water which the geysers hurl in air.

In the northeastern part of the Yellowstone a large central crater was surrounded by smaller volcanoes. You can easily trace the conformation from Mount Washburn which stood upon its southeastern rim, heaped there, doubtless, by some explosion of more than common violence. This volcanic period was of long duration, perhaps hundreds of thousands of years. In the northeastern part of the park the erosion of a hill has exposed the petrified remains of thirteen large forests in layers one on top of the other, the deep intervening spaces filled with thick deposits of ashes. Thirteen consecutive times were great forests here smothered in the products of eruption. Thirteen times did years enough elapse between eruptions for soil to make and forests to grow again, each perhaps of many generations of great trees.

Yellowstone's mountains, then, are decayed volcanoes, its rock is lava, its soil is ash and disintegrated lava. The resulting outline is soft and waving, with a tendency to levels. There are no pinnacled heights, no stratified, minareted walls, no precipiced cirques and glacier-shrouded peaks. Yet glaciers visited the region. The large granite boulder brought from afar and left near the west rim of the Grand Canyon with thousands of feet of rhyolite and other products of volcanism beneath it is alone sufficient proof of that.

Between the periods from volcano to glacier and from glacier to to-day, stream erosion has performed its miracles. The volcanoes have been rounded and flattened, the plateaus have been built up and levelled, and the canyons of the Yellowstone, Gibbon, and Madison Rivers have been dug. Vigorous as its landscape still remains, it has thus become the natural playground for a multitude of people unaccustomed to the rigors of a powerfully accented mountain country.

The fact is that, in spite of its poverty of peaks and precipices, the Yellowstone country is one of the most varied and beautiful wildernesses in the world. Among national parks it gains rather than loses by its difference. While easily penetrated, it is wild in the extreme, hinting of the prairies in its broad opens, pasture for thousands of wild ruminants, and of the loftier mountains in its distant ranges, its isolated peaks and its groups of rugged, rolling summits. In the number, magnitude, and variety of its waters it stands quite alone. It contains no less than three watersheds of importance, those of the Yellowstone, Madison, and Snake Rivers, flowing respectively north, west, and south. The waters of the Yellowstone and Madison make it an important source of the Missouri. There are minor rivers of importance in the park and innumerable lesser streams. It is a network of waterways. Its waterfalls are many, and two of them are large and important. Its lakes are many, and several are large. Yellowstone Lake is the largest of its altitude in the world.

As a wilderness, therefore, the Yellowstone is unequalled. Its innumerable waters insure the luxuriance of its growths. Its forested parts are densely forested; its flower-gardens are unexcelled in range, color, and variety, and its meadows grow deep in many kinds of rich grass. If it were only for the splendor of its wilderness, it still would be worth the while. Imagine this wilderness heavily populated with friendly wild animals, sprinkled with geysers, hot springs, mud volcanoes, painted terraces and petrified groves, sensational with breath-taking canyons and waterfalls, penetrable over hundreds of miles of well built road and several times the mileage of trails, and comfortable because of its large hotels and public camps located conveniently for its enjoyment, and you have a pleasure-ground of extraordinary quality. Remember that one may camp out almost anywhere, and that all waters are trout waters. Yellowstone offers the best fishing easily accessible in the continent.

Another advantage possessed by the Yellowstone is a position near the centre of the country among great railroad systems. The Northern Pacific reaches it on the north, the Burlington on the east, and the Union Pacific on the west. One can take it coming or going between oceans; it is possible to buy tickets in by any one railroad and out by either of the others. An elaborate system of automobile-coaches swings the passenger where he pleases, meeting all incoming trains and delivering at all outgoing trains. It is much easier now to see the Yellowstone than in the much-vaunted stage-coach times previous to 1915, times sorely lamented by the romantic because their passing meant the passing of the picturesque old horse-drawn stage-coach from its last stand in the United States; times when a tour of the Yellowstone meant six and a half days of slow, dusty travel, starting early and arriving late, with a few minutes or hours at each "sight" for the soiled and exhausted traveller to gape in ignorant wonder, watch in hand.

To-day one travels swiftly and comfortably in entire leisure, stopping at hotels or camps as he pleases, and staying at each as long as he likes. The runs between the lingering places are now a pleasure. If hurried, one can now accomplish the stage-coach trip of the past in two days, while the old six and a half days now means a leisurely and delightful visit.

With the new order of travel began a new conception of the Yellowstone's public usefulness. It ceased to be a museum of wonders and began to be a summer pleasure-ground. Instead of the fast automobile-stage decreasing the average length of visit, the new idea which it embodied has lengthened it. This new idea is a natural evolution which began with the automobile and spread rapidly. The railroads had been bringing tourists principally on transcontinental stop-overs. Automobiles brought people who came really to see the Yellowstone, who stayed weeks at public camps to see it, or who brought outfits and camped out among its spectacles. The first Ford which entered the park on the morning of August 1, 1915, the day when private cars were first admitted, so loaded with tenting and cooking utensils that the occupants scarcely could be seen, was the herald of the new and greater Yellowstone. Those who laughed and those who groaned at sight of it, and there were both, were no seers; for that minute Yellowstone entered upon her destiny.

The road scheme is simple and effective. From each entrance a road leads into an oblong loop road enclosing the centre of the park and touching the principal points of scenic interest. This loop is connected across the middle for convenience. From it several short roads push out to special spectacles, and a long road follows Lamar Creek through a northeastern entrance to a mining town which has no other means of communication with the world outside. This is the road to Specimen Ridge with its thirteen engulfed forests, to the buffalo range, and, outside the park boundaries, to the Grasshopper Glacier, in whose glassy embrace may be seen millions of grasshoppers which have lain in very cold storage indeed from an age before man. All are automobile roads.

II

The hot-water phenomena are scattered over a large area of the park. The Mammoth Hot Springs at the northern entrance are the only active examples of high terrace-building. The geysers are concentrated in three adjoining groups upon the middle-west side. But hot springs occur everywhere at widely separated points; a steam jet is seen emerging even from the depths of the Grand Canyon a thousand feet below the rim.

The traveller is never long allowed to forget, in the silent beauty of the supreme wilderness, the park's uncanny nature. Suddenly encountered columns of steam rising from innocent meadows; occasional half-acres of dead and discolored brush emerging from hot and yellow mud-holes within the glowing forest heart; an unexpected roaring hillside running with smoking water; irregular agitated pools of gray, pink, or yellow mud, spitting, like a pot of porridge, explosive puffs of steam; the warm vaporing of a shallow in a cold forest-bound lake; a continuous violent bellowing from the depths of a ragged roadside hole which at intervals

vomits noisily quantities of thick brown and purple
liquid; occasional groups of richly colored hot springs
in an acre or more of dull yellows, the whole steaming
vehemently and interchanging the pinks and blues of
its hot waters as the passing traveller changes his angle
of vision—these and other uncouth phenomena in
wide variety and frequent repetition enliven the tourist's way. They are more numerous in geyser neighborhoods, but some of them are met singly, always with
a little shock of surprise, in every part of the park.

The terrace-building springs in the north of the
park engulf trees. The bulky growing mounds of
white and gray deposit are edged with minutely carven
basins mounted upon elaborately fluted supports of
ornate design, over whose many-colored edges flows a
shimmer of hot water. Basin rises upon basin, tier
upon tier, each in turn destined to clog and dry and
merge into the mass while new basins and new tiers
form and grow and glow awhile upon their outer flank.
The material, of course, is precipitated by the water
when it emerges from the earth's hot interior. The
vivid yellows and pinks and blues in which these terraces clothe themselves upon warm days result from
minute vegetable algæ which thrive in the hot saturated lime-water but quickly die and fade to gray and
shining white on drying. The height of some of these
shapeless masses of terrace-built structures is surprising. But more surprising yet is the vividness of color
assumed by the limpid springs in certain lights and at
certain angles.

Climbing the terraces at the expense of wet feet, one stands upon broad, white, and occasionally very damp plateaus which steam vigorously in spots. These spots are irregularly circular and very shallow pools of hot water, some of which bubble industriously with a low, pleasant hum. They are not boiling springs; the bubbling is caused by escaping gases; but their waters are extremely hot. The intense color of some of these pools varies or disappears with the changing angle of vision; the water itself is limpid.

Elsewhere throughout the park the innumerable hot springs seem to be less charged with depositable matter; elsewhere they build no terraces, but bubble joyously up through bowls often many feet in depth and diameter. Often they are inspiringly beautiful. The blue Morning Glory Spring is jewel-like rather than flower-like in its color quality, but its bowl remarkably resembles the flower which gives it name. Most springs are gloriously green. Some are the sources of considerable streams. Some stir slightly with the feeling rather than the appearance of life; others are perpetually agitated, several small springs betraying their relationship to the geysers by a periodicity of activity.

When the air is dry and the temperature low, the springs shoot thick volumes of steam high in air. To the incomer by the north or west entrance who has yet to see a geyser, the first view of the Lower Geyser Basin brings a shock of astonishment no matter what his expectation. Let us hope it is a cool, bracing, breezy morning when the broad yellow plain emits hundreds of columns of heavy steam to unite in a wind-tossed cloud overlying and setting off the uncanny spectacle. Several geysers spout vehemently and one or more roaring vents bellow like angry bulls in a nightmare. This is appropriately the introduction to the greater geyser basins which lie near by upon the south.

Who shall describe the geysers? What pen, what brush, shall do justice to their ghostly glory, the eager vehemence of their assaults upon the sky, their joyful gush and roar, their insistence upon conscious personality and power, the white majesty of their fluted columns at the instant of fullest expansion, the supreme loveliness of their feathery florescence at the level of poise between rise and fall, their graciousness of form, their speedy airiness of action, their giant convolutions of sun-flecked steam rolling aloft in ever-expanding volume to rejoin the parent cloud?

Perhaps there have been greater geyser basins somewhere in the prehistoric past. There may be greater still to come; one or two promising possibilities are in Alaska. But for the lapse of geologic time in which man has so far lived, Yellowstone has cornered the world's geyser market. There are only two other places where one may enjoy the spectacle of large geysers. One of these is New Zealand and the other Iceland; but both displays combined cannot equal Yellowstone's either in the number or the size of the geysers.

Yellowstone has dozens of geysers of many kinds. They range in size from the little spring that spurts a few inches every minute to the monster that hurls hundreds of tons of water three hundred feet in air every six or eight weeks. Many spout at fairly regular intervals of minutes or hours or days. Others are notably irregular, and these include most of the largest. Old Faithful won its name and reputation by its regularity; it is the only one of the group of monsters which lives up to its time-table. Its period ranges from intervals of about fifty-five minutes in seasons following winters of heavy snow to eighty or eighty-five minutes in seasons following winters of light snow. Its eruptions are announced in the Old Faithful Inn a few minutes in advance of action and the population of the hotel walks out to see the spouting. At night a searchlight is thrown upon the gushing flood.

After all, Old Faithful is the most satisfactory of geysers. Several are more imposing. Sometimes enthusiasts remain in the neighborhood for weeks waiting for the Giant to play and dare not venture far away for fear of missing the spectacle; while Old Faithful, which is quite as beautiful and nearly as large, performs hourly for the pleasure of thousands. Even the most hurried visitor to the Upper Basin is sure, between stages, of seeing several geysers in addition to one or more performances of Old Faithful.

The greatest of known geysers ceased playing in 1888. I have found no authentic measurements or other stated records concerning the famous Excelsior. It hurled aloft an enormous volume of water, with a fury of action described as appalling. Posterity is fortunate in the existence of a striking photograph of this monster taken at the height of its play by F. Jay Haynes, then official photographer of the park.

"The first photographs I made were in the fall of 1881," Mr. Haynes writes me. "The eruptions continued during the winter at increasing intervals from two hours, when the series began, to four hours when it ceased operations before the tourist season of 1882. Not having the modern photographic plates for instantaneous work in 1881, it was impossible to secure instantaneous views then, but in the spring of 1888, I made the view which you write about. It was taken at the fulness of its eruption.

"The explosion was preceded by a rapid filling of the crater and a great overflow of water. The column was about fifty feet wide and came from the centre of the crater. Pieces of formation were torn loose and were thrown out during each eruption; large quantities eventually were removed from the crater, thus enlarging it to its present size."

Here we have a witness's description of the process which clouds the career of the Excelsior Geyser. The enlargement of the vent eventually gave unrestrained passage to the imprisoned steam. The geyser ceased to play. To-day the Excelsior Spring is one of the largest hot springs in the Yellowstone and the world; its output of steaming water is constant and voluminous. Thus again we find relationship between the hot spring and the geyser; it is apparent that the same vent, except perhaps for differences of internal shaping, might serve for both. It was the removal of restraining walls which changed the Excelsior Geyser to the Excelsior Spring.

For many years geyser action remained a mystery balanced among conflicting theories, of which at last Bunsen's won general acceptance. Spring waters, or surface waters seeping through porous lavas, gather thousands of feet below the surface in some pocket located in strata which internal pressures still keep hot. Boiling as they gather, the waters rise till they fill the long vent-hole to the surface. Still the steam keeps making in the deep pocket, where it is held down by the weight of the water in the vent above. As it accumulates this steam compresses more and more. The result is inevitable. There comes a moment when the expansive power of the compressed steam overcomes the weight above. Explosion follows. The steam, expanding now with violence, drives the water up the vent and out; nor is it satisfied until the vent is emptied.

Upon the surface, as the geyser lapses and dies, the people turn away to the Inn and luncheon. Under the surface, again the waters gather and boil in preparation for the next eruption. The interval till then will depend upon the amount of water which reaches the deep pocket, the size of the pocket, and the length and shape of the vent-hole. If conditions permit the upward escape of steam as fast as it makes in the pocket, we have a hot spring. If the steam makes faster than it can escape, we have a geyser.

From a photograph by Haynes

THE EXCELSIOR GEYSER WHICH BLEW OUT IN 1888; YELLOWSTONE

From a photograph by Haynes

ONE OF THE TERRACES AT MAMMOTH HOT SPRINGS; YELLOWSTONE

III

So interesting are the geysers and their kin that, with their splendid wilderness setting, other glories seem superfluous. I have had my moments of impatience with the Grand Canyon of the Yellowstone for being in the Yellowstone. Together, the canyon and the geysers are almost too much for one place, even perhaps for one visit. One can only hold so much, even of beauty, at once. Spectacles of this quality and quantity need assimilation, and assimilation requires time. Nevertheless, once enter into sympathetic relations with the canyon, once find its heart and penetrate its secret, and the tables are quickly turned. Strangely, it now becomes quite easy to view with comparative coolness the claims of mere hot-water wonders.

The canyon cannot be considered apart from its river any more than a geyser apart from its environment of hot spring and basin, and any consideration of the Yellowstone River begins with its lake. As compared with others of scenic celebrity, Yellowstone Lake is unremarkable. Its shores are so low and the mountains of its southern border so flat and unsuggestive that it curiously gives the impression of surface altitude—curiously because it actually has the altitude; its surface is more than seven thousand seven hundred feet above tide. If I have the advertisement right, it is the highest water in the world that floats a line of steamboats.

The lake is large, twenty miles north and south by fifteen miles east and west; it is irregular with deep indentations. It is heavily wooded to the water's edge. All its entering streams are small except the Yellowstone River, which, from its source in the Absarokas just south of the park boundary, enters the Southeast Arm through the lowland wilderness home of the moose and the wild buffalo. The lake is the popular resort of thousands of large white pelicans, its most picturesque feature.

That part of the Yellowstone River which interests us emerges from the lake at its most northerly point. It is here a broad swift stream of some depth and great clarity, so swarming with trout that a half-dozen or more usually may be seen upon its bottom at any glance from boat or bridge. A number of boats usually are anchored above the bridge from which anglers are successfully trailing artificial flies and spinners in the fast current; and the bridge is usually lined with anglers who, in spite of crude outfits, frequently hook good trout which they pull up by main strength much as the phlegmatic patrons of excursion-steamers to the Banks yank flopping cod from brine to basket on the top deck.

The last time I crossed the Fishing Bridge and paused to see the fun, a woman whose face beamed with happiness held up a twenty-inch trout and said:

"Just look! My husband caught this and he is seventy-six years old—last month. It's the first fish he ever caught, for he was brought up in Kansas, you know, where there isn't any fishing. My! but he's a proud man! We're going to get the camp to cook it for us. He's gone now to look for a board to draw its measurements to show the folks at home."

From here to the river's emergence from the park the fishing is not crude. In fact, it taxes the most skilful angler's art to steer his fighting trout through boiling rapids to the net. For very soon the Yellowstone narrows and pitches down sharper slants to the climax of the falls and the mighty canyon.

This intermediate stretch of river is beautiful in its quietude. The forests often touch the water's edge. And ever it narrows and deepens and splashes higher against the rocks which stem its current; forever it is steepening to the plunge. Above the Upper Fall it pinches almost to a mill-race, roars over low sills, swings eastward at right angles, and plunges a hundred and nine feet. I know of no cataract which expresses might in action so eloquently as the Upper Fall of the Yellowstone. Pressed as it is within narrow bounds, it seems to gush with other motive power than merely gravity. Seen from above looking down, seen sideways from below, or looked at straight on from the camp site on the opposite rim, the water appears hurled from the brink.

Less than a mile south of the Upper Fall, the river again falls, this time into the Grand Canyon.

Imposing as the Great Fall is, it must chiefly be considered as a part of the Grand Canyon picture.

The only separate view of it looks up from the river's edge in front, a view which few get because of the difficult climb; every other view poses it merely as an element in the canyon composition. Compared with the Upper Fall, its more than double height gives it the great superiority of majesty without detracting from the Upper Fall's gushing personality. In fact, it is the King of Falls. Comparison with Yosemite's falls is impossible, so different are the elements and conditions. The Great Fall of the Yellowstone carries in one body, perhaps, a greater bulk of water than all the Yosemite Valley's falls combined.

And so we come to the canyon. In figures it is roughly a thousand feet deep and twice as wide, more or less, at the rim. The supremely scenic part reaches perhaps three miles below the Great Fall. Several rock points extend far into the canyon, from which the gorgeous spectacle may be viewed as from an aeroplane. Artists' Point, which is reached from the east side, displays the Great Fall as the centre of a noble composition. It was Moran's choice. Inspiration Point, which juts far in from the west side, shows a deeper and more comprehensive view of the canyon and only a glimpse of the Great Fall. Both views are essential to any adequate conception. From Artists' Point the eye loses detail in the overmastering glory of the whole. From Inspiration Point the canyon reveals itself in all the intimacy of its sublime form and color. Both views dazzle and astonish. Neither can be looked at very long at one time.

YELLOWSTONE VALLEY FROM THE UPPER FALL TO THE LOWER FALL

THE LOWER FALL AND THE GRAND CANYON OF THE YELLOWSTONE

It will help comprehension of the picture quality of this remarkable canyon to recall that it is carved out of the products of volcanism; its promontories and pinnacles are the knobbed and gnarled decomposition products of lava rocks left following erosion; its sides are gashed and fluted lava cliffs flanked by long straight slopes of coarse volcanic sand-like grains; its colors have the distinctness and occasional luridness which seem natural to fused and oxidized disintegrations. Geologically speaking, it is a young canyon. It is digging deeper all the time.

Yellow, of course, is the prevailing color. Moran was right. His was the general point of view, his message the dramatic ensemble. But, even from Artists' Point, closer looking reveals great masses of reds and grays, while Inspiration Point discloses a gorgeous palette daubed with most of the colors and intermediate tints that imagination can suggest. I doubt whether there is another such kaleidoscope in nature. There is apparently every gray from purest white to dull black, every yellow from lemon to deep orange, every red, pink, and brown. These tints dye the rocks and sands in splashes and long transverse streaks which merge into a single joyous exclamation in vivid color whose red and yellow accents have something of the Oriental. Greens and blues are missing from the dyes, but are otherwise supplied. The canyon is edged with lodge-pole forests, and growths of lighter greens invade the sandy slants, at times nearly to the frothing river; and the river is a chain of emeralds and pearls. Blue completes the color gamut from the inverted bowl of sky.

No sketch of the canyon is complete without the story of the great robbery. I am not referring to the several hold-ups of the old stage-coach days, but to a robbery which occurred long before the coming of man —the theft of the waters of Yellowstone Lake; for this splendid river, these noble falls, this incomparable canyon, are the ill-gotten products of the first of Yellowstone's hold-ups.

Originally Yellowstone Lake was a hundred and sixty feet higher and very much larger than it is to-day. It extended from the headwaters of the present Yellowstone River, far in the south, northward past the present Great Fall and Inspiration Point. It included a large part of what is now known as the Hayden Valley. At that time the Continental Divide, which now cuts the southwest corner of the park, encircled the lake on its north, and just across the low divide was a small flat-lying stream which drained and still drains the volcanic slopes leading down from Dunraven Peak and Mount Washburn.

This small stream, known as Sulphur Creek, has the honor, or the dishonor if you choose, of being the first desperado of the Yellowstone, but one so much greater than its two petty imitators of human times that there is no comparison of misdeeds. Sulphur Creek stole the lake from the Snake River and used it to create the Yellowstone River, which in turn created the wonderful canyon. Here at last is a crime in which all will agree that the end justified the means.

How this piracy was accomplished is written on the rocks; even the former lake outlet into the Snake River is plainly discernible to-day. At the lake's north end, where the seeping waters of Sulphur Creek and the edge of the lake nearly met on opposite sides of what was then the low flat divide, it only required some slight disturbance indirectly volcanic, some unaccustomed rising of lake levels, perhaps merely some special stress of flood or storm to make the connection. Perhaps the creek itself, sapping back in the soft lava soils, unaided found the lake. Connection once made, the mighty body of lake water speedily deepened a channel northward and Sulphur Creek became sure of its posterity.

At that time, hidden under the lake's surface, two rhyolite dikes, or upright walls of harder rock, extended crosswise through the lake more than half a mile apart. As the lake-level fell, the nearer of these dikes emerged and divided the waters into two lakes, the upper of which emptied over the dike into the lower. This was the beginning of the Great Fall. And presently, as the Great Fall cut its breach deeper and deeper into the restraining dike, it lowered the upper-lake level until presently the other rhyolite dike emerged from the surface carrying another cataract. And thus began the Upper Fall.

Meantime the stream below kept digging deeper the canyon of Sulphur Creek, and there came a time when the lower lake drained wholly away. In its place was left a bottom-land which is now a part of the Hayden Valley, and, running through it, a river. Forthwith this river began scooping, from the Great Fall to Inspiration Point, the scenic ditch which is world-celebrated to-day as the Grand Canyon of the Yellowstone.

IV

Now imagine this whole superlative wilderness heavily populated with wild animals in a state of normal living. Imagine thirty thousand elk, for instance, roaming about in bands of half a dozen to half a thousand. Imagine them not friendly, perhaps, but fearless, with that entire indifference which most animals show to creatures which neither help nor harm them—as indifferent, say, as the rabbits in your pasture or the squirrels in your oak woods. Imagine all the wild animals, except the sneaking, predatory kind, proportionally plentiful and similarly fearless—bear, antelope, mountain-sheep, deer, bison, even moose in the fastnesses, to say nothing of the innumerable smaller beasts. There has been no hunting of harmless animals in the Yellowstone since 1894, and this is one result.

It is true that comparatively few visitors see many animals, but that is the fault of their haste or their temperament or their inexperience of nature. One must seek in sympathy to find. Tearing over the wilderness roads in noisy motors smelling of gasolene is not the best way to find them, although the elk and deer became indifferent to automobiles as soon as they discovered them harmless. One may see them not infrequently from automobiles and often from horse-drawn wagons; and one may see them often and intimately who walks or rides horseback on the trails.

The admission of the automobile to Yellowstone roads changed seeing conditions materially. In five days of quiet driving in 1914 with Colonel L. M. Brett, then superintendent of the park, in a direction opposite to the stages, I saw more animals from my wagon-seat than I had expected to see wild in all my life. We saw bear half a dozen times, elk in numbers, black-tailed and white-tailed deer so frequently that count was lost the second morning, four bands of antelope, buffalo, foxes, coyotes, and even a bull moose. Once we stopped so as not to hurry a large bear and two cubs which were leisurely crossing the road. Deer watched us pass within a hundred yards. Elk grazed at close quarters, and our one bull moose obligingly ambled ahead of us along the road. There was never fear, never excitement (except my own), not even haste. Even the accustomed horses no more than cocked an ear or two while waiting for three wild bears to get out of the middle of the road.

Of course scenic completeness is enough in itself to justify the existence of these animals in the marvellous wilderness of the Yellowstone. Their presence in normal abundance and their calm at-homeness perfects nature's spectacle. In this respect, also, Yellowstone's unique place among the national parks is secure.

The lessons of the Yellowstone are plain. It is now too late to restore elsewhere the great natural possession which the thoughtless savagery of a former generation destroyed in careless ruth, but, thanks to this early impulse of conservation, a fine example still remains in the Yellowstone. But it is not too late to obliterate wholly certain misconceptions by which that savagery was then justified. It is not too late to look upon wild animals as fellow heritors of the earth, possessing certain natural rights which men are glad rather than bound to respect. It is not too late to consider them, with birds and forests, lakes, rivers, seas, and skies, a part of nature's glorious gift for man's manifold satisfaction, a gift to carefully conserve for the study and enjoyment of to-day, and to develop for the uses of larger and more appreciative generations to come.

Of course if this be brought to universal accomplishment (and the impulse has been advancing fast of late), it must be Yellowstone's part to furnish the exhibit, for we have no other.

To many the most surprising part of Yellowstone's wild-animal message is man's immunity from hatred and harm by predatory beasts. To know that wild bears if kindly treated are not only harmless but friendly, that grizzlies will not attack except in self-defense, and that wolves, wild cats, and mountain-lions fly with that instinctive dread which is man's dependable protection, may destroy certain romantic illusions of youth and discredit the observation if not the conscious verity of many an honest hunter; but it imparts a modern scientific fact which sets the whole wild-animal question in a new light. In every case of assault by bears where complete evidence has been obtainable, the United States Biological Survey, after fullest investigation, has exonerated the bear; he has always been attacked or has had reason to believe himself attacked. In more than thirty summers of field-work Vernon Bailey, Chief Field-Naturalist of the Biological Survey, has slept on the ground without fires or other protection, and frequently in the morning found tracks of investigating predatory beasts. There are reports but no records of human beings killed by wolves or mountain-lions in America. Yet, for years, all reports susceptible of proof have been officially investigated.

One of Yellowstone's several manifest destinies is to become the well-patronized American school of wild-life study. Already, from its abundance, it is supplying wild animals to help in the long and difficult task of restoring here and there, to national parks and other favorable localities, stocks which existed before the great slaughter.

V

Thirty miles south of this rolling volcanic interlude the pristine Rockies, as if in shame of their moment of gorgeous softness, rear in contrast their sharpest and most heroic monument of bristling granite.

Scarcely over the park's southern boundary, the foot-hills of the Teton Mountains swell gently toward their Gothic climax. The country opens and roughens. The excellent road, which makes Jackson's Hole a practical part of the Yellowstone pleasure-ground, winds through a rolling, partly wooded grazing-ground of elk and deer. The time was when these wild herds made living possible for the nation's hunted despera-does, for Jackson's Hole was the last refuge to yield to law and order.

At the climax of this sudden granite protest, the Grand Teton rises 7,014 feet in seeming sheerness from Jackson Lake to its total altitude of 13,747 feet. To its right is Mount Moran, a monster only less. The others, clustering around them, have no names.

All together, they are few and grouped like the units of some fabulous barbaric stronghold. Fitted by size and majesty to be the climax of a mighty range, the Tetons concentrate their all in this one giant group. Quickly, north and south, they subside and pass. They are a granite island in a sea of plain.

Seen across the lake a dozen miles which seem but three, these clustered steepled temples rise sheer from the water. Their flanks are snow-streaked still in August, their shoulders hung with glaciers, their spires bare and shining. A greater contrast to the land from which we came and to which we presently return cannot be imagined. Geologically, the two have nothing in common. Scenically, the Tetons set off and complete the spectacle of the Yellowstone.

From a photograph by Charles D. Walcott

THE TETON MOUNTAIN FROM JACKSON HOLE, SOUTH OF YELLOWSTONE

From a photograph by Haynes

THE LAVA LANDSCAPE OF THE YELLOWSTONE AND GIBBON FALLS

XI

THREE MONSTERS OF HAWAII

IF this chapter is confined to the three volcano tops which Congress reserved on the islands of Hawaii and Maui in 1917, wonderful though these are, it will describe a small part indeed of the wide range of novelty, charm, and beauty which will fall to the lot of those who visit the Hawaii National Park. One of the great advantages enjoyed by this national park, as indeed by Mount McKinley's, is its location in a surrounding of entire novelty, so that in addition to the object of his visit, itself so supremely worth while, the traveller has also the pleasure of a trip abroad.

In novelty at least the Hawaii National Park has the advantage over the Alaskan park because it involves the life and scenery of the tropics. We can find snow-crowned mountains and winding glaciers at home, but not equatorial jungles, sandalwood groves, and surf-riding.

Enormous as this element of charm unquestionably is, this is not the place to sing the pleasures of the Hawaiian Islands. Their palm-fringed horizons, surf-edged coral reefs, tropical forests and gardens, plantations of pineapple and sugar-cane are as celebrated as their rainbows, earthquakes, and graceful girls dancing under tropical stars to the languorous ukelele.

Leaving these and kindred spectacles to the steamship circulars and the library shelf, it is our part to

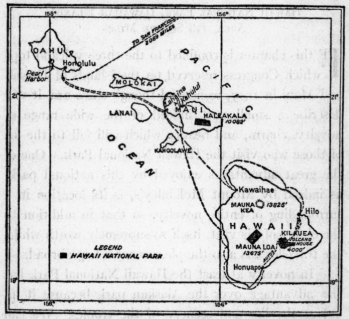

MAP OF HAWAII NATIONAL PARK

note that the Hawaii National Park possesses the fourth largest volcanic crater in the world, whose aspect at sunrise is one of the world's famous spectacles, the largest active volcano in the world, and a lake of turbulent, glowing, molten lava, "the House of Everlasting Fire," which fills the beholder with awe.

It was not at all, then, the gentle poetic aspects
of the Hawaiian Islands which led Congress to create
a national park there, though these form its romantic,
contrasted setting. It was the extraordinary volcanic
exhibit, that combination of thrilling spectacles of
Nature's colossal power which for years have drawn
travellers from the four quarters of the earth. The
Hawaii National Park includes the summits of Haleakala, on the island of Maui, and Mauna Loa and
Kilauea, on the island of Hawaii.

Spain claims the discovery of these delectable
isles by Juan Gaetano, in 1555, but their formal discovery and exploration fell to the lot of Captain James
Cook, in 1778. The Hawaiians thought him a god
and loaded him with the treasures of the islands, but
on his return the following year his illness and the conduct of his crew ashore disillusioned them; they killed
him and burned his flesh, but their priests deified his
bones, nevertheless. Parts of these were recovered
later and a monument was erected over them. Then
civil wars raged until all the tribes were conquered,
at the end of the eighteenth century, by one chieftain,
Kamehameha, who became king. His descendants
reigned until 1874 when, the old royal line dying out,
Kalakaua was elected his successor.

From this time the end hastened. A treaty with
the United States ceded Pearl Harbor as a coaling-sta-
tion and entered American goods free of duty, in return
for which Hawaiian sugar and a few other products entered the United States free. This established the

sugar industry on a large and permanent scale and brought laborers from China, Japan, the Azores, and Madeira. More than ten thousand Portuguese migrated to the islands, and the native population began a comparative decrease which still continues.

After Kalakaua's death, his sister Liliuokalani succeeding him in 1891, the drift to the United States became rapid. When President Cleveland refused to annex the islands, a republic was formed in 1894, but the danger from Japanese immigration became so imminent that in 1898, during the Spanish-American War, President McKinley yielded to the Hawaiian request and the islands were annexed to the United States by resolution of Congress.

The setting for the picture of our island-park will be complete with several facts about its physical origin. The Hawaiian Islands rose from the sea in a series of volcanic eruptions. Originally, doubtless, the greater islands were simple cones emitting lava, ash, and smoke, which coral growths afterward enlarged and enriched. Kauai was the first to develop habitable conditions, and the island southeast of it followed in order. Eight of the twelve are now habitable.

The most eastern island of the group is Hawaii. It is also much the largest. This has three volcanoes. Mauna Loa, greatest of the three, and also the greatest volcanic mass in the world, is nearly the centre of the island; Kilauea lies a few miles east of it; the summits of both are included in the national park. Mauna Kea, a volcanic cone of great beauty in the north centre of the island, forming a triangle with the other two, is not a part of the national park.

Northwest of Hawaii across sixty miles or more of salt water is the island of Maui, second largest of the group. In its southern part rises the distinguished volcano of Haleakala, whose summit and world-famous crater is the third member of the national park. The other habited islands, in order westward, are Kahoolawe, Lanai, Molokai, Oahu, Kauai, and Niihau; no portions of these are included in the park. Kahoolawe, Lanai, and Niihau are much the smallest of the group.

HALEAKALA

Of the three volcanic summits which concern us, Haleakala is nearest the principal port of Honolulu, though not always the first visited. Its slopes nearly fill the southern half of the island of Maui.

The popular translation of the name Haleakala is "The House of the Sun"; literally the word means "The House Built by the Sun." The volcano is a monster of more than ten thousand feet, which bears upon its summit a crater of a size and beauty that make it one of the world's show-places. This crater is seven and a half miles long by two and a third miles wide. Only three known craters exceed Haleakala's in size. Aso san, the monster crater of Japan, largest by far in the world, is fourteen miles long by ten wide and contains many farms. Lago di Bolseno, in Italy, next in size, measures eight and a half by seven and a half miles; and Monte Albano, also in Italy, eight by seven miles.

Exchanging your automobile for a saddle-horse at the volcano's foot, you spend the afternoon in the ascent. Wonderful indeed, looking back, is the growing arc of plantation and sea, islands growing upon the horizon, Mauna Kea and Mauna Loa lifting distant snow-tipped peaks. You spend the night in a rest-house on the rim of the crater, but not until you have seen the spectacle of sunset; and in the gray of the morning you are summoned to the supreme spectacle of sunrise. Thousands have crossed seas for Haleakala's sunrise.

That first view of the crater from the rim is one never to be forgotten. Its floor lies two thousand feet below, an enormous rainless, rolling plain from which rise thirteen volcanic cones, clean-cut, as regular in form as carven things. Several of these are seven hundred feet in height. "It must have been awe-inspiring," writes Castle, "when its cones were spouting fire, and rivers of scarlet molten lava crawled along the floor."

The stillness of this spot emphasizes its emotional effect. A word spoken ordinarily loud is like a shout. You can hear the footsteps of the goats far down upon the crater floor. Upon this floor grow plants known nowhere else; they are famous under the name of Silver Swords—yucca-like growths three or four feet high whose drooping filaments of bloom gleam like polished silver stilettos.

When Mark Twain saw the crater, "vagrant white clouds came drifting along, high over the sea and valley; then they came in couples and groups; then in imposing squadrons; gradually joining their forces, they banked themselves solidly together a thousand feet under us and totally shut out land and ocean; not a vestige of anything was left in view, but just a little of the rim of the crater circling away from the pinnacle whereon we sat, for a ghostly procession of wanderers from the filmy hosts without had drifted through a chasm in the crater wall and filed round and round, and gathered and sunk and blended together till the abyss was stored to the brim with a fleecy fog. Thus banked, motion ceased, and silence reigned. Clear to the horizon, league on league, the snowy folds, with shallow creases between, and with here and there stately piles of vapory architecture lifting themselves aloft out of the common plain—some near at hand, some in the middle distances, and others relieving the monotony of the remote solitudes. There was little conversation, for the impressive scene overawed speech. I felt like the Last Man, neglected of the judgment, and left pinnacled in mid-heaven, a forgotten relic of a vanished world."

The extraordinary perfection of this desert crater is probably due to two causes. Vents which tapped it far down the volcano's flanks prevented its filling with molten lava; absence of rain has preserved its walls intact and saved its pristine beauty from the deface- ment of erosion.

Haleakala has its legend, and this Jack London has sifted to its elements and given us in "The Cruise of the *Snark*." I quote:

"It is told that long ago, one Maui, the son of Hina, lived on what is now known as West Maui. His mother, Hina, employed her time in the making of kapas. She must have made them at night, for her days were occupied in trying to dry the kapas. Each morning, and all morning, she toiled at spreading them out in the sun. But no sooner were they out than she began taking them in in order to have them all under shelter for the night. For know that the days were shorter then than now. Maui watched his mother's futile toil and felt sorry for her. He decided to do something—oh, no, not to help her hang out and take in the kapas. He was too clever for that. His idea was to make the sun go slower. Perhaps he was the first Hawaiian astronomer. At any rate, he took a series of observations of the sun from various parts of the island. His conclusion was that the sun's path was directly across Haleakala. Unlike Joshua, he stood in no need of divine assistance. He gathered a huge quantity of cocoanuts, from the fibre of which he braided a stout cord, and in one end of which he made a noose, even as the cowboys of Haleakala do to this day.

"Next he climbed into the House of the Sun. When the sun came tearing along the path, bent on completing its journey in the shortest time possible, the valiant youth threw his lariat around one of the

sun's largest and strongest beams. He made the sun
slow down some; also, he broke the beam short off.
And he kept on roping and breaking off beams till the
sun said it was willing to listen to reason. Maui set
forth his terms of peace, which the sun accepted,
agreeing to go more slowly thereafter. Wherefore
Hina had ample time in which to dry her kapas, and
the days are longer than they used to be, which last
is quite in accord with the teachings of modern as-
tronomy."

MAUNA LOA

Sixty miles south of Maui, Hawaii, largest of the
island group, contains the two remaining parts of our
national park. From every point of view Mauna
Loa and Mauna Kea, both snow-crowned monsters
approaching fourteen thousand feet of altitude, dom-
inate the island. But Mauna Kea is not a part of the
national park; Kilauea, of less than a third its height,
shares that honor with Mauna Loa. Of the two,
Kilauea is much the older, and doubtless was a conspicuous figure in the old landscape. It has been
largely absorbed in the immense swelling bulk of
Mauna Loa, which, springing later from the island
soil near by, no doubt diverting Kilauea's vents far
below sea-level, has sprawled over many miles. So
nearly has the younger absorbed the older, that
Kilauea's famous pit of molten lava seems almost to
lie upon Mauna Loa's slope.

Mauna Loa soars 13,675 feet. Its snowy dome

shares with Mauna Kea, which rises even higher, the summit honors of the islands. From Hilo, the principal port of the island of Hawaii, Mauna Loa suggests the back of a leviathan, its body hidden in the mists. The way up, through forests of ancient mahogany and tangles of giant tree-fern, then up many miles of lava slopes, is one of the inspiring tours in the mountain world. The summit crater, Mokuaweoweo, three-quarters of a mile long by a quarter mile wide, is as spectacular in action as that of Kilauea.

This enormous volcanic mass has grown of its own output in comparatively a short time. For many decades it has been extraordinarily frequent in eruption. Every five or ten years it gets into action with violence, sometimes at the summit, oftener of recent years since the central vent has lengthened, at weakened places on its sides. Few volcanoes have been so regularly and systematically studied.

KILAUEA

The most spectacular exhibit of the Hawaii National Park is the lake of fire in the crater of Kilauea.

Kilauea is unusual among volcanoes. It follows few of the popular conceptions. Older than the towering Mauna Loa, its height is only four thousand feet. Its lavas have found vents through its flanks, which they have broadened and flattened. Doubtless its own lavas have helped Mauna Loa's to merge the two mountains into one. It is no longer explosive like the usual volcano; since 1790, when it destroyed a native

THE KILAUEA PIT OF FIRE, HAWAII NATIONAL PARK

Photographed at night by the light of its flaming lavas

WITHIN THE CRATER OF KILAUEA

army, it has ejected neither rocks nor ashes. Its crater is no longer definitely bowl-shaped. From the middle of a broad flat plain, which really is what is left of the ancient great crater, drops a pit with vertical sides within which boil its lavas.

The pit, the lake of fire, is Halemaumau, commonly translated "The House of Everlasting Fire"; the correct translation is "The House of the Maumau Fern," whose leaf is twisted and contorted like some forms of lava. Two miles and a little more from Halemaumau, on a part of the ancient crater wall, stands the Hawaiian Volcano Observatory, which is under the control of the Massachusetts Institute of Technology. The observatory was built for the special purpose of studying the pit of fire, the risings and fallings of whose lavas bear a relationship toward the volcanism of Mauna Loa which is scientifically important, but which we need not discuss here.

The traveller enters Hawaii by steamer through Hilo. He reaches the rim of Kilauea by automobile, an inspiring run of thirty-one miles over a road of volcanic glass, bordered with vegetation strange to eyes accustomed only to that of the temperate zone—brilliant hibiscus, native hardwood trees with feathery pompons for blossoms, and the giant ferns which tower overhead. On the rim are the hotels and the observatory. Steam-jets emerge at intervals, and hot sulphur banks exhibit rich yellows. From there the way descends to the floor of the crater and unrolls a ribbon of flower-bordered road seven miles long to the pit of fire. By trail, the distance is only two miles and a half across long stretches of hard lava congealed in ropes and ripples and strange contortions. Where else is a spectacle one-tenth as appalling so comfortably and quickly reached?

Halemaumau is an irregular pit a thousand feet long with perpendicular sides. Its depth varies. Sometimes one looks hundreds of feet down to the boiling surface; sometimes its lavas overrun the top. The fumes of sulphur are very strong, with the wind in your face. At these times, too, the air is extremely hot. There are cracks in the surrounding lava where you can scorch paper or cook a beefsteak.

Many have been the attempts to describe it. Not having seen it myself, I quote two here; one a careful picture by a close student of the spectacle, Mr. William R. Castle, Jr., of Honolulu; the other a rapid sketch by Mark Twain.

"By daylight," writes Castle, "the lake of fire is a greenish-yellow, cut with ragged cracks of red that look like pale streaks of stationary lightning across its surface. It is restless, breathing rapidly, bubbling up at one point and sinking down in another; throwing up sudden fountains of scarlet molten lava that play a few minutes and subside, leaving shimmering mounds which gradually settle to the level surface of the lake, turning brown and yellow as they sink.

"But as the daylight fades the fires of the pit shine more brightly. Mauna Loa, behind, becomes a pale, gray-blue, insubstantial dome, and overhead stars

begin to appear. As darkness comes the colors on
the lake grow so intense that they almost hurt. The
fire is not only red; it is blue and purple and orange
and green. Blue flames shimmer and dart about the
edges of the pit, back and forth across the surface of
the restless mass. Sudden fountains paint blood-red
the great plume of sulphur smoke that rises constantly, to drift away across the poisoned desert of
Kau. Sometimes the spurts of lava are so violent, so
exaggerated by the night, that one draws back terrified lest some atom of their molten substance should
spatter over the edge of the precipice. Sometimes the
whole lake is in motion. Waves of fire toss and battle with each other and dash in clouds of bright vermilion spray against the black sides of the pit. Sometimes one of these sides falls in with a roar that echoes
back and forth, and mighty rocks are swallowed in
the liquid mass of fire that closes over them in a whirl-
pool, like water over a sinking ship.

"Again everything is quiet, a thick scum forms
over the surface of the lake, dead, like the scum on
the surface of a lonely forest pool. Then it shivers.
Flashes of fire dart from side to side. The centre
bursts open and a huge fountain of lava twenty feet
thick and fifty high, streams into the air and plays for
several minutes, waves of blinding fire flowing out
from it, dashing against the sides until the black rocks
are starred all over with bits of scarlet. To the spec-
tator there is, through it all, no sense of fear. So intense, so tremendous is the spectacle that silly little

human feelings find no place. All sensations are submerged in a sense of awe."

Mark Twain gazed into Halemaumau's terrifying depths. "It looked," he writes, "like a colossal railroad-map of the State of Massachusetts done in chain lightning on a midnight sky. Imagine it—imagine a coal-black sky shivered into a tangled network of angry fire!

"Here and there were gleaming holes a hundred feet in diameter, broken in the dark crust, and in them the melted lava—the color a dazzling white just tinged with yellow—was boiling and surging furiously; and from these holes branched numberless bright torrents in many directions, like the spokes of a wheel, and kept a tolerably straight course for a while and then swept round in huge rainbow curves, or made a long succession of sharp worm-fence angles, which looked precisely like the fiercest jagged lightning. Those streams met other streams, and they mingled with and crossed and recrossed each other in every conceivable direction, like skate-tracks on a popular skating-ground. Sometimes streams twenty or thirty feet wide flowed from the holes to some distance without dividing—and through the opera-glasses we could see that they ran down small, steep hills and were genuine cataracts of fire, white at their source, but soon cooling and turning to the richest red, grained with alternate lines of black and gold. Every now and then masses of the dark crust broke away and floated slowly down these streams like rafts down a river.

"Occasionally, the molten lava flowing under the superincumbent crust broke through—split a dazzling streak, from five hundred to a thousand feet long, like a sudden flash of lightning, and then acre after acre of the cold lava parted into fragments, turned up edgewise like cakes of ice when a great river breaks up, plunged downward, and were swallowed in the crimson caldron. Then the wide expanse of the 'thaw' maintained a ruddy glow for a while, but shortly cooled and became black and level again. During a 'thaw' every dismembered cake was marked by a glittering white border which was superbly shaded inward by aurora borealis rays, which were a flaming yellow where they joined the white border, and from thence toward their points tapered into glowing crimson, then into a rich, pale carmine, and finally into a faint blush that held its own a moment and then dimmed and turned black. Some of the streams preferred to mingle together in a tangle of fantastic circles, and then they looked something like the confusion of ropes one sees on a ship's deck when she has just taken in sail and dropped anchor—provided one can imagine those ropes on fire.

"Through the glasses, the little fountains scattered about looked very beautiful. They boiled, and coughed, and spluttered, and discharged sprays of stringy red fire—of about the consistency of mush, for instance—from ten to fifteen feet into the air, along with a shower of brilliant white sparks—a quaint and unnatural mingling of gouts of blood and snowflakes."

One can descend the sides and approach surprisingly close to the flaming surface, the temperature of which, by the way, is 1750 degrees Fahrenheit.

Such is "The House of Everlasting Fire" to-day. But who can say what it will be a year or a decade hence? A clogging or a shifting of the vents below sea-level, and Kilauea's lake of fire may become again explosive. Who will deny that Kilauea may not soar even above Mauna Loa? Stranger things have happened before this in the Islands of Surprise.

THE SEDIMENTARY NATIONAL PARKS

THE SEDIMENTARY NATIONAL PARKS

XII

ON SEDIMENTARY ROCK IN SCENERY

THE national parks which are wrought in sedimentary rocks are Glacier, Mesa Verde, Hot Springs, Platt, Wind Cave, Sully's Hill, and Grand Canyon. Zion National Monument is carved from sedimentary rock; also several distinguished reservations in our southwest which conserve natural bridges and petrified forests.

Sedimentary rocks have highly attractive scenic quality. Lying in strata usually horizontal but often inclined by earth movements, sometimes even standing on end, they form marked and pleasing contrasts with the heavy massing of the igneous rocks and the graceful undulations and occasional sharp-pointed summits of the lavas.

As distinguished from igneous rocks, which form under pressure in the earth's hot interior, and from lava, which results from volcanic eruption when fluid igneous rocks are released from pressure, sedimentary rocks are formed by the solidification of precipitations in water, like limestone; or from material resulting from rock disintegrations washed down by streams, like sandstone and shale. The beds in which they lie one above another exhibit a wide range of tint and texture, often forming spectacles of surpassing beauty and grandeur.

These strata tend to cleave vertically, sometimes producing an appearance suggestive of masonry, frequently forming impressive cliffs; but often they lie in unbroken beds of great area. When a number of well-defined strata cleave vertically, and one end of the series sags below the other, or lifts above it, the process which geologists call faulting, the scenic effect is varied and striking; sometimes, as in Glacier National Park, it is puzzling and amazing.

Many granitic and volcanic landscapes are variegated in places by accidental beds of sedimentary rock; and conversely occasional sedimentary landscapes are set off by intrusions of igneous rocks.

Besides variety of form, sedimentary rocks furnish a wide range of color derived from mineral dyes dissolved out of rocks by erosion. The gorgeous tint of the Vermilion Cliff in Utah and Arizona, the reds and greens of the Grand Canyon and Glacier National Park, the glowing cliffs of the Canyon de Chelly, and the variegated hues of the Painted Desert are examples which have become celebrated.

Geologists distinguish many kinds of sedimentary rocks. Scenically, we need consider only four: limestone, conglomerate, sandstone, and shale.

Limestone is calcium carbonate derived principally from sea-water, sometimes from fresh water, either by the action of microscopic organisms which absorb it for their shells, or occasionally by direct precipitation from saturated solutions. The sediment from organisms, which is the principal source of American scenic limestones, collects as ooze in shallow lakes or seas, and slowly hardens when lifted above the water-level. Limestone is a common and prominent scenic rock; generally it is gray or blue and weathers pale yellow. Moisture seeping in from above often reduces soluble minerals which drain away, leaving caves which sometimes have enormous size.

The other sedimentary rocks which figure prominently in landscape are products of land erosion which rivers sweep into seas or lakes, where they are promptly deposited. The coarse gravels which naturally fall first become conglomerate when cemented by the action of chemicals in water. The finer sandy particles become sandstone. The fine mud, which deposits last, eventually hardens into shale.

Shale has many varieties, but is principally hardened clay; it tends to split into slate-like plates each the thickness of its original deposit. It is usually dull brown or slate color, but sometimes, as in Glacier National Park and the Grand Canyon, shows a variety of more or less brilliant colors and, by weathering, a wide variety of kindred tints.

Sandstone, which forms wherever moving water or wind has collected sands, and pressure or chemical action has cemented them, is usually buff, but sometimes is brilliantly colored.

The processes of Nature have mixed the earth's scenic elements in seemingly inextricable confusion, and the task of the geologist has been colossal. Fortunately for us, the elements of scenery are few, and their larger combinations broad and simple. Once the mind has grasped the outline and the processes, and the eye has learned to distinguish elements and recognize forms, the world is recreated for us.

XIII

GLACIERED PEAKS AND PAINTED SHALES

GLACIER NATIONAL PARK, NORTHWESTERN MONTANA.
AREA, 1,534 SQUARE MILES

I

TO say that Glacier National Park is the Canadian Rockies done in Grand Canyon colors is to express a small part of a complicated fact. Glacier is so much less and more. It is less in its exhibit of ice and snow. Both are dying glacial regions, and Glacier is hundreds of centuries nearer the end; no longer can it display snowy ranges in August and long, sinuous Alaska-like glaciers at any time. Nevertheless, it has its glaciers, sixty or more of them perched upon high rocky shelves, the beautiful shrunken reminders of one-time monsters. Also it has the precipice-walled cirques and painted, lake-studded valleys which these monsters left for the enjoyment of to-day.

It is these cirques and valleys which constitute Glacier's unique feature, which make it incomparable of its kind. Glacier's innermost sanctuaries of grandeur are comfortably accessible and intimately enjoyable for more than two months each summer. The greatest places of the Canadian Rockies are never accessible comfortably; alpinists may clamber over their icy crevasses and scale their slippery heights in August, but the usual traveller will view their noblest spectacles from hotel porches or valley trails.

This comparison is useful because both regions are parts of the same geological and scenic development in which Glacier may be said to be scenically, though by no means geologically, completed and the Canadian Rockies still in the making. A hundred thousand years or more from now the Canadian Rockies may have reached, except for coloring, the present scenic state of Glacier.

Glacier National Park hangs down from the Canadian boundary-line in northwestern Montana, where it straddles the continental divide. Adjoining it on the north is the Waterton Lakes Park, Canada. The Blackfeet Indian Reservation borders it on the east. Its southern boundary is Marias Pass, through which the Great Northern Railway crosses the crest of the Rocky Mountains. Its western boundary is the North Fork of the Flathead River. The park contains fifteen hundred and thirty-four square miles.

Communication between the east and west sides within the park is only by trail across passes over the continental divide.

There are parts of America quite as distinguished as Glacier: Mount McKinley, for its enormous snowy mass and stature; Yosemite, for the quality of its valley's beauty; Mount Rainier, for its massive radiating glaciers; Crater Lake, for its color range in pearls and blues; Grand Canyon, for its stupendous painted gulf. But there is no part of America or the Americas,

or of the world, to match it of its kind. In respect to
the particular wondrous thing these glaciers of old
left behind them when they shrank to shelved trifles,
there is no other. At Glacier one sees what he never
saw elsewhere and never will see again—except at
Glacier. There are mountains everywhere, but no
others carved into shapes quite like these; cirques in
all lofty ranges, but not cirques just such as these;
and because of these unique bordering highlands there
are nowhere else lakes having the particular kind of
charm possessed by Glacier's lakes.

Visitors seldom comprehend Glacier; hence they
are mute, or praise in generalities or vague superlatives. Those who have not seen other mountains
find the unexpected and are puzzled. Those who have
seen other mountains fail to understand the difference
in these. I have never heard comparison with any
region except the Canadian Rockies, and this seldom
very intelligent. "I miss the big glaciers and snowy
mountain-tops," says the traveller of one type. "You
can really see something here besides snow, and how
stunning it all is!" says the traveller of another type.
"My God, man, where are your artists?" cried an
Englishman who had come to St. Mary Lake to spend
a night and was finishing his week. "They ought to
be here in regiments. Not that this is the greatest
thing in the world, but that there's nothing else in
the world like it." Yet this emotional traveller, who
had seen the Himalayas, Andes, and Canadian Rockies,
could not tell me clearly why it was different. Neither

could the others explain why they liked it better than the Canadian Rockies, or why its beauty puzzled and disturbed them. It is only he whom intelligent travel has educated to analyze and distinguish who sees in the fineness and the extraordinary distinction of Glacier's mountain forms the completion of the more heroic undevelopment north of the border.

II

The elements of Glacier's personality are so unusual that it will be difficult, if not impossible, to make phrase describe it. Comparison fails. Photographs will help, but not very efficiently, because they do not convey its size, color, and reality; or perhaps I should say its unreality, for there are places like Two Medicine Lake in still pale mid-morning, St. Mary Lake during one of its gold sunsets, and the cirques of the South Fork of the Belly River under all conditions which never can seem actual.

To picture Glacier as nearly as possible, imagine two mountain ranges roughly parallel in the north, where they pass the continental divide between them across a magnificent high intervening valley, and, in the south, merging into a wild and apparently planless massing of high peaks and ranges. Imagine these mountains repeating everywhere huge pyramids, enormous stone gables, elongated cones, and many other unusual shapes, including numerous saw-toothed edges which rise many thousand feet upward from swelling sides, and suggest nothing so much as overturned keel-boats. Imagine ranges glacier-bitten alternately on either side with cirques of three or four thousand feet of precipitous depth. Imagine these cirques often so nearly meeting that the intervening walls are knife-like edges; miles of such walls carry the continental divide, and occasionally these cirques meet and the intervening wall crumbles and leaves a pass across the divide. Imagine places where cirque walls have been so bitten outside as well as in that they stand like amphitheatres builded up from foundations instead of gouged out of rock from above.

Imagine these mountains plentifully snow-spattered upon their northern slopes and bearing upon their shoulders many small and beautiful glaciers perched upon rock-shelves above and back of the cirques left by the greater glaciers of which they are the remainders. These glaciers are nearly always wider than they are long; of these I have seen only three with elongated lobes. One is the Blackfeet Glacier, whose interesting west lobe is conveniently situated for observation south of Gunsight Lake, and another, romantically beautiful Agassiz Glacier, in the far northwest of the park, whose ice-currents converge in a tongue which drops steeply to its snout. These elongations are complete miniatures, each exhibiting in little more than half a mile of length all usual glacial phenomena, including caves and ice-falls. Occasionally, as on the side of Mount Jackson at Gunsight Pass and east of it, one notices small elongated glaciers occupying clefts in steep slopes. The largest and most striking of these tongued glaciers is the westernmost of the three Carter Glaciers on the slopes of Mount Carter. It cascades its entire length into Bowman Valley, and Marius R. Campbell's suggestion that it should be renamed the Cascading Glacier deserves consideration.

Imagine deep rounded valleys emerging from these cirques and twisting snakelike among enormous and sometimes grotesque rock masses which often are inconceivably twisted and tumbled, those of each drainage-basin converging fanlike to its central valley. Sometimes a score or more of cirques, great and small, unite their valley streams for the making of a river; seven principal valleys, each the product of such a group, emerge from the east side of the park, thirteen from the west.

Imagine hundreds of lakes whose waters, fresh-run from snow-field and glacier, brilliantly reflect the odd surrounding landscape. Each glacier has its lake or lakes of robin's-egg blue. Every successive shelf of every glacial stairway has its lake—one or more. And every valley has its greater lake or string of lakes. Glacier is pre-eminently the park of lakes. When all is said and done, they constitute its most distinguished single element of supreme beauty. For several of them enthusiastic admirers loudly claim world pre-eminence.

And finally imagine this picture done in soft glowing colors—not only the blue sky, the flowery meadows, the pine-green valleys, and the innumerable many-hued waters, but the rocks, the mountains, and the cirques besides. The glaciers of old penetrated the most colorful depths of earth's skin, the very ancient Algonkian strata, that from which a part of the Grand Canyon also was carved. At this point, the rocks appear in four differently colored layers. The lowest of these is called the Altyn limestone. There are about sixteen hundred feet of it, pale blue within, weathering pale buff. Whole yellow mountains of this rock hang upon the eastern edge of the park. Next above the Altyn lies thirty-four hundred feet of Appekunny argillite, or dull-green shale. The tint is pale, deepening to that familiar in the lower part of the Grand Canyon. It weathers every darkening shade to very dark greenish-brown. Next above that lies twenty-two hundred feet of Grinnell argillite, or red shale, a dull rock of varying pinks which weathers many shades of red and purple, deepening in places almost to black. There is some gleaming white quartzite mixed with both these shales. Next above lies more than four thousand feet of Siyeh limestone, very solid, very massive, iron-gray with an insistent flavor of yellow, and weathering buff. This heavy stratum is the most impressive part of the Glacier landscape. Horizontally through its middle runs a dark broad ribbon of diorite, a rock as hard as granite, which once, while molten, burst from below and forced its way between horizontal beds of limestone; and occasionally, as in the Swiftcurrent and Triple Divide Passes, there are dull iron-black lavas in heavy twisted masses. Above all of these colored strata once lay still another shale of very brilliant red. Fragments of this, which geologists call the Kintla formation, may be seen topping mountains here and there in the northern part of the park.

Imagine these rich strata hung east and west across the landscape and sagging deeply in the middle, so that a horizontal line would cut all colors diagonally.

Now imagine a softness of line as well as color resulting probably from the softness of the rock; there is none of the hard insistence, the uncompromising definiteness of the granite landscape. And imagine further an impression of antiquity, a feeling akin to that with which one enters a mediæval ruin or sees the pyramids of Egypt. Only here is the look of immense, unmeasured, immeasurable age. More than at any place except perhaps the rim of the Grand Canyon does one seem to stand in the presence of the infinite; an instinct which, while it baffles analysis, is sound, for there are few rocks of the earth's skin so aged as these ornate shales and limestones.

And now, at last, you can imagine Glacier!

III

But, with Glacier, this is not enough. To see, to realize in full its beauty, still leaves one puzzled. One of the peculiarities of the landscape, due perhaps to its differences, is its insistence upon explanation. How came this prehistoric plain so etched with cirques and valleys as to leave standing only worm-like crests, knife-edged walls, amphitheatres, and isolated peaks? The answer is the story of a romantic episode in the absorbing history of America's making.

Somewhere between forty and six hundred million years ago, according to the degree of conservatism controlling the geologist who does the calculating, these lofty mountains were deposited in the shape of muddy sediments on the bottom of shallow fresh-water lakes, whose waves left many ripple marks upon the soft muds of its shores, fragments of which, hardened now to shale, are frequently found by tourists. So ancient was the period that these deposits lay next above the primal Archean rocks, and marked, therefore, almost the beginning of accepted geological history. Life was then so nearly at its beginnings that the forms which Walcott found in the Siyeh limestone were not at first fully accepted as organic.

Thereafter, during a time so long that none may even estimate it, certainly for many millions of years, the history of the region leaves traces of no extraordinary change. It sank possibly thousands of feet beneath the fresh waters tributary to the sea which once swept from the Gulf of Mexico to the Arctic, and accumulated there sediments which to-day are scenic limestones and shales, and doubtless other sediments above these which have wholly passed away. It may have alternated above and below water-level many times, as our southwest has done. Eventually, under earth-pressures concerning whose cause many theories have lived and died, it rose to remain until our times.

Then, millions of years ago, but still recently as compared with the whole vast lapse we are considering, came the changes which seem dramatic to us as we look back upon them accomplished; but which came to pass so slowly that no man, had man then lived, could have noticed a single step of progress in the course of a long life. Under earth-pressures the skin buckled and the Rocky Mountains rose. At some stage of this process the range cracked along its crest from what is now Marias Pass to a point just over the Canadian border, and, a couple of hundred miles farther north, from the neighborhood of Banff to the northern end of the Canadian Rockies.

Then the great overthrust followed. Side-pressures of inconceivable power forced upward the western edge of this crack, including the entire crust from the Algonkian strata up, and thrust it over the eastern edge. During the overthrusting, which may have taken a million years, and during the millions of years since, the frosts have chiselled open and the rains have washed away all the overthrust strata, the accumulations of the geological ages from Algonkian times down, except only that one bottom layer. This alone remained for the three ice invasions of the Glacial Age to carve into the extraordinary area which is called to-day the Glacier National Park.

The Lewis Overthrust, so called because it hap-

pened to the Lewis Range, is ten to fifteen miles wide.
The eastern boundary of the park roughly defines its
limit of progress. Its signs are plain to the eye taught
to perceive them. The yellow mountains on the eastern edge near the gateway to Lake McDermott lie
on top of the Blackfeet Indian Reservation, whose
surface is many millions of years younger and quite
different in coloring. Similarly, Chief Mountain, at
the entrance of the Belly River Valley, owes much of
its remarkable distinction to the incompatibility of its
form and color with the prairie upon which it lies
but out of which it seems to burst. The bottom of
McDermott Falls at Many Glacier Hotel is plainly a
younger rock than the colored Algonkian limestones
which form its brink.

Perhaps thousands of years after the overthrust
was accomplished another tremendous faulting still
further modified the landscape of to-day. The overthrust edge cracked lengthwise, this time west of the
continental divide all the way from the Canadian line
southward nearly to Marias Pass. The edge of the
strata west of this crack sank perhaps many thousands
of feet, leaving great precipices on the west side of the
divide similar to those on the east side. There was
this great difference, however, in what followed: the
elongated gulf or ditch thus formed became filled with
the deposits of later geologic periods.

This whole process, which also was very slow in
movement, is important in explaining the conformation and scenic peculiarities of the west side of the

park, which, as the tourist sees it to-day, is remarkably different from those of the east side. Here, the great limestone ranges, glaciered, cirqued, and precipiced as on the east side, suddenly give place to broad, undulating plains which constitute practically the whole of the great west side from the base of the mountains on the east to the valley of the Flathead which forms the park's western boundary. These plains are grown thickly with splendid forests. Cross ranges, largely glacier-built, stretch west from the high mountains, subsiding rapidly; and between these ranges lie long winding lakes, forest-grown to their edges, which carry the western drainage of the continental divide through outlet streams into the Flathead.

The inconceivable lapse of time covered in these titanic operations of Nature and their excessive slowness of progress rob them of much of their dramatic quality. Perhaps an inch of distance was an extraordinary advance for the Lewis Overthrust to make in any ordinary year, and doubtless there were lapses of centuries when no measurable advance was made. Yet sometimes sudden settlings, accompanied by more or less extended earthquakes, must have visibly altered local landscapes.

Were it possible, by some such mental foreshortening as that by which the wizards of the screen compress a life into a minute, for imagination to hasten this progress into the compass of a few hours, how overwhelming would be the spectacle! How tremendously would loom this advancing edge, which

at first we may conceive as having enormous thickness!
How it must have cracked, crumbled, and fallen in
frequent titanic crashes as it moved forward. It does
not need the imagination of Doré to picture this advance, thus hastened in fancy, grim, relentless as death,
its enormous towering head lost in eternal snows, its
feet shaken by earthquakes, accumulating giant glaciers only to crush them into powder; resting, then
pushing forward in slow, smashing, reverberating
shoves. How the accumulations of all periods may
be imagined crashing together into the depths! Si-
lurian gastropods, strange Devonian fishes, enormous
Triassic reptiles, the rich and varied shells of the
Jurassic, the dinosaurs and primitive birds of Cretaceous, the little early horses of Eocene, and Mi-
ocene's camels and mastodons mingling their fossil
remnants in a democracy of ruin to defy the eternal
ages!

It all happened, but unfortunately for a romantic
conception, it did not happen with dramatic speed.
Hundreds, thousands, sometimes millions of years in-
tervened between the greater stages of progress which,
with intervening lesser stages, merged into a seldom-
broken quietude such as that which impresses to-day's
visitor to the mountain-tops of Glacier National Park.
And who can say that the landscape which to-day's
visitor, with the inborn arrogance of man, looks upon
as the thing which the ages have completed for his
pleasure, may not merely represent a minor stage in a
progress still more terrible?

The grist of Creation's past milling has disappeared. The waters of heaven, collected and stored in snow-fields and glaciers to be released in seasonal torrents, have washed it all away. Not a sign remains to-day save here and there perhaps a fragment of Cretaceous coal. All has been ground to powder and carried off by flood and stream to enrich the soils and upbuild later strata in the drainage basins of the Saskatchewan, the Columbia, and the Mississippi.

It is probable that little remained but the Algonkian shales and limestones when the Ice Age sent southward the first of its three great invasions. Doubtless already there were glaciers there of sorts, but the lowering temperatures which accompanied the ice-sheets developed local glaciers so great of size that only a few mountain-tops were left exposed. It was then that these extraordinary cirques were carved. There were three such periods during the Ice Age, between which and after which stream erosion resumed its untiring sway. The story of the ice is written high upon Glacier's walls and far out on the eastern plains.

IV

Into this wonderland the visitor enters by one of two roads. Either he leaves the railroad at Glacier Park on the east side of the continental divide or at Belton on the west side. In either event he can cross to the other side only afoot or on horseback over passes. The usual way in is through Glacier Park.

There is a large hotel at the station from which automobile-stages run northward to chalets at Two Medicine Lake, the Cut Bank Valley, and St. Mary Lake, and to the Many Glacier Hotel and chalets at Lake McDermott. A road also reaches Lake McDermott from Canada by way of Babb, and Canadian visitors can reach the trails at the head of Waterton Lake by boat from their own Waterton Lakes Park. Those entering at Belton, where the park headquarters are located, find chalets at the railroad-station and an excellent hotel near the head of Lake McDonald. There is also a comfortable chalet close to the Sperry Glacier.

To see Glacier as thoroughly as Glacier deserves and to draw freely on its abundant resources of pleasure and inspiration, one must travel the trails and pitch his tent where day's end brings him. But that does not mean that Glacier cannot be seen and enjoyed by those to whom comfortable hotel accommodations are a necessity, or even by those who find trail-travelling impossible.

Visitors, therefore, fall into three general classes, all of whom may study scenery which quite fully covers the range of Glacier's natural phenomena and peculiar beauty. The largest of these classes consists of those who can travel, or think they can travel, only in vehicles, and can find satisfactory accommodations only in good hotels. The intermediate class includes those who can, at a pinch, ride ten or twelve miles on comfortably saddled horses which walk the trails at two or three miles an hour, and who do not object to the somewhat primitive but thoroughly comfortable overnight accommodations of the chalets. Finally comes the small class, which constantly will increase, of those who have the time and inclination to leave the beaten path with tent and camping outfit for the splendid wilderness and the places of supreme magnificence which are only for those who seek.

The man, then, whose tendency to gout, let us say, forbids him ride a horse or walk more than a couple of easy miles a day may, nevertheless, miss nothing of Glacier's meaning and magnificence provided he takes the trouble to understand. But he must take the trouble; he must comprehend the few examples that he sees; this is his penalty for refusing the rich experience of the trail, which, out of its very fulness, drives meaning home with little mental effort. His knowledge must be got from six places only which may be reached by vehicle, at least three of which, however, may be included among the world's great scenic places. He can find at Two Medicine, St. Mary, and McDermott superb examples of Glacier's principal scenic elements.

Entering at Glacier Park, he will have seen the range from the plains, an important beginning; already, approaching from the east, he has watched it grow wonderfully on the horizon. So suddenly do these painted mountains spring from the grassy plain that it is a relief to recognize in them the advance guard of the Lewis Overthrust, vast fragments of the upheavals of the depths pushed eastward by the cen-

turies to their final resting-places upon the surface of
the prairie. From the hotel porches they glow gray
and yellow and purple and rose and pink, according to
the natural coloring of their parts and the will of the
sun—a splendid ever-changing spectacle.

THE TWO MEDICINE COUNTRY

An hour's automobile-ride from Glacier Park
Hotel will enable our traveller to penetrate the range
at a point of supreme beauty and stand beside a chalet
at the foot of Two Medicine Lake. He will face what
appears to be a circular lake in a densely forested valley from whose shore rises a view of mountains which
will take his breath. In the near centre stands a cone
of enormous size and magnificence—Mount Rockwell
—faintly blue, mistily golden, richly purple, dull silver,
or red and gray, according to the favor of the hour and
the sky. Upon its left and somewhat back rises a
smaller similar cone, flatter but quite as perfectly
proportioned, known as Grizzly Mountain, and upon
its right less regular masses. In the background, connecting all, are more distant mountains flecked with
snow, the continental divide. Towering mountains
close upon him upon both sides, that upon his right a
celebrity in red argillite known as Rising Wolf. He
sees all this from a beach of many-colored pebbles.

Few casual visitors have more than a midday
view of Two Medicine Lake, for the stage returns in
the afternoon. The glory of the sunset and the wonder before sunrise are for the few who stay over at the

chalet. The lover of the exquisite cannot do better, for, though beyond lie scenes surpassing this in the qualities which bring to the lips the shout of joy, I am convinced that nothing elsewhere equals the Two Medicine canvas in the perfection of delicacy. It is the Meissonier of Glacier.

Nor can the student of Nature's processes afford to miss the study of Two Medicine's marvellously complete and balanced system of cirques and valleys —though this of course is not for the rheumatic traveller but for him who fears not horse and tent. Such an explorer will find thrills with every passing hour. Giant Mount Rockwell will produce one when a sideview shows that its apparent cone is merely the smaller eastern end of a ridge two miles long which culminates in a towering summit on the divide; Pumpelly Piller, with the proportions of a monument when seen from near the lake, becomes, seen sideways, another long and exceedingly beautiful ridge; striking examples, these, of the leavings of converging glaciers of old. Two Medicine Lake proves to be long and narrow, the chalet view being the long way, and Upper Two Medicine Lake proves to be an emerald-encircled pearl in a silvery-gray setting. The climax of such a several days' trip is a night among the coyotes at the head of the main valley and a morning upon Dawson Pass overlooking the indescribable tangle of peak, precipice, and canyon lying west of the continental divide.

Taken as a whole, the Two Medicine drainage-basin is an epitome of Glacier in miniature. To those entering the park on the east side and seeing it first it becomes an admirable introduction to the greater park. To those who have entered on the west side and finish here it is an admirable farewell review, especially as its final picture sounds the note of scenic perfection. Were there nothing else of Glacier, this spot would become in time itself a world celebrity. Incidentally, exceedingly lively Eastern brook-trout will afford an interesting hour to one who floats a fly down the short stream into the lakelet at the foot of Two Medicine Lake not far below the chalet. There are also fish below Trick Falls.

THE SPECTACLE OF ST. MARY

St. Mary Lake, similarly situated in the outlet valley of a much greater group of cirques north of Two Medicine, offers a picture as similar in kind as two canvases are similar which have been painted by the same hand; but they widely differ in composition and magnificence; Two Medicine's preciousness yields to St. Mary's elemental grandeur. The steamer which brings our rheumatic traveller from the motor-stage at the foot of the lake lands him at the upper chalet group, appropriately Swiss, which finds vantage on a rocky promontory for the view of the divide. Gigantic mountains of deep-red argillite, grotesquely carved, close in the sides, and with lake and sky wonderfully frame the amazing central picture of pointed pyramids, snow-fields, hanging glaciers, and silvery ridges merging into sky. Seen on the way into Glacier,

St. Mary is a prophecy which will not be fulfilled elsewhere in charm though often far exceeded in degree.
Seen leaving Glacier, it combines with surpassing
novelty scenic elements whose possibilities of further
gorgeous combination the trip through the park has
seemed to exhaust.

The St. Mary picture is impossible to describe.
Its colors vary with the hours and the atmosphere's
changing conditions. It is silver, golden, mauve, blue,
lemon, misty white, and red by turn. It is seen clearly
in the morning with the sun behind you. Afternoons
and sunsets offer theatrical effects, often baffling,
always lovely and different. Pointed Fusillade and
peaked Reynolds Mountains often lose their tops in
lowering mists. So, often, does Going-to-the-Sun
Mountain in the near-by right foreground. So, not
so often, does keel-shaped Citadel Mountain on the
near-by left; also, at times, majestic Little Chief, he
of lofty mien and snow-dashed crown, and stolid Red
Eagle, whose gigantic reflection reddens a mile of
waters. It is these close-up monsters even more than
the colorful ghosts of the Western horizon which stamp
St. Mary's personality.

From the porches of the chalets and the deck of
the steamer in its evening tour of the lake-end the
traveller will note the enormous size of those upper
valleys which once combined their glaciers as now they
do their streams. He will guess that the glacier which
once swept through the deep gorge in whose bottom
now lies St. Mary Lake was several thousand feet in

thickness. He will long to examine those upper valleys and reproduce in imagination the amazing spectacle of long ago. But they are not for him. That vision is reserved for those who ride the trails.

The Scenic Climax of the Swiftcurrent

Again passing north, the automobile-stage reaches road's end at McDermott Lake, the fan-handle of the Swiftcurrent drainage-basin. Overlooking a magnifi-cent part of each of its contributing valleys, the lake, itself supremely beautiful, may well deserve its repu-tation as Glacier's scenic centre. I have much sym-pathy with the thousands who claim supremacy for McDermott Lake. Lake McDonald has its wonder-fully wooded shores, its majestic length and august vista; Helen Lake its unequalled wildness; Bowman Lake its incomparable view of glacier-shrouded divide. But McDermott has something of everything; it is a composite, a mosaic masterpiece with every stone a gem. There is no background from which one looks forward to "the view." Its horizon contains three hundred and sixty degrees of view. From the towering south gable of that rock-temple to God the Creator, which the map calls Mount Gould, around the circle, it offers an unbroken panorama in superlative.

In no sense by way of comparison, which is ab-surd between scenes so different, but merely to help realization by contrast with what is well known, let us recall the Yosemite Valley. Yosemite is a valley, Swiftcurrent an enclosure. Yosemite is gray and shining, Swiftcurrent richer far in color. Yosemite's walls are rounded, peaked, and polished, Swiftcurrent's toothed, torn, and crumbling; the setting sun shines through holes worn by frost and water in the living rock. Yosemite guards her western entrance with a shaft of gray granite rising thirty-six hundred feet from the valley floor, and her eastern end by granite domes of five thousand and six thousand feet; Swiftcurrent's rocks gather round her central lake—Altyn, thirty-two hundred feet above the lake's level; Henkel, thirty-eight hundred feet; Wilbur, forty-five hundred feet; Grinnell, four thousand; Gould, forty-seven hundred; Allen, forty-five hundred—all of colored strata, green at base, then red, then gray. Yosemite has its winding river and waterfalls, Swiftcurrent its lakes and glaciers.

Swiftcurrent has the repose but not the softness of Yosemite. Yosemite is unbelievably beautiful. Swiftcurrent inspires wondering awe.

McDermott Lake, focus point of all this natural glory, is scarcely a mile long, and narrow. It may be vivid blue and steel-blue and milky-blue, and half a dozen shades of green and pink all within twice as many minutes, according to the whim of the breeze, the changing atmosphere, and the clouding of the sun. Often it suggests nothing so much as a pool of dull-green paint. Or it may present a reversed image of mountains, glaciers, and sky in their own coloring. Or at sunset it may turn lemon or purple or crimson or orange, or a blending of all. Or, with rushing storm-

From a photograph by A. J. Baker

THE CIRQUE AT THE HEAD OF CUT BANK CREEK

Fine examples of glacier cirques throughout the park. The peak is
Mount Morgan; Glacier National Park

From a photograph by Bailey Willis

THE GREAT GABLE OF GOULD MOUNTAIN

The water is McDermott Lake, one of the most beautiful in
Glacier National Park

clouds, it may quite suddenly lose every hint of any color, and become a study in black, white, and intermediate grays.

There are times when, from hotel porch, rock, or boat, the towering peaks and connecting limestone walls become suddenly so fairylike that they lose all sense of reality, seeming to merge into their background of sky, from which, nevertheless, they remain sharply differentiated. The rapidity and the variety of change in the appearance of the water is nothing to that in the appearance of these magical walls and mountains. Now near, now distant; now luring, now forbidding; now gleaming as if with their own light; now gloomy in threat, they lose not their hold on the eye for a moment. The unreality of McDermott Lake, the sense it often imparts of impossibility, is perhaps its most striking feature. One suspects he dreams, awake.

The Scenic Circle

To realize the spot as best we may, let us pause on the bridge among those casting for trout below the upper fall and glance around. To our left rises Allen Mountain, rugged, irregular, forest-clothed half-way up its forty-five hundred feet of elevation above the valley floor. Beyond it a long gigantic wall sets in at right angles, blue, shining, serrated, supporting, apparently on the lake edge, an enormous gable end of gray limestone banded with black diorite, a veritable personality comparable with Yosemite's most famous rocks. This is Mount Gould. Next is the Grinnell

Glacier, hanging glistening in the air, dripping water-falls, backgrounded by the gnawed top of the venerable Garden Wall. Then comes in turn the majestic mass of Mount Grinnell, four miles long, culminating at the lakeside in an enormous parti-colored pyramid more impressive from the hotel than even Rockwell is from Two Medicine chalets. Then, upon its right, appears a wall which is the unnamed continuation of the Garden Wall, and, plastered against the side of Swift-current Mountain, three small hanging glaciers, seeming in the distance like two long parallel snow-banks. Then Mount Wilbur, another giant pyramid, gray, towering, massively carved, grandly proportioned, kingly in bearing! Again upon its right emerges still another continuation, also unnamed, of the Garden Wall, this section loftiest of all and bitten deeply by the ages. A part of it is instantly recognized from the hotel window as part of the sky-line surrounding famous Iceberg Lake. Its right is lost behind the nearer slopes of red Mount Henkel, which swings back upon our right, bringing the eye nearly to its starting-point. A glance out behind between mountains, upon the limitless lake-dotted plain, completes the scenic circle.

McDermott Lake, by which I here mean the Swift-current enclosure as seen from the Many Glacier Hotel, is illustrative of all of Glacier. There are wilder spots, by far, some which frighten; there are places of nobler beauty, though as I write I know I shall deny it the next time I stand on McDermott's shores; there are supreme places which at first glance seem to have

no kinship with any other place on earth. Nevertheless, McDermott contains all of Glacier's elements, all
her charm, and practically all her combinations. It
is the place of places to study Glacier. It is also a
place to dream away idle weeks.

So he who cannot ride or walk the trails may still
see and understand Glacier in her majesty. Besides
the places I have mentioned he may see, from the Cut
Bank Chalet, a characteristic forested valley of great
beauty, and at Lewis's hotel on Lake McDonald the
finest spot accessible upon the broad west side, the
playground, as the east side is the show-place, of hundreds of future thousands.

So many are the short horseback trips from
Many Glacier Hotel to places of significance and beauty
that it is hard for the timid to withstand the temptation of the trail. Four miles will reach Grinnell Lake
at the foot of its glacier, six miles will penetrate the
Cracker Lake Gorge at the perpendicular base of
Mount Siyeh, eight miles will disclose the astonishing
spectacle of Iceberg Lake, and nine miles will cross the
Swiftcurrent Pass to the Granite Park Chalet.

ICEBERG LAKE TYPICAL OF ALL

In some respects Iceberg Lake is Glacier's supreme
spectacle. There are few spots so wild. There may
be no easily accessible spot in the world half so wild.
Imagine a horseshoe of perpendicular rock wall, twenty-
seven hundred to thirty-five hundred feet high, a glacier in its inmost curve, a lake of icebergs in its centre.

The back of the tower-peak of Mount Wilbur is the southern end of this horseshoe. This enclosure was not built up from below, as it looks, but bitten down within and without; it was left. On the edge of the lake in early July the sun sets at four o'clock.

Stupendous as Iceberg Lake is as a spectacle, its highest purpose is illustrative. It explains Glacier. Here by this lakeside, fronting the glacier's floating edge and staring up at the jagged top in front and on either side, one comprehends at last. The appalling story of the past seems real.

The Climax at Granite Park

It is at Granite Park that one realizes the geography of Glacier. You have crossed the continental divide and emerged upon a lofty abutment just west of it. You are very nearly in the park's centre, and on the margin of a forested canyon of impressive breadth and depth, lined on either side by mountain monsters, and reaching from Mount Cannon at the head of Lake McDonald northward to the Alberta plain. The western wall of this vast avenue is the Livingston Range. Its eastern wall is the Lewis Range. Both in turn carry the continental divide, which crosses the avenue from Livingston to Lewis by way of low-crowned Flattop Mountain, a few miles north of where you stand, and back to Livingston by way of Clements Mountain, a few miles south. Opposite you, across the chasm, rises snowy Heavens Peak. Southwest lies Lake McDonald, hidden by Heavens' shoulder.

From a photograph by Haynes

PTARMIGAN LAKE AND MOUNT WILBUR, GLACIER NATIONAL PARK

From a photograph by A. J. Thiri

SCOOPED BOTH SIDES BY GIANT GLACIERS

Wall on the left encloses Iceberg Lake; on the right is the Belly River abyss; Glacier National Park

South is Logan Pass, carrying another trail across the divide, and disclosing hanging gardens beyond on Reynolds' eastern slope. Still south of that, unseen from here, is famous Gunsight Pass.

It is a stirring spectacle. But wait. A half-hour's climb to the summit of Swiftcurrent Mountain close at hand (the chalet is most of the way up, to start with) and all of Glacier lies before you like a model in relief. Here you see the Iceberg Cirque from without and above. The Belly River chasm yawns enormously. Mount Cleveland, monarch of the region, flaunts his crown of snow among his near-by court of only lesser monsters. The Avenue of the Giants deeply splits the northern half of the park, that land of extravagant accent, mysterious because so little known; the Glacier of tourists lying south. A marvellous spectacle, this, indeed, and one which clears up many misconceptions. The Canadian Rockies hang on the misty northern horizon, the Montana plains float eastward, the American Rockies roll south and west.

OVER GUNSIGHT PASS

To me one of the most stirring sights in all Glacier is the view of Gunsight Pass from the foot of Gunsight Lake. The immense glaciered uplift of Mount Jackson on the south of the pass, the wild whitened sides of Gunsight Mountain opposite dropping to the up-turned strata of red shale at the water's edge, the pass itself—so well named—perched above the dark precipice at the lake's head, the corkscrew which the trail makes up Jackson's perpendicular flank and its passage across a mammoth snow-bank high in air—these in contrast with the silent black water of the sunken lake produce ever the same thrill however often seen. The look back, too, once the pass is gained, down St. Mary's gracious valley to Going-to-the-Sun Mountain and its horizon companions! Sun Mountain (for short), always a personality, is never from any other point of view so undeniably the crowned majesty as from Gunsight Pass. And finally, looking forward, which in this speaking means westward, the first revelation of Lake Ellen Wilson gives a shock of awed astonishment whose memory can never pass.

Truly, Gunsight is a pass of many sensations, for, leaving Lake Ellen Wilson and its eighteen hundred feet of vertical frothing outlet, the westward trail crosses the shoulder of Lincoln Peak to the Sperry Glacier and its inviting chalet (where the biggest hoary marmot I ever saw sat upon my dormitory porch), and, eight miles farther down the mountain, beautiful Lake McDonald.

DESTINY OF THE WEST SIDE

Although it was settled earlier, Glacier's west side is less developed than its east side; this because, for the most part, its scenery is less sensational though no less gorgeously beautiful. Its five long lakes, of which McDonald is much the longest and largest, head up toward the snowy monsters of the divide; their thin bodies wind leisurely westward among superbly forested slopes. Its day is still to come. It is the land of the bear, the moose, the deer, the trout, and summer leisure. Its destiny is to become Glacier's vacation playground.

THE COMING SPLENDORS OF THE NORTH

The wild north side of Glacier, its larger, bigger-featured, and occasionally greater part, is not yet for the usual tourist; for many years from this writing, doubtless, none will know it but the traveller with tent and pack-train. He alone, and may his tribe increase, will enjoy the gorgeous cirques and canyons of the Belly River, the wild quietude of the Waterton Valley, the regal splendors of Brown Pass, and the headwater spectacles of the Logging, Quartz, Bowman, and Kintla valleys. He alone will realize that here is a land of greater power, larger measures, and bigger horizons.

And yet with Kintla comes climax. Crossing the border the mountains subside, the glaciers disappear. Canada's Waterton Lakes Park begins at our climax and merges in half a dozen miles into the great prairies of Alberta. It is many miles northwest before the Canadian Rockies assume proportions of superlative scenic grandeur.

THE BELLY RIVER VALLEYS

To realize the growing bigness of the land north-ward one has only to cross the wall from Iceberg Lake into the Belly River canyon. "Only," indeed! In 1917 it took us forty miles of detour outside the park, even under the shadow of Chief Mountain, to cross the wall from Iceberg Lake, the west-side precipice of which is steeper even than the east. The Belly River drainage-basin is itself bigger, and its mountains bulk in proportion. Eighteen glaciers contribute to the making of perhaps as many lakes. The yellow mountains of its northern slopes invade Canada. The borders of its principal valley are two monster mountains, Cleveland, the greatest in the park for mass and height and intricate outline; the other, Merritt, in some respects the most interesting of Glacier's abundant collection of majestic peaks.

There are three valleys. The North Fork finds its way quickly into Canada. The Middle Fork rises in a group of glaciers high under the continental divide and descends four giant steps, a lake upon each step, to two greater lakes of noble aspect in the valley bottom. The South Fork emerges from Helen Lake deep in the gulf below the Ahern Glacier across the Garden Wall from Iceberg Lake. Between the Middle and South Forks Mount Merritt rises 9,944 feet in altitude, minareted like a mediæval fort and hollow as a bowl, its gaping chasm hung with glaciers.

This is the valley of abundance. The waters are large, their trout many and vigorous; the bottoms are extravagantly rich in grasses and flowers; the forests are heavy and full-bodied; there is no open place, even miles beyond its boundaries, which does not offer views of extraordinary nobility. Every man who enters it becomes enthusiastically prophetic of its future. After all, the Belly River country is easily visited. A leisurely horseback journey from McDermott, that is all; three days among the strange yellow mountains of the overthrust's eastern edge, including two afternoons among the fighting trout of Kennedy Creek and Slide Lake, and two nights in camp among the wild bare arroyos of the Algonkian invasion of the prairie—an interesting prelude to the fulness of wilderness life to come.

I dwell upon the Belly valleys because their size, magnificence, and accessibility suggest a future of public use; nothing would be easier, for instance, than a road from Babb to join the road already in from Canada. The name naturally arouses curiosity. Why Belly? Was it not the Anglo-Saxon frontier's pronunciation of the Frenchman's original Belle? The river, remember, is mainly Canadian. Surely in all its forks and tributaries it was and is the Beautiful River.

THE AVENUE OF THE GIANTS

The Avenue of the Giants looms in any forecast of Glacier's future. It really consists of two valleys joined end on at their beginnings on Flattop Mountain; McDonald Creek flowing south, Little Kootenai flowing north. The road which will replace the present trail up this avenue from the much-travelled south to Waterton Lake and Canada is a matter doubtless of a distant future, but it is so manifestly destiny that it must be accepted as the key to the greater Glacier to come. Uniting at its southern end roads from both sides of the divide, it will reach the Belly valleys by way of Ahern Pass, the Bowman and Kintla valleys by way of Brown Pass, and will terminate at the important tourist settlement which is destined to grow at the splendid American end of Waterton Lake. Incidentally it will become an important motor-highway between Canada and America. Until then, though all these are now accessible by trail, the high distinction of the Bowman and the Kintla valleys' supreme expression of the glowing genius of this whole country will remain unknown to any considerable body of travellers.

The Climax of Bowman and Kintla

And, after all, the Bowman and Kintla regions are Glacier's ultimate expression, Bowman of her beauty, Kintla of her majesty. No one who has seen the foaming cascades of Mount Peabody and a lost outlet of the lofty Boulder Glacier emerging dramatically through Hole-in-the-Wall Fall, for all the world like a horsetail fastened upon the face of a cliff, who has looked upon the Guardhouse from Brown Pass and traced the distant windings of Bowman Lake between the fluted precipice of Rainbow Peak and the fading slopes of Indian Ridge; or has looked upon the mighty monolith of Kintla Peak rising five thousand feet from the lake in its gulf-like valley, spreading upon its shoulders, like wings prepared for flight, the broad gleaming glaciers known as Kintla and Agassiz, will withhold his guerdon for a moment.

SHOWING THE AGAZZIZ GLACIER

Kintla Peak, Glacier National Park, 5,000 feet above the lake, spreads glaciers out either
way like wings

BEAUTIFUL BOWMAN LAKE, GLACIER NATIONAL PARK

It heads close up under the Continental Divide, where is found some of the most striking
scenery of America

Here again we repeat, for the hundredth or more time in our leisurely survey of the park, what the Englishman said of the spectacle of St. Mary: "There is nothing like it in the world."

XIV

ROCK RECORDS OF A VANISHED RACE

<small>MESA VERDE NATIONAL PARK, SOUTHWESTERN COLORADO.
AREA, 77 SQUARE MILES</small>

I

MANY years, possibly centuries, before Columbus discovered America, a community of cliff-dwellers inhabiting a group of canyons in what is now southwestern Colorado entirely disappeared.

Many generations before that, again possibly centuries, the founders of this community, abandoning the primitive pueblos of their people elsewhere, had sought new homes in the valleys tributary to the Mancos River. Perhaps they were enterprising young men and women dissatisfied with the poor and unprogressive life at home. Perhaps they were dissenters from ancient religious forms, outcasts and pilgrims, for there is abundant evidence that the prehistoric sun-worshippers of our southwest were deeply religious, and human nature is the same under skins of all colors in every land and age. More likely they were merely thrifty pioneers attracted to the green cedar-grown mesas by the hope of better conditions.

Whatever the reason for their pilgrimage, it is a fair inference that, like our own Pilgrim Fathers, they were sturdy of body and progressive of spirit, for they

284

had a culture which their descendants carried beyond that of other tribes and communities of prehistoric people in America north of the land of the Aztecs.

Beginning with modest stone structures of the usual cliff-dwellers' type built in deep clefts in the mesa's perpendicular cliff, safe from enemies above and below, these enterprising people developed in time a complicated architecture of a high order; they advanced the arts beyond the practice of their forefathers and their neighbors; they herded cattle upon the mesas; they raised corn and melons in clearings in the forests, and watered their crops in the dry seasons by means of simple irrigation systems as soundly scientific, so far as they went, as those of to-day; outgrowing their cliff homes, they invaded the neighboring mesas, where they built pueblos and more ambitious structures.

Then, apparently suddenly, for they left behind them many of their household goods, and left unfinished an elaborate temple to their god, the sun, they vanished. There is no clew to the reason or the manner of their going.

Meantime European civilization was pushing in all directions. Columbus discovered America; De Soto explored the southeast and ascended the Mississippi; Cortez pushed into Mexico and conquered the Aztecs; Spanish priests carried the gospel north and west from the Antilles to the continent; Raleigh sent explorers to Virginia; the Pilgrim Fathers landed in Massachusetts; the white man pushed the Indian aside, and at last the European pioneer sought a precarious living on the sands of the southwest.

One December day in 1888 Richard and Alfred Wetherill hunted lost cattle on the top of one of the green mesas north and west of the Mancos River. They knew this mesa well. Many a time before had they rounded up their herds and stalked the deer among the thin cedar and pinyon forests. Often, doubtless, in their explorations of the broad Mancos Valley below, they had happened upon ruins of primitive isolated or grouped stone buildings hidden by sagebrush, half buried in rock and sand. No doubt, around their ranch fire, they had often speculated concerning the manner of men that had inhabited these lowly structures so many years before that sometimes aged cedars grew upon the broken walls.

But this December day brought the Wetherills the surprise of their uneventful lives. Some of the cattle had wandered far, and the search led to the very brink of a deep and narrow canyon, across which, in a long deep cleft under the overhang of the opposite cliff, they saw what appeared to be a city. Those who have looked upon the stirring spectacle of Cliff Palace from this point can imagine the astonishment of these ranchmen.

Whether or not the lost cattle were ever found is not recorded, but we may assume that living on the mesa was not plentiful enough to make the Wetherills forget them in the pleasure of discovering a ruin. But they lost no time in investigating their find, and soon after crossed the canyon and climbed into this prehistoric city. They named it Cliff Palace, most inappropriately, by the way, for it was in fact that most democratic of structures, a community dwelling. Pushing their explorations farther, presently they discovered also a smaller ruin, which they named Spruce Tree House, because a prominent spruce grew in front of it. These are the largest two cliff-dwellings in the Mesa Verde National Park, and, until Doctor J. Walter Fewkes unearthed Sun Temple in 1915, among the most extraordinary prehistoric buildings north of Mexico.

There are thousands of prehistoric ruins in our southwest, and many besides those of the Mesa Verde are examples of an aboriginal civilization. Hundreds of canyons tell the story of the ancient cliff-dwellers; and still more numerous are the remains of communal houses built of stone or sun-dried brick under the open sky. These pueblos in the open are either isolated structures like the lesser cliff-dwellings, or are crowded together till they touch walls, as in our modern cities; often they were several stories high, the floors connected by ladders. Sometimes, for protection against the elements, whole villages were built in caves. Pueblos occasionally may be seen from the car-window in New Mexico. The least modified of the prehistoric type which are occupied to-day are the eight villages of the Hopi near the Grand Canyon in Arizona; a suggestive reproduction of a model pueblo, familiar to many thousands who have visited the canyon, stands near the El Tovar Hotel.

It was not therefore because of the rarity of prehistoric dwellings of either type that the cliff villages of the Mesa Verde were conserved as a national park, nor only because they are the best preserved of all North American ruins, but because they disclose a type of this culture in advance of all others.

The builders and inhabitants of these dwellings were Indians having physical features common to all American tribes. That their accomplishment differed in degree from that of the shiftless war-making tribes north and east of them, and from that of the cultured and artistic Mayas of Central America, was doubtless due to differences in conditions of living. The struggle for bare existence in the southwest, like that of the habitats of other North American Indians, was intense; but these were agriculturalists and protected by environment. The desert was a handicap, of course, but it offered opportunity in many places for dry farming; the Indian raised his corn. The winters, too, were short. It is only in the southwest that enterprise developed the architecture of stone houses which distinguish pueblo Indians from others in North America.

The dwellers in the Mesa Verde were more fortunate even than their fellow pueblo dwellers. The forested mesas, so different from the arid cliffs farther south and west, possessed constant moisture and fertile soil. The grasses lured the deer within capture. The Mancos River provided fish. Above all, the remoteness of these fastness canyons from the trails of raiders and traders and their ease of defense made for long generations of peace. The enterprise innate in the spirit of man did the rest.

II

The history of the Mesa Verde National Park began with the making of America. All who have travelled in the southwest have seen mesas from the car-window. New Mexico, Arizona, and parts of Colorado and Utah, the region of the pueblos, constitute an elevated plateau largely arid. Many millions of years ago all was submerged in the intercontinental sea; in fact the region was sea many times, for it rose and fell alternately, accumulating thousands of feet of sands and gravels much of which hardened into stone after the slow great uplifting which made it the lofty plateau of to-day. Erosion did its work. For a million years or more the floods of spring have washed down the sands and gravels, and the rivers have carried them into the sea. Thousands of vertical feet have disappeared in this way from the potential altitude of the region. The spring floods are still washing down the sands and gravels, and the canyons, cliffs, and mesas of the desert are disclosed to-day as stages in the eternal levelling.

Thus were created the canyons and mesas of the Mesa Verde. Mesa, by the way, is Spanish for table, and verde for green. These, then, are the green table-lands, forest-covered and during the summer grown scantily with grass and richly with flowers.

The Mesa Verde National Park was created by act of Congress in June, 1906, and enlarged seven years later. The Mancos River, on its way to the San Juan and thence to the Colorado and the passage of the Grand Canyon, forms its southern boundary. Scores of canyons, large and small, nearly all dry except at the spring floods, are tributary. All of these trend south; in a general way they are parallel. Each of the greater stems has its lesser tributaries and each of these its lesser forks. Between the canyons lie the mesas. Their tops, if continued without break, would form a more or less level surface; that is, all had been a plain before floods cut the separating canyons.

The region has a wonderful scenic charm. It is markedly different in quality from other national parks, but in its own way is quite as startling and beautiful. Comparison is impossible because of the lack of elements in common, but it may be said that the Mesa Verde represents our great southwest in one of its most fascinating phases, combining the fundamentals of the desert with the flavor of the near-by mountains. The canyons, which are seven or eight hundred feet deep and two or three times as wide where the cliff-dwellings gather, are prevailingly tawny yellow. Masses of sloping talus reach more than half-way up; above them the cliffs are perpendicular; it is in cavities in these perpendiculars that the cliff-dwellings hide. Above the cliffs are low growths of yellowish-green cedar with pinyons and other conifers of darker foliage. Beneath the trees and covering the many

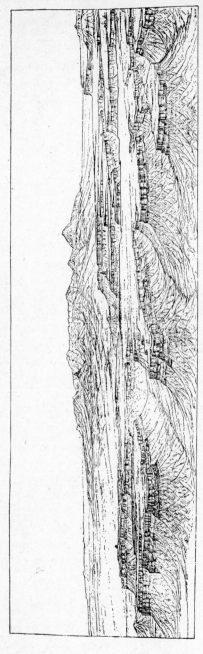

OUTLINE OF THE MESA VERDE FORMATION

Showing the manner in which water erosion is reducing the plains to canyons and mesas. The Mesa Verde cliff-dwellers built their homes in caves in the perpendicular cliffs above the sloping talus

opens grows the familiar sage of the desert, a gray which hints at green and yellow both but realizes neither. But the sage-brush shelters desert grasses, and, around the occasional springs and their slender outlets, grass grows rank and plenteous; a little water counts for a great deal in the desert.

Summer, then, is delightful on the Mesa Verde. The plateau is high and the air invigorating, warm by day in midsummer, always cool at night. The atmosphere is marvellously clear, and the sunsets are famous. The winter snows, which reach three or four feet in depth, disappear in April. From May to Thanksgiving the region is in its prime. It is important to realize that this land has much for the visitor besides its ruins. It has vigor, distinction, personality, and remarkable charm. It is the highest example of one of America's most distinctive and important scenic phases, and this without reference to its prehistoric dwellings. No American traveller knows his America, even the great southwest, who does not know the border-land where desert and forest mingle.

The Southern Ute Indian Reservation bites a large rectangle from the southeast corner of the park, but its inhabitants are very different in quality of mind and spirit from the ancient and reverent builders of Sun Temple. Reservation Indians frequently enter the park, but they cannot be persuaded to approach the cliff-dwellings. The "little people," they tell you, live there, and neither teaching nor example will convince them that these invisible inhabitants will not injure intruders. Some of these Indians allege that it was their own ancestors who built the cliff-dwellings, but there is neither record nor tradition to support such a claim. The fact appears to be that the Utes were the ancient enemies of this people. There is a Ute tradition of a victory over the ancient pueblo-dwellers at Battle Rock in McElmo Canyon.

There are, on the other hand, many reasons for the opinion that the Hopi Indians of the present day, so far at least as culture goes, are descendants of this remarkable prehistoric people. Besides the many similarities between the architectural types of the Mesa Verde and the pueblos of the modern Hopi, careful investigators have found suggestive points of similarity in their utensils, their art forms, and their customs. Doctor Fewkes cites a Hopi tradition to that effect by mentioning the visit of a Hopi courier a few years ago to prehistoric ruins in the Navajo National Monument to obtain water from an ancestral spring for use in a Hopi religious ceremonial. If these traditions are founded in fact, the promising civilization of the Mesa Verde has sadly retrograded in its transplanting. Hopi architecture and masonry shows marked retrogression from the splendid types of the Mesa Verde.

When the telephone-line was under construction to connect the park with the outside world, the Indians from the adjoining Ute reservation became suspicious and restless. Upon hearing its purpose, they begged the superintendent not to go on with the work, which was certain to bring evil to the neighborhood.

"The little people," they solemnly declared, "will not like it."

They assured the superintendent that the wires would not talk.

"The little people will not let them talk," they told him.

But the line was completed and the wires talked.

The park is reached by motor and rail. From Denver, Salt Lake City, and Santa Fé railroad routes offer choice of some of the biggest country of the Rockies. From either direction a night is spent en route in a mountain mining-town, an experience which has its usefulness in preparation for the contrasted and unusual experience to come. Entrance is through Mancos, from which motor-stages thread the maze of canyons and mesas from the highlands of the northern border to the deep canyons of the south where cluster the ruins of distinction.

This entry is delightful. The road crosses the northern boundary at the base of a lofty butte known as Point Lookout, the park's highest elevation. Encircling its eastern side and crossing the Morefield Canyon the road perches for several miles upon the sinuous crest of a ridge more than eight thousand feet in altitude, whose north side plunges eighteen hundred feet into the broad Montezuma Valley, and whose gentle southern slope holds the small beginnings of the great canyons of the cliff-dwellers. Both north and south the panorama unfolds in impressive grandeur, eloquent of the beautiful scanty land and of the difficult conditions of living which confronted the sturdy builders whose ancient masterpieces we are on our way to see. At the northern end of Chapin Mesa we swing sharply south and follow its slope, presently entering the warm, glowing, scented forests, through which we speed to the hotel-camp perched upon a bluff overlooking the depths of Spruce Canyon.

Upon the top and under the eaves of this mesa are found very fine types of prehistoric civilization. At Mummy Lake, half-way down the mesa, we passed on the way a good example of pueblo architecture, and within an easy walk of our terminal camp we find some of the noblest examples of cliff-dwellings in existence. Here it was, near the head of this remote, nearly inaccessible, canyon, guarded by nature's ramparts, that aboriginal American genius before the coming of the Anglo-Saxon found its culminating expression.

In this spirit the thoughtful American of to-day enters the Mesa Verde National Park and examines its precious memorials.

III

Although the accident of the road brings the traveller first to the mesa-top pueblos of the Mummy Lake district, historical sequence suggests that examination begin with the cliff-dwellings.

Of the many examples of these remains in the park, Cliff Palace, Spruce Tree House, and Balcony House are the most important because they concisely and completely cover the range of life and the fulness

of development. This is not the place for detailed
descriptions of these ruins. The special publications
of the National Park Service and particularly the writings of Doctor J. Walter Fewkes of the Smithsonian
Institution, who has devoted many years of brilliant
investigation to American prehistoric remains, are
obtainable from government sources. Here we shall
briefly consider several types.

It is impossible, without reference to photographs,
to convey a concise adequate idea of Cliff Palace.
Seen from across its canyon the splendid crescent-
shaped ruin offers to the unaccustomed eye little that
is common to modern architecture. Prominently in
the foreground, large circular wells at once challenge
interest. These were the kivas, or ceremonial rooms of
the community, centres of the religious activities which
counted so importantly in pueblo life. Here it was
that men gathered monthly to worship their gods. In
the floors of some kivas are small holes representing
symbolically the entrance to the underworld, and
around these from time to time priests doubtless performed archaic ceremonies and communicated with
the dead. Each family or clan in the community is
supposed to have had its own kiva.

The kiva walls of Cliff Palace show some of the
finest prehistoric masonry in America. All are subterranean, which in a few instances necessitated excavation in floors of solid rock. The roofs were supported by pedestals rising from mural banquettes,
usually six pedestals to a kiva; the kiva supposed to

have belonged to the chief's clan had eight pedestals, and one, perhaps belonging to a clan of lesser prominence, had only two. Several kivas which lack roof-supports may have been of different type or used for lesser ceremonials. All except these have fireplaces and ventilators. Entrance was by ladder from the roof.

Other rooms identified are living-rooms, storage-rooms, milling-rooms, and round and square towers, besides which there are dark rooms of unknown use and several round rooms which are neither kivas nor towers. Several of the living-rooms have raised benches evidently used for beds, and in one of them pegs for holding clothing still remain in the walls. The rooms are smoothly plastered or painted.

Mills for grinding corn were found in one room in rows; in others, singly. The work was done by women, who rubbed the upper stone against the lower by hand. The rests for their feet while at work still remain in place; also the brushes for sweeping up the meal. The small storage-rooms had stone doors, carefully sealed with clay to keep out mice and prevent moisture from spoiling the corn and meal.

One of the most striking buildings in Cliff Palace is the Round Tower, two stories high, which not only was an observatory, as is indicated by its peep-holes, but also served purposes in religious festivals. Its masonry belongs to the finest north of Mexico. The stones are beautifully fitted and dressed. The Square Tower which stands at the southern end of the village is four stories high, reaching the roof of the cave. The inner walls of its third story are elaborately painted with red and white symbols, triangles, zigzags, and parallels, the significance of which is not known.

The ledge under which Cliff Palace is built forms a roof that overhangs the structure. An entrance, probably the principal one, came from below to a court at a lower level than the floor, from which access was by ladder.

Spruce Tree House, which may have been built after Cliff Palace, has a circular room with windows which were originally supposed to have been portholes for defense. Doctor Fewkes, however, suggests a more probable purpose, as the position of the room does not specially suggest a fortress. Through the openings in this room the sun-priest may have watched the setting sun to determine the time for ceremonies. The room was entered from above, like a kiva. Another room, differing from any in other cliff-dwellings, has been named the Warriors' Room because, unlike sleeping-rooms, its bench surrounds three sides, and because, unlike any other room, it is built above a kiva. Only the exigencies of defense, it is supposed, would warrant so marked a departure from the prescribed religious form of room.

Balcony House has special interest, apart from its commanding location, perfection of workmanship and unusual beauty, and because of the ingenuity of the defenses of its only possible entrance. At the top of a steep trail a cave-like passage between rocks is walled so as to leave a door capable of admitting only one at a time, behind which two or three men could strike down, one by one, an attacking army.

Out of these simple architectural elements, together with the utensils and weapons found in the ruins, the imagination readily constructs a picture of the austere, laborious, highly religious, and doubtless happy lives led by the earnest people who built these ancient dwellings in the caves.

When all the neighborhood caves were filled to overflowing with increasing population, and generations of peace had wrought a confidence which had not existed when the pioneers had sought safety in caves, these people ventured to move out of cliffs and to build upon the tops of the mesa. Whether all the cave-dwellers were descended from the original pilgrims or whether others had joined them afterward is not known, but it seems evident that the separate communities had found some common bond, probably tribal, and perhaps evolved some common government. No doubt they intermarried. No doubt the blood of many cliff-dwelling communities mingled in the new communities which built pueblos upon the mesa. In time there were many of these pueblos, and they were widely scattered; there are mounds at intervals all over the Mesa Verde. The largest group of pueblos, one infers from the number of visible mounds, was built upon the Chapin Mesa several miles north of the above-mentioned cliff-dwelling near a reservoir known to-day as Mummy Lake. It is there, then, that we shall now go in continuation of our story.

PREHISTORIC POTTERY FROM MESA VERDE

Coloring and design as well as form show high artistic sense and clean workmanship

Mummy Lake is not a lake and no mummies were ever found there. This old-time designation applies to an artificial depression surrounded by a low rude stone wall, much crumbled, which was evidently a storage reservoir for an irrigation system of some size. A number of conspicuous mounds in the neighborhood suggest the former existence of a village of pueblos dependent upon the farms for which the irrigation system had been built. One of these, from which a few stones protruded, was excavated in 1916 by Doctor Fewkes, and has added a new and important chapter to the history of this people. This pueblo has been named Far View House. Its extensive vista includes four other groups of similar mounds. Each cluster occurs in the fertile sage-brush clearings which bloom in summer with asters and Indian paint-brush; there is no doubt that good crops of Indian corn could still be raised from these sands to-day by dry-farming methods.

Far View House is a pueblo, a hundred and thirteen feet long by more than fifty feet wide, not including a full-length plaza about thirty-five feet wide in which religious dances are supposed to have taken place. The differences between this fine structure and the cliff-cities are considerable. The most significant evidence of progress, perhaps, is the modern regularity of the ground-plan. The partitions separating the secular rooms are continuous through the building, and the angles are generally accurately right angles.

The pueblo had three stories. It is oriented approximately to the cardinal points and was terraced southward to secure a sunny exposure. The study of the solar movements became an advanced science with these people in the latter stages of their development. It must be remembered that they had no compasses; knowing nothing of the north or any other fixed point, nevertheless there is evidence that they successfully worked out the solstices and planned their later buildings accurately according to cardinal points of their own calculation.

Another difference indicating development is the decrease in the number of kivas, and the construction of a single very large kiva in the middle of the building. Its size suggests at once that the individual clan organization of cliff-dwelling days had here given place to a single priestly fraternity, sociologically a marked advance. Drawing parallels with the better-known customs of other primitive people, we are at liberty, if we please, to infer similar progress in other directions. The original primitive communism was developing naturally, though doubtless very slowly, into something akin to organized society, probably involving more complicated economic relationships in all departments of living.

While their masonry did not apparently improve in proportion, Far View House shows increase in the number and variety of the decorative figures incised on hewn stones. The spiral, representing the coiled serpent, appears a number of times, as do many combinations of squares, curves, and angles arranged in fanciful design, which may or may not have had symbolic meanings.

A careful examination of the neighborhood discloses few details of the irrigation system, but it shows a cemetery near the southeast corner of the building in which the dead were systematically buried.

Large numbers of minor antiquities were found in this interesting structure. Besides the usual stone implements of the mason and the housekeeper, many instruments of bone, such as needles, dirks, and bodkins, were found. Figurines of several kinds were unearthed, carved from soft stone, including several intended to symbolize Indian corn; all these may have been idols. Fragments of pottery were abundant, in full variety of form, decoration, and color, but always the most ancient types. Among the bones of animals, the frequency of those of rabbits, deer, antelope, elk, and mountain-sheep indicate that meat formed no inconsiderable part of the diet. Fabrics and embroideries were not discovered, as in the cliff-dwellings, but they may have disappeared in the centuries through exposure to the elements.

Far View House may not show the highest development of the Mummy Lake cluster of pueblos, and further exhumations here and in neighboring groups may throw further light upon this interesting people in their gropings from darkness to light. Meantime, however, returning to the neighborhood of the cliff-dwellings, let us examine a structure so late in the history of these people that they left it unfinished.

Sun Temple stands on a point of Chapin Mesa, somewhat back from the edge of Cliff Canyon, commanding an extraordinary range of country. It is within full view of Cliff Palace and other cliff-dwellings of importance and easy of access. From it, one can look southward to the Mancos River. On every side a wide range of mesa and canyon lies in full view. The site is unrivalled for a temple in which all could worship with devotion.

When Doctor Fewkes, in the early summer of 1915, attacked the mound which had been designated Community House under the supposition that it covered a ruined pueblo, he had no idea of the extraordinary nature of the find awaiting him, although he was prepared from its shape and other indications for something out of the usual. So wholly without parallel was the disclosure, however, that it was not till it was entirely uncovered that he ventured a public conjecture as to its significance. The ground-plan of Sun Temple is shaped like the letter D. It encloses another D-shaped structure occupying nearly two-thirds of its total area, within which are two large kivas. Between the outer and the inner D are passages and rooms, and at one end a third kiva is surrounded by rooms, one of which is circular.

Sun Temple is also impressive in size. It is a hundred and twenty-one feet long and sixty-four feet wide. Its walls average four feet in thickness, and are double-faced, enclosing a central core of rubble; they are built of the neighborhood sandstone. The masonry

SUN TEMPLE, MESA VERDE NATIONAL PARK

Built by prehistoric people to their god, the sun, and unfinished when they suddenly disappeared

SPRUCE TREE HOUSE FROM ACROSS THE CANYON

Showing the overhanging rock roof and the forest which tops the Mesa Verde

is of fine quality. This, together with its symmetrical architectural design, its fine proportions, and its many decorated stones, mark it the highest type of Mesa Verde architecture.

It was plainly unfinished. Walls had risen in some places higher than in others. As yet there was no roofing. No rooms had been plastered. Of internal finishing little was completed, and of contents, of course, there was none. The stone hammers and other utensils of the builders were found lying about as if thrown down at day's close.

The kivas, although circular, are unlike those of Cliff Palace, inasmuch as they are above ground, not subterranean. The mortar used in pointing shows the impress of human hands; no trowels were used. The walls exhibit many stones incised with complicated designs, largely geometric; some may be mason's marks; others are decorative or symbolic. These designs indicate a marked advance over those in Far View House; in fact they are far more complicated and artistic than any in the southwest.

Bare and ineloquent though its unfinished condition left it, the religious purposes of the entire building are clear to the archæologist in its form. And, as if to make conjecture certainty, a shrine was uncovered on the corner-stone of the outer wall which frames in solid stone walls a large fossil palm-leaf whose rays strongly suggest the sun!

It requires no imagination to picture the effect which the original discovery of this image of their god must have had upon a primitive community of sun-worshippers. It must have seemed to them a divine gift, a promise, like the Ark of the Covenant, of the favor of the Almighty. It may even have first suggested the idea of building this temple to their deity.

This is all the story. Go there and study it in detail. Enlightened, profoundly impressed, nevertheless you will finish at this point. The tale has no climax. It just stops.

What happened to the people of the Mesa Verde?

Some archæologists believe that they emigrated to neighboring valleys southwest. But why should they have left their prosperous farms and fine homes for regions which seem to us less desirable? And why, a profoundly religious people, should they have left Sun Temple unfinished?

What other supposition remains?

Only, I think, that, perhaps because of their prosperity and the unpreparedness that accompanies long periods of peace, they were suddenly overwhelmed by enemies.

XV

THE HEALING WATERS

Hot Springs Reservation, Arkansas.   Platt National
Park, Oklahoma

I

FROM a hillside on the edge of the Ozark Mountains in central Arkansas issue springs of hot
water which are effective in the alleviation of rheumatic and kindred ills. Although chemical analysis
fails to explain the reason, the practice of many years
has abundantly proved their worth. Before the coming of the white man they were known to the Indians,
who are said to have proclaimed them neutral territory in time of war. Perhaps it was rumor of their
fame upon which Ponce de Leon founded his dream of
a Fountain of Youth.

In the early years of the last century hundreds of
settlers toiled many miles over forest trails to camp
beside them and bathe daily in their waters. The
bent and suffering were carried there on stretchers.
So many and so striking were the cures that the fame
of these springs spread throughout the young nation,
and in 1832, to prevent their falling into hands outstretched to seize and exploit them for private gain,
Congress created them a national reservation. The
Hot Springs Reservation was our first national park.

Previous to this a couple of log houses built by visitors served for shelter for the pilgrims at the shrine of health. Soon after, other buildings quite as primitive were erected. A road was constructed through the forests from the settled portions of the State, and many drove laboriously in with tents and camping outfits. I have seen a copy of a photograph which was taken when photographs were new, showing several men and women in the odd conventional costume of that period sitting solemnly upon the banks of a steaming spring, their clothes drawn up, their bare legs calf deep in the hot water.

Once started, Hot Springs grew rapidly. Unfortunately, this first act of national conservation failed to foresee the great future of these springs, and the reservation line was drawn so that it barely enclosed the brook of steaming vapors which was their outlet. To-day, when the nation contemplates spending millions to beautify the national spa, it finds the city built solidly opposite.

Railroads soon pushed their way through the Ozark foot-hills and landed thousands yearly beside the healing waters. Hotels became larger and more numerous. The government built a public bath-house into which the waters were piped for the free treatment of the people. Concessioners built more elaborate structures within the reservation to accommodate those who preferred to pay for pleasanter surroundings or for private treatment. The village became a town and the town a city. Boarding-houses sprang up everywhere with accommodations to suit the needs of purses of all lengths. Finally, large and costly hotels were built for the prosperous and fashionable who began to find rare enjoyment in the beautiful Ozark country while they drank their hot water and took their invigorating baths. Hot Springs became a national resort.

It will be seen that, in its way, Hot Springs has reflected the social development of the country. It has passed through the various stages that marked the national growth in taste and morals. During the period when gambling was a national vice it was noted for its high play, and then gamblers of all social grades looked forward to their season in the South. During the period of national dissipation, when polite drunkenness was a badge of class and New Year's day an orgy, it became the periodic resort of inebriates, just as later, with the elevation of the national moral sense, it became instead the most conservative of resorts, the periodic refuge of thousands of work-worn business and professional men seeking the astonishing recuperative power of its water.

True again to the spirit of the times, Hot Springs reflects to the full the spirit of to-day. It is a Southern mountain resort of quiet charm and wonderful natural beauty set on the edge of a broad region of hills, ravines, and sweet-smelling pines, a paradise for the walker, the hiker, and the horseback rider. Down on the street a long row of handsome modern bath-houses, equipped with all the scientific luxuries, and more besides, of the most elaborate European spa, concentrates the business of bath and cure. Back of this rise directly the beautiful Ozark hills. One may have exactly what he wishes at Hot Springs. He may live with the sick if that is his bent, or he may spend weeks of rich enjoyment of the South in holiday mood, and have his baths besides, without a suggestion of the sanitarium or even of the spa.

Meantime the mystery of the water's potency seems to have been solved. It is not chemical in solution which clears the system of its ills and restores the jaded tissues to buoyancy, but the newly discovered principle of radioactivity. Somewhere deep in Nature's laboratory these waters become charged with an uplifting power which is imparted to those who bathe according to the rules which many years of experience have prescribed. Many physicians refuse to verify the waters' virtues; some openly scoff. But the fact stands that every year hundreds who come helpless cripples walk jauntily to the station on their departure, and many thousands of sufferers from rheumatic ills and the wear and tear of strenuous living return to their homes restored. I myself can testify to the surprising recuperative effect of only half a dozen daily baths, and I know business men who habitually go there whenever the stress of overwork demands measures of quick relief.

It is not surprising that more than a hundred thousand persons visit Hot Springs every year. The recognized season begins after the winter holidays;

ON HOT SPRINGS MOUNTAIN, HOT SPRINGS OF ARKANSAS

BATH HOUSE ROW, HOT SPRINGS OF ARKANSAS

then it is that gayety and pleasuring, riding, driving, motoring, golfing, and the social life of the fashionable hotels reach their height. But, for sheer enjoyment of the quieter kind, the spring, early summer, and the autumn are unsurpassed; south though it lies, Hot Springs is delightful even in midsummer.

Two railroads land the visitor almost at the entrance of the reservation. A fine road brings the motorist sixty miles from the lively city of Little Rock. The elaborate bath-houses line the reservation side of the principal street, opposite the brick city. But back of them rises abruptly the beautiful forested mountain from whose side gush the healing waters, and back of this roll the beautiful pine-grown Ozarks. The division is sharply drawn. He who chooses may forget the city except at the hour of his daily bath.

The plans for realizing in stone and landscape gardening the ideal of the great American spa, which this spot is in fact, contemplate the work of years.

II

In southern Oklahoma not far from the Texas boundary, a group of thirty healing springs, these of cold sparkling water, were set apart by Congress in 1904 under the title of the Platt National Park. Most of them are sulphur springs; others are impregnated with bromides and other mineral salts. Many thousands visit yearly the prosperous bordering city of Sulphur to drink these waters; many camp in or near the reservation; the bottled waters bring relief to thousands at home.

Through the national park, from its source in the east to its entry into Rock Creek, winds Travertine Creek, the outlet of most of these springs. Rock Creek outlines the park's western boundary, and on its farther bank lies the city. Springs of importance within the park pour their waters directly into its current. All these Platt springs, like those of Hot Springs, Arkansas, were known to the Indians for their curative properties for many generations before the coming of the white settler.

The park is the centre of a region of novelty and charm for the visitor from the North and East. The intimate communion of prairie and rich forested valley, the sophistication of the bustling little city in contrast with the rough life of the outlying ranches, the mingling in common intercourse of such differing human elements as the Eastern tourist, the free and easy Western townsman, the cowboy and the Indian, give rare spice to a visit long enough to impart the spirit of a country of so many kinds of appeal. The climate, too, contributes to enjoyment. The long spring lasts from February to June. During the short summer, social life is at its height. The fall lingers to the holidays before it gives way to a short winter, which the Arbuckle Mountains soften by diverting the colder winds.

The pleasures are those of prairie and valley. It is a great land for riding. There is swimming, rowing, and excellent black-bass fishing in the larger lakes.

It is a region of deer and many birds. Its altitude is about a thousand feet.

The rolling Oklahoma plateau attains in this neighborhood its pleasantest outline and variety. Broad plains of grazing-land alternate with bare rocky heights and low mountains. The creeks and rivers which accumulate the waters of the springs scattered widely among these prairie hills are outlined by winding forested belts and flowered thickets of brush. Great areas of thin prairie yield here and there to rounded hills, some of which bear upon their summits columns of flat rocks heaped one upon the other high enough to be seen for miles against the low horizon.

These, which are known as the Chimney Hills, for many years have been a cause of speculation among the settlers who have nearly replaced the Indians since the State of Oklahoma replaced the Indian Territory with which we became familiar in the geographies of earlier days. Who were the builders of these chimneys and what was their purpose?

"At a hearing in Ardmore a few years ago before a United States court taking testimony upon some ancient Indian depredation claims," writes Colonel R. A. Sneed, for years the superintendent of the Platt National Park, "practically all the residents of the Chickasaw Nation, Indian and negro, whose memories of that country extend back fifty years or more, were in attendance. In recounting his recollections of a Comanche raid in which his master's horses were stolen, one old negro incidentally gave a solution of the Chimney Hills which is the only one the writer ever heard, and which probably accounts for all of them.

"He said that his master lived at Big Sulphur Springs, farthest west of any of the Chickasaws; that the Kiowas and Comanches raided the country every summer and drove out horses or cattle wherever they could find them unprotected; that he had often gone with his master to find these stolen cattle; that these forages were so frequent that the Chickasaws had never undertaken to occupy any of their lands west of Rock Creek, north of Big Sulphur Springs, nor west of the Washita River south of the springs; that the country west of Sulphur Springs was dry, and water was hard to find unless one knew just where to look; and that the Comanches had a custom of marking all the springs they could find by building rock chimneys on the hills nearest to the springs. Only one chimney would be built if the spring flowed from beneath the same hill, but if the spring was distant from the hill two chimneys would be built, either upon the same hill or upon two distant hills, and a sight along the two chimneys would indicate a course toward the spring.

"The old man said that every hill in their pasture had a Comanche chimney on it and that his master would not disturb them because he did not want to make the wild Indians mad. There never was open war between the Chickasaws and the Comanches, but individual Chickasaws often had trouble with Comanche hunting-parties.

"The Big Sulphur Springs on Rock Creek in the Chickasaw Nation afterward became the centre around which the city of Sulphur was built, and after the town was grown to a population of two thousand or more it was removed bodily to make room for the Platt National Park, around which has been built the new city of Sulphur, which now has a population of forty-five hundred.

"Many of the Comanche monuments are extant and the great bluff above the Bromide Springs of the national park looks out toward the north and west over a prairie that extends to the Rocky Mountains; the monument that stood on the brow of that bluff must have been visible for many miles to the keen vision of the Comanche who knew how to look for it."

The Indian Territory became the State of Oklahoma in 1907; the story of the white man's peaceful invasion is one of absorbing interest; the human spectacle of to-day is complex, even kaleidoscopic. In the thirties and forties the government had established in the territory the five civilized Indian nations, the Cherokees, Chickasaws, Choctaws, Creeks, and Seminoles, each with its allotted boundaries, its native government, its legislatures, and its courts. In many respects these were foreign nations within our boundaries. Besides them, the Osage Indians had their reservation in the north, and fragments of no less than seventeen other tribes lived on assigned territory.

Gradually white men invaded the land, purchased

holdings from the Indian nations, built cities, established businesses of many kinds, ran railroads in all directions. In time, the nations were abolished and their remaining lands were divided up among the individuals composing them; the Indians of these nations became American citizens; their negro slaves, for they had been large slaveholders, received each his portion of the divided land. Then came Oklahoma.

To-day there is only one Indian reservation in the State, that of the Osages. Oil has been found on their land and they are the wealthiest people in the world to-day, the average cash income of each exceeding five thousand dollars a year. In a state with a total population of two and a quarter millions live 336,000 Indians representing twenty-three tribes and 110,000 negroes descended from slaves. There has been much intermarrying between Indians and whites, and some between Indians and blacks. Here is a mixture of races to baffle the keenest eye.

Elsewhere than in the Osage Reservation, wealth also has come to the Indians. Many have very large incomes, large even for the rich of our Eastern cities. Asphalt also has enriched many. Cotton is raised extensively in the southern counties. Grazing on a large scale has proved profitable. Many Indians own costly and luxurious homes, ride in automobiles, and enter importantly into business, politics, and the professions; these usually have more or less white blood. Many full-bloods who have grown rich without effort possess finely furnished bedrooms, and sleep on the floor in blankets; elaborate dining-rooms with costly table equipments, and eat cross-legged on the kitchen floor; gas-ranges, and cook over chip fires out-of-doors; automobiles, and ride blanketed ponies. Many wealthy men are deeply in debt because of useless luxuries which they have been persuaded to buy.

Platt National Park lies about the centre of what was once the Chickasaw nation. It is a grazing and a cotton country. There are thousands of Indians, many of them substantial citizens, some men of local influence. Native dress is seldom seen.

Quoting again from my correspondence with Colonel Sneed, here is the legend of the last of the Delawares:

"Along about 1840, a very few years after the Chickasaws and Choctaws had arrived in Indian Territory, a small band of about sixty Delaware Indians arrived in the Territory, having roved from Alabama through Mississippi and Missouri, and through the northwest portion of Arkansas. Being a small band, they decided to link their fortunes with those of some other tribe of Indians, and they first pitched their tepees with those of the Cherokees. But the Cherokee Chief and old Chief Wahpanucka of the Delawares did not agree. So the little band of Delawares continued rambling until they reached the Choctaw Nation, where they again tried to make terms with the Chief of the tribe. Evidently no agreement was reached between that Chief and Wahpanucka, for the Delawares continued their roving until they reached the Chickasaw Nation, where they remained.

"Old Chief Wahpanucka had a beautiful daughter whose name was Deerface; two of the Delaware braves were much in love with her, but Deerface could not decide which one of these warriors she should take to become Chief after the death of Wahpanucka.

"Chief Wahpanucka called the two warriors before him and a powwow was agreed upon. The council was held around the Council Rocks (which is now a point of interest within the Platt National Park), and a decision was reached to the effect that at a certain designated time the Delawares should all assemble on the top of the Bromide Cliff, at the foot of which flow the now famous Bromide and Medicine Springs, and that the two braves should ride their Indian ponies to the edge of the cliff, which was at that time known as Medicine Bluff, and jump off to the bed of the creek about two hundred feet below. The one who survived was to marry Deerface, and succeed Wahpanucka as Chief of the Delawares.

"The race was run and both Indian braves made the jump from the bluff, but both were killed. When Deerface saw this she threw herself from the bluff and died at the foot of the cliff where her lovers had met their death. To-day her image may be seen indelibly fixed on one of the rocks of the cliff where she fell, and the water of the Medicine Spring is supposed to be the briny tears of the old Chief when he saw the havoc his decision had wrought. These tears, filtering down through the cliff where the old Chief stood, are credited with being so purified that the water of the spring which they form is possessed with remedial qualities which make it a cure for all human ailments."

THE GRAND CANYON AND OUR
NATIONAL MONUMENTS

ON THE SCENERY OF THE SOUTHWEST

TO most Americans the southwest means the desert, and it is true that most of Arizona, New Mexico, and Utah, and portions of Colorado and southern California, are arid or semiarid lands, relieved, however, by regions of fertility and agricultural prosperity. In popular conception the desert has been the negative of all that means beauty, richness, and sublimity; it has been the synonym of poverty and death. Gradually but surely the American public is learning that again popular conception is wrong, that the desert is as positive a factor in scenery as the mountain, that it has its own glowing beauty, its own intense personality, and occasionally, in its own amazing way, a sublimity as gorgeous, as compelling, and as emotion-provoking as the most stupendous snow-capped range.

The American desert region includes some of the world's greatest scenery. The Grand Canyon of the Colorado River is sunk in a plateau which, while sprinkled with scant pine, is nearly rainless. Zion Canyon is a palette of brilliant color lying among golden sands. A score of national monuments conserve large natural bridges, forests of petrified trees, interesting volcanic or other phenomena of prehistoric times, areas of strange cactus growths, deposits of the bones of monstrous reptiles, and remains of a civilization which preceded the discovery of America; and, in addition to these, innumerable places of remarkable magnificence as yet unknown except to the geologist, the topographer, the miner, the Indian, and the adventurer in unfrequented lands.

This arid country consists of rolling sandy plains as broad as seas, dotted with gray sage-brush and relieved by bare craggy monadnocks and naked ranges which the rising and the setting sun paints unbelievable colors. Here and there thin growths of cottonwood outline thin ribbons of rivers, few and far between. Here and there alkali whitens the edges of stained hollows where water lies awhile after spring cloudbursts. Here and there are salt ponds with no outlet. Yet even in the desolation of its tawny monotony it has a fascination which is insistent and cumulative.

But the southwest is not all desert. There are great areas of thin grazing ranges and lands where dry farming yields fair crops. There are valleys which produce fruits and grains in abundance. There are hamlets and villages and cities which are among the oldest in America, centres of fertile tracts surrounded by deserts which need only water to become the richest lands on the continent. There are regions reclaimed by irrigation where farming has brought prosperity. In other places the plateau covers itself for hundreds of square miles with scrubby pine and cedar.

All in all, it is a land of rare charm and infinite variety.

To appreciate a region which more and more will enter into American consciousness and divide travel with the mountains, the reader should know something of its structural history.

The southwestern part of the United States rose above sea-level and sank below it many times during the many thousands of centuries preceding its present state, which is that of a sandy and generally desert plateau, five to ten thousand feet in altitude. How many times it repeated the cycle is not fully known. Some portions of it doubtless were submerged oftener than others. Some were lifting while others were lowering. And, meantime, mountains rose and were carried away by erosion to give place to other mountains which also wore away; river systems formed and disappeared, lakes and inland seas existed and ceased to exist. The history of our southwest would have been tempestuous indeed had it been compassed within say the life of one man; but, spread over a period of time inconceivable to man, there may have been no time when it might have seemed to be more active in change than its still hot deserts seem to-day to the traveller in passing trains.

Other parts of the continent, no doubt, have undergone as many changes; our southwest is not singular in that. But nowhere else, perhaps, has the change left evidences so plain and so interesting to the unscientific observer. The page of earth's history is more easily read upon the bare deserts of our southwest than on the grass-concealed prairies of the Mississippi

Valley or the eroded and forested ranges of the Appalachians.

Before the Rockies and the Sierra even existed, in the shallow sea which covered this part of the continent were deposited the ooze which later, when this region rose above the sea, became the magnificent limestones of the Grand Canyon. Muds accumulated which to-day are seen in many highly colored shales. Long ages of erosion from outlying mountain regions spread it thick with gravels and sands which now appear in rocky walls of deep canyons. A vast plain was built up and graded by these deposits. The trunks of trees washed down by the floods from far distant uplands were buried in these muds and sands, where, in the course of unnumbered centuries, they turned to stone. They are the petrified forests of to-day.

Mountains, predecessors of our modern Sierra, lifted in the south and west, squeezed the moisture from the Pacific winds, and turned the region into desert. This was in the Jurassic Period. Sands thousands of feet deep were accumulated by the desert winds which are to-day the sandstones of the giant walls of Zion Canyon.

But this was not the last desert, for again the region sank below the sea. Again for half a million years or more ooze settled upon the sands to turn to limestone millions of years later. In this Jurassic sea sported enormous marine monsters whose bones settled to the bottom to be unearthed in our times, and great flying reptiles crossed its water.

Again the region approached sea-level and accumulated, above its new limestones, other beds of sands. New river systems formed and brought other accumulations from distant highlands. It was then a low swampy plain of enormous size, whose northern limits reached Montana, and which touched what now is Kansas on its east. Upon the borders of its swamps, in Cretaceous times, lived gigantic reptiles, the Dinosaurs and their ungainly companions whose bones are found to-day in several places.

For the last time the region sank and a shallow sea swept from the Gulf of Mexico to the Arctic Ocean. Again new limestones formed, and as the surface very slowly rose for the last time at the close of the Cretaceous Period many new deposits were added to the scenic exhibit of to-day.

Meantime other startling changes were making which extended over a lapse of time which human mind cannot grasp. Responding to increasing pressures from below, the continent was folding from north to south. The miracle of the making of the Rockies was enacting.

During all of Tertiary times earth movements of tremendous energy rocked and folded the crust and hastened change. The modern Sierra rose upon the eroded ruins of its predecessor, again shutting off the moisture-laden western winds and turning the southwest again into a desert. One of the mountain-building impulses spread eastward from the Sierra to the Wasatch Mountains, but Nature's project for this vast granite-cored table-land never was realized, for continually its central sections caved and fell. And so it happened that the eastern edge of the Sierra and the western edge of the Wasatch Mountains became the precipitous edges, thousands of feet high, of a mountain-studded desert which to-day is called the Great Basin. It includes southeastern Oregon, nearly all of Nevada, the western half of Utah, and a large area in the south of California, besides parts of Idaho and Wyoming. It is 880 miles north and south and 572 miles wide. Its elevation is five thousand feet, more or less, and its area more than two hundred thousand square miles.

This enormous bowl contained no outlet to the sea, and the rivers which flowed into it from all its mountainous borders created a prehistoric lake with an area of fifty-four thousand square miles which was named Lake Bonneville after the army officer whose adventures in 1833 were narrated by Washington Irving; but it was Frémont who first clearly described it. Lake Bonneville has evaporated and disappeared, but in its place are many salty lakes, the greatest of which is Great Salt Lake in Utah. Attenuated rivers still flow into the Great Basin, but are lost in their sands. The greatest of these, the Mohave River, is a hundred miles long, but is not often seen because it hides its waters chiefly under the surface sands. Lake Bonneville's prehistoric beaches exist to-day. Transcontinental passengers by rail cross its ancient bed, but few know it.

The Great Basin to-day is known to travellers principally by the many lesser deserts which compose it, deserts separated from each other by lesser mountain ranges and low divides. Its southern and southeastern boundaries are the plateaus and mountains which form the northern watershed of the muddy Colorado River and its confluents. South of the Colorado, the plateaus of New Mexico, Arizona, and southern California gradually subside to the Rio Grande.

During this period and the Quaternary which followed it, volcanoes appeared in many places; their dead cones diversify our modern landscape. It was during the Quaternary Period, in whose latter end lives man, that erosion dug the mighty canyons of our great southwest. The Colorado was sweeping out the Grand Canyon at the same time that, far in the north, the glaciers of the Great Ice Age were carving from Algonkian shales and limestones the gorgeous cirques and valleys of Glacier National Park.

XVI

A PAGEANT OF CREATION

Grand Canyon National Park, Arizona. Area, 958
Square Miles

THERE is only one Grand Canyon. It lies in
northern Arizona, and the Colorado River, one
of the greatest of American rivers, flows through its
inner gorge. It must not be confused with the Grand
Canyon of the Yellowstone, or with any of the *grande
cañons* which the Spaniards so named because they
were big canyons.

The Grand Canyon is 217 miles long, 8 to 12 miles
wide at the rim, and more than a mile deep. It is
the Colossus of canyons, by far the hugest example of
stream erosion in the world. It is gorgeously colored.
It is by common consent the most stupendous spectacle
in the world. It may be conceived as a mountain
range reversed. Could its moulded image, similarly
colored, stand upon the desert floor, it would be a
spectacle second only to the vast mould itself.

More than a hundred thousand persons visit the
Grand Canyon each year. In other lands it is our
most celebrated scenic possession. It was made a
national park in 1919.

I

The Grand Canyon is not of America but of the
world. Like the Desert of Sahara and the monster

group of the Himalayas, it is so entirely the greatest example of its kind that it refuses limits. This is true of it also as a spectacle; far truer, in fact, for, if it is possible to compare things so dissimilar, in this respect certainly it will lead all others. None see it without being deeply moved—all to silence, some even to tears. It is charged to the rim with emotion; but the emotion of the first view varies. Some stand astounded at its vastness. Others are stupefied and search their souls in vain for definition. Some tremble. Some are uplifted with a sense of appalling beauty. For a time the souls of all are naked in the presence.

This reaction is apparent in the writings of those who have visited it; no other spectacle in America has inspired so large a literature. Joaquin Miller found it fearful, full of glory, full of God. Charles Dudley Warner pronounced it by far the most sublime of earthly spectacles. William Winter saw it a pageant of ghastly desolation. Hamlin Garland found its lines chaotic and disturbing but its combinations of color and shadow beautiful. Upon John Muir it bestowed a new sense of earth's beauty.

Marius R. Campbell, whose geological researches have familiarized him with Nature's scenic gamut, told me that his first day on the rim left him emotionally cold; it was not until he had lived with the spectacle that realization slowly dawned. I think this is the experience of very many, a fact which renders still more tragic a prevailing public assumption that the Grand Canyon is a one-day stop in a transcontinental journey.

It is not surprising that wonder is deeply stirred by its vastness, its complexity, and the realization of Nature's titanic labor in its making. It is far from strange that extreme elation sometimes follows upon a revelation so stupendous and different. That beauty so extraordinary should momentarily free emotion from control is natural enough. But why the expressions of repulsion not infrequently encountered upon the printed pages of the past? I have personally inquired of many of our own day without finding one, even among the most sensitive, whom it repelled. Perhaps a clew is discovered in the introductory paragraphs of an inspired word-picture which the late Clarence E. Dutton hid in a technical geological paper of 1880. "The lover of nature," he wrote, "whose perceptions have been trained in the Alps, in Italy, Germany, or New England, in the Appalachians or Cordilleras, in Scotland or Colorado, would enter this strange region with a shock and dwell there with a sense of oppression, and perhaps with horror. Whatsoever things he had learned to regard as beautiful and noble he would seldom or never see, and whatsoever he might see would appear to him as anything but beautiful or noble. Whatsoever might be bold or striking would seem at first only grotesque. The colors would be the very ones he had learned to shun as tawdry or bizarre. The tones and shades, modest and tender, subdued yet rich, in which his fancy had always taken special delight, would be the ones which are conspicuously absent."

I suspect that this repulsion, this horror, as several have called it, was born of the conventions of an earlier generation which bound conceptions of taste and beauty, as of art, dress, religion, and human relations generally, in shackles which do not exist in these days of individualism and broad horizons. To-day we see the Grand Canyon with profound astonishment but without prejudice. Its amazing size, its bewildering configuration, its unprecedented combinations of color affect the freed and elated consciousness of our times as another and perhaps an ultimate revelation in nature of law, order, and beauty.

In these pages I shall make no attempt to describe the Grand Canyon. Nature has written her own description, graving it with a pen of water in rocks which run the series of the eternal ages. Her story can be read only in the original; translations are futile. Here I shall try only to help a little in the reading.

II

The Grand Canyon was cut by one of the great rivers of the continent, the Colorado, which enters Arizona from the north and swings sharply west; thence it turns south to form most of Arizona's western boundary, and a few miles over the Mexican border empties into the head of the Gulf of California. It drains three hundred thousand square miles of Arizona, Utah, Wyoming, and Colorado. It is formed in Utah by the confluence of the Green and the Grand Rivers.

Including the greater of these, the Green River, it makes a stream fifteen hundred miles in length which collects the waters of the divide south and east of the Great Basin and of many ranges of the Rocky Mountain system. The Grand River, for its contribution, collects the drainage of the Rockies' mighty western slopes in Colorado.

The lower reaches of these great tributaries and practically all of the Colorado River itself flow through more than five hundred miles of canyons which they were obliged to dig through the slowly upheaving sandstone plateaus in order to maintain their access to the sea. Succeeding canyons bear names designating their scenic or geologic character. Progressively southward they score deeper into the strata of the earth's crust until, as they approach their climax, they break through the bottom of the Paleozoic limestone deep into the heart of the Archean gneiss. This limestone trench is known as the Marble Canyon, the Archean trench as the Granite Gorge. The lower part of the Marble Canyon and all the Granite Gorge, together with their broad, vividly colored and fantastically carved upper canyon ten miles across from rim to rim, a mile high from water to rim-level, the climax of the world of canyons and the most gorgeous spectacle on earth, is the Grand Canyon of the Colorado. It lies east and west in the northern part of the State.

To comprehend it, recall one of those ditches which we all have seen crossing level fields or bordering country roads. It is broad from rim to rim and deeply indented by the side washes which follow heavy showers. Its sides descend by terraces, steep in places with gentle slopes between the steeps, and on these slopes are elevations of rock or mud which floods have failed to wash away. Finally, in the middle, is the narrow trench which now, in dry weather, carries a small trickling stream. Not only does this ditch roughly typify the Grand Canyon, reproducing in clumsy, inefficient miniature the basic characteristics of its outline, but it also is identical in the process of its making.

Imagining it in cross-section, we find its sides leading down by successive precipices to broad intermediate sloping surfaces. We find upon these broad surfaces enormous mesas and lofty, ornately carved edifices of rock which the floods have left standing. We find in its middle, winding snakelike from side to side, the narrow gorge of the river.

The parallel goes further. It is not at all necessary to conceive that either the wayside ditch or the Grand Canyon was once brimful of madly dashing waters. On the contrary, neither may ever have held much greater streams than they hold to-day. In both cases the power of the stream has been applied to downward trenching; the greater spreading sides were cut by the erosion of countless side streamlets resulting temporarily from periods of melting snow or of local rainfall. It was these streamlets which cut the side canyons and left standing between them the bold promontories of the rim. It was these streamlets, working from the surface, which separated portions of these promontories from the plateau and turned them into isolated mesas. It was the erosion of these mesas which turned many of them into the gigantic and fantastic temples and towers which rise from the canyon's bowl.

Standing upon the rim and overlooking miles of these successive precipices and intermediate templed levels, we see the dark gorge of the granite trench, and, deep within it, wherever its windings permit a view of its bottom, a narrow ribbon of brown river. This is the Colorado—a rill; but when we have descended six thousand feet of altitude to its edge we find it a rushing turbulent torrent of muddy water. Its average width is three hundred feet; its average depth thirty feet. It is industriously digging the Grand Canyon still deeper, and perhaps as rapidly as it ever dug since it entered the granite.

Developing the thought in greater detail, let us glance at the illustrations of this chapter and at any photographs which may be at hand, and realization will begin. Let imagination dart back a million years or more to the time when this foreground rim and that far rim across the vast chasm are one continuous plain; perhaps it is a pine forest, with the river, no greater than to-day, perhaps not so great, winding through it close to the surface level. As the river cuts downward, the spring floods following the winter snows cave in its banks here and there, forming sharply slanted valleys which enclose promontories between them.

Spring succeeds spring, and these side valleys deepen and eat backward while the promontories lengthen and grow. The harder strata resist the disintegration of alternate heat and cold, and, while always receding, hold their form as cliffs; the softer strata between the cliffs crumbles and the waste of spring waters spreads them out in long flattened slopes. The centuries pass. The ruin buries itself deep in the soft sandstone. The side valleys work miles back into the pine forest. Each valley acquires its own system of erosion; into each, from either side, enter smaller valleys which themselves are eating backward into the promontories.

The great valley of the Colorado now has broad converging cliff-broken sides. Here and there these indentations meet far in the background behind the promontories, isolating island-like mesas.

The rest of the story is simple repetition. Imagine enough thousands of centuries and you will imagine the Grand Canyon. Those myriad temples and castles and barbaric shrines are all that the rains and melting snows have left of noble mesas, some of which, when originally isolated, enclosed, as the marble encloses the future statue, scores of the lesser but mighty structures which compose the wonder city of the depths.

These architectural operations of Nature may be seen to-day in midway stages. Find on the map the Powell Plateau in the northwest of the canyon. Once it was continuous with the rim, a noble promontory. It was cut out from the rim perhaps within the existence of the human race. A few hundred thousand years from now it will be one or more Aladdin palaces.

Find on the map the great Walhalla Plateau in the east of the canyon. Note that its base is nearly separated from the parental rim; a thousand centuries or so and its isolation will be complete. Not long after that, as geologists reckon length of time, it will divide into two plateaus; it is easy to pick the place of division. The tourist of a million years hence will see, where now it stands, a hundred glowing castles.

Let us look again at our photographs, which now we can see with understanding. To realize the spectacle of the canyon, let imagination paint these strata their brilliant colors. It will not be difficult; but here again we must understand.

It is well to recall that these strata were laid in the sea, and that they hardened into stone when the earth's skin was pushed thousands of feet in air. Originally they were the washings of distant highlands brought down by rivers; the coloring of the shales and sandstones is that of the parent rock modified, no doubt, by chemical action in sea-water. The limestone, product of the sea, is gray.

As these differently colored strata were once continuous across the canyon, it follows that their sequence is practically identical on both sides of the canyon. That the colors seem confused is because, viewing the spectacle from an elevation, we see the enormous indentations of the opposite rim in broken and disorganized perspective. Few minds are patient and orderly enough to fully disentangle the kaleidoscopic disarray, but, if we can identify the strata by form as well as color, we can at least comprehend without trouble our principal outline; and comprehension is the broad highway to appreciation.

To identify these strata, it is necessary to call them by name. The names that geologists have assigned them have no scientific significance other than identity; they are Indian and local.

Beginning at the canyon rim we have a stalwart cliff of gray limestone known as the Kaibab Limestone, or, conversationally, the Kaibab; it is about seven hundred feet thick. Of this product of a million years of microscopic life and death on sea-bottoms is formed the splendid south-rim cliffs from which we view the chasm. Across the canyon it is always recognizable as the rim.

Below the talus of the Kaibab is the Coconino sandstone, light yellowish-gray, coarse of grain, the product of swift currents of untold thousands of centuries ago. This stratum makes a fine bright cliff usually about four hundred feet in thickness, an effective roofing for the glowing reds of the depths.

Immediately below the Coconino are the splendid red shales and sandstones known as the Supai formation. These lie in many strata of varying shades, qualities, and thicknesses, but all, seen across the canyon, merging into a single enormous horizontal body of gorgeous red. The Supai measures eleven hundred

feet in perpendicular thickness, but as it is usually
seen in slopes which sometimes are long and gentle,
it presents to the eye a surface several times as broad.
This is the most prominent single mass of color in the
canyon, for not only does it form the broadest feature
of the opposite wall and of the enormous promontories
which jut therefrom, but the main bodies of Buddha,
Zoroaster, and many others of the fantastic temples
which rise from the floor.

Below the Supai, a perpendicular wall of intense
red five hundred feet high forces its personality upon
every foot of the canyon's vast length. This is the
famous Redwall, a gray limestone stained crimson
with the drip of Supai dye from above. Harder than
the sloping sandstone above and the shale below, it
pushes aggressively into the picture, squared, perpendicular, glowing. It winds in and out of every bay
and gulf, and fronts precipitously every flaring promontory. It roofs with overhanging eaves many a noble
palace and turns many a towering monument into a
pagoda.

Next below in series is the Tonto, a deep, broad,
shallow slant of dull-green and yellow shale, which,
with the thin broad sandstone base on which it rests,
forms the floor of the outer canyon, the tessellated
pavement of the city of flame. Without the Tonto's
green the spectacle of the Grand Canyon would have
missed its contrast and its fulness.

Through this floor the Granite Gorge winds its
serpentine way, two thousand feet deep, dark with

shadows, shining in places where the river swings in view.

These are the series of form and color. They occur with great regularity except in several spots deep in the canyon where small patches of gleaming quartzites and brilliant red shales show against the dark granite; the largest of these lies in the depths directly opposite El Tovar. These rocks are all that one sees of ancient Algonkian strata which once overlay the granite to a depth of thirteen thousand feet— more than twice the present total depth of the canyon. The erosion of many thousands of centuries wore them away before the rocks that now compose the floor, the temples and the precipiced walls of the great canyon were even deposited in the sea as sand and limestone ooze, a fact that strikingly emphasizes the enormous age of this exhibit. Geologists speak of these splashes of Algonkian rocks as the Unkar group, another local Indian designation. There is also a similar Chuar group, which need not concern any except those who make a close study of the canyon.

This is the picture. The imagination may realize a fleet, vivid impression from the photograph. The visitor upon the rim, outline in hand, may trace its twisting elements in a few moments of attentive observation, and thereafter enjoy his canyon as one only enjoys a new city when he has mastered its scheme and spirit, and can mentally classify its details as they pass before him.

To one thus prepared, the Grand Canyon ceases

to be the brew-pot of chaotic emotion and becomes the orderly revelation of Nature, the master craftsman and the divine artist.

III

Entrance is from the south. The motor-road to Grand View is available for most of the year. The railroad to the El Tovar Hotel serves the year around, for the Grand Canyon is an all-year resort. There is a short winter of heavy snows on the rim, but not in the canyon, which may be descended at all seasons. Both routes terminate on the rim. Always dramatic, the Grand Canyon welcomes the pilgrim in the full panoply of its appalling glory. There is no waiting in the anteroom, no sounding of trumpets, no ceremony of presentation. He stands at once in the presence.

Most visitors have bought tickets at home which permit only one day's stay. The irrecoverable sensation of the first view is broken by the necessity for an immediate decision upon how to spend that day, for if one is to descend horseback to the river he must engage his place and don his riding-clothes at once. Under this stress the majority elect to remain on the rim for reasons wholly apart from any question of respective merit.

After all, if only one day is possible, it is the wise decision. With the rim road, over which various drives are scheduled, and several commanding points to whose precipices one may walk, it will be a day to remember

From a photograph copyright by Fred Harvey

SUNSET FROM GRAND VIEW, GRAND CANYON NATIONAL PARK

All the strata from the rim to the river may be seen in this picture

for a lifetime. One should not attempt too much in this one day. It is enough to sit in the presence of the spectacle. Fortunate is he who may stay another day and descend the trail into the streets of this vast city; many times fortunate he who may live a little amid its glories.

Because of this general habit of "seeing" the Grand Canyon between sunrise and sunset, the admirable hotel accommodations are not extensive, but sufficient. There are cottage accommodations also at cheaper rates. Hotels and cottages are well patronized summer and winter. Upon the rim are unique rest-houses, in one of which is a high-power telescope. There is a memorial altar to John Wesley Powell, the first explorer of the canyon. There is an excellent reproduction of a Hopi house. There is an Indian camp. The day's wanderer upon the rim will not lack entertainment when his eyes turn for rest from the chasm.

From the hotel, coaches make regular trips daily to various view-points. Hopi Point, Mohave Point, Yavapai Point, and Grandeur Point may all be visited; the run of eight miles along the famous Hermit Rim Road permits brief stops at Hopi, Mohave, and Pima Points. Automobiles also make regular runs to the gorgeous spectacle from Grand View. Still more distant points may be made in private or hired cars. Navajo Point offers unequalled views up and down the full length of the canyon, and an automobile-road will bring the visitor within easy reach of Bass Camp near Havasupai Point in the far west of the reservation.

Many one-day visitors take none of these stage and automobile trips, contented to dream the hours away upon Yavapai or Hopi Points near by. After all, it is just as well. A single view-point cannot be mastered in one's first day, so what's the use of others? On the other hand, seeing the same view from different view-points miles apart will enrich and elaborate it. Besides, one should see many views in order to acquire some conception, however small, of the intricacy and grandeur of the canyon. Besides, these trips help to rest the eyes and mind. It is hard indeed to advise the unlucky one-day visitor. It is as if a dyspeptic should lead you to an elaborate banquet of a dozen courses, and say: "I have permission to eat three bites. Please help me choose them."

Wherever he stands upon the rim the appalling silence hushes the voice to whispers. No cathedral imposes stillness so complete. It is sacrilege to speak, almost to move. And yet the Grand Canyon is a moving picture. It changes every moment. Always shadows are disappearing here, appearing there; shortening here, lengthening there. With every passing hour it becomes a different thing. It is a sun-dial of monumental size.

In the early morning the light streams down the canyon from the east. Certain promontories shoot miles into the picture, gleaming in vivid color, backed by dark shadows. Certain palaces and temples stand in magnificent relief. The inner gorge is brilliantly outlined in certain places. As the day advances these prominences shift positions; some fade; some disappear; still others spring into view.

As midday approaches the shadows fade; the promontories flatten; the towering edifices move bodily backward and merge themselves in the opposite rim. There is a period of several hours when the whole canyon has become a solid wall; strata fail to match; eye and mind become confused; comprehension is baffled by the tangle of disconnected bands of color; the watcher is distressed by an oppressive sense of helplessness.

It is when afternoon is well advanced that the magician sun begins his most astonishing miracles in the canyon's depths. Out from the blazing wall, one by one, step the mighty obelisks and palaces, defined by ever-changing shadows. Unsuspected promontories emerge, undreamed-of gulfs sink back in the perspective. The serpentine gorge appears here, fades there, seems almost to move in the slow-changing shadows. I shall not try even to suggest the soul-uplifting spectacle which culminates in sunset.

Days may be spent upon the rim in many forms of pleasure; short camping trips may be made to distant points.

The descent into the canyon is usually made from El Tovar down the Bright Angel Trail, so called because it faces the splendid Bright Angel Canyon of the north side, and by the newer Hermit Trail which starts a few miles west. There are trails at Grand View, eight miles east, and at Bass Camp, twenty-four miles west of El Tovar, which are seldom used now. All go to the bottom of the Granite Gorge. The commonly used trails may be travelled afoot by those physically able, and on mule-back by any person of any age who enjoys ordinary health. The Bright Angel trip returns the traveller to the rim at day's end. The Hermit Trail trip camps him overnight on the floor of the canyon at the base of a magic temple. The finest trip of all takes him down the Hermit Trail, gives him a night in the depths, and returns him to the rim by the Bright Angel Trail. Powell named Bright Angel Creek during that memorable first passage through the Canyon. He had just named a muddy creek Dirty Devil, which suggested, by contrast, the name of Bright Angel for a stream so pure and sparkling.

The Havasupai Indian reservation may be visited in the depths of Cataract Canyon by following the trail from Bass Camp.

The first experience usually noted in the descent is the fine quality of the trail, gentle in slope and bordered by rock on the steep side. The next experience is the disappearance of the straight uncompromising horizon of the opposite rim, which is a distinctive feature of every view from above. As soon as the descent fairly begins, even the smaller bluffs and promontories assume towering proportions, and, from the Tonto floor, the mighty elevations of Cheops, Isis, Zoroaster, Shiva, Wotan, and the countless other temples of the abyss become mountains of enormous height.

From a photograph copyright by Fred Harvey

DOWN HERMIT TRAIL FROM RIM TO RIVER

Grand Canyon National Park

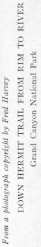

From a photograph copyright by Fred Harvey

CAMPING PARTY ON THE SOUTH RIM

This is within a few hundred feet of the Grand Canyon abyss

From the river's side the elevations of the Granite Gorge present a new series of precipitous towers, back of which in places loom the tops of the painted palaces, and back of them, from occasional favored view-spots, the far-distant rim. Here, and here only, does the Grand Canyon reveal the fulness of its meaning.

IV

The Grand Canyon was discovered in 1540 by El Tovar, one of the captains of Cardenas, in charge of one of the expeditions of the Spanish explorer, Diaz, who was hunting for seven fabled cities of vast wealth. "They reached the banks of a river which seemed to be more than three or four leagues above the stream that flowed between them." It was seen in 1776 by a Spanish priest who sought a crossing and found one at a point far above the canyon; this still bears the name Vado de los Padres.

By 1840 it was probably known to the trappers who overran the country. In 1850 Lieutenant Whipple, surveying for a Pacific route, explored the Black Canyon and ascended the Grand Canyon to Diamond Creek.

In 1857 Lieutenant Ives, sent by the War Department to test the navigability of the Colorado, ascended as far as the Virgin River in a steamboat which he had shipped in pieces from Philadelphia. From there he entered the Grand Canyon afoot, climbed to the rim, and, making a detour, encountered the river again higher up. In 1867 James White was picked up below the Virgin River lashed to floating logs. He said that his hunting-party near the head of the Colorado River, attacked by Indians, had escaped upon a raft. This presently broke up in the rapids and his companions were lost. He lashed himself to the wreckage and was washed through the Grand Canyon.

About this time Major John Wesley Powell, a school-teacher who had lost an arm in the Civil War, determined to explore the great canyons of the Green and Colorado Rivers. Besides the immense benefit to science, the expedition promised a great adventure. Many lives had been lost in these canyons and wonderful were the tales told concerning them. Indians reported that huge cataracts were hidden in their depths and that in one place the river swept through an underground passage.

Nevertheless, with the financial backing of the State institutions of Illinois and the Chicago Academy of Science, Powell got together a party of ten men with four open boats, provisions for ten months, and all necessary scientific instruments. He started above the canyons of the Green River on May 24, 1869.

There are many canyons on the Green and Colorado Rivers. They vary in length from eight to a hundred and fifty miles, with walls successively rising from thirteen hundred to thirty-five hundred feet in height. The climax of all, the Grand Canyon, is two hundred and seventeen miles long, with walls six thousand feet in height.

WHEN MORNING MISTS LIFT FROM THE DEPTHS OF
THE GRAND CANYON

THROUGH THE GRANITE GORGE SURGES THE MUDDY
COLORADO

On August 17, when Powell and his adventurers reached the Grand Canyon, their rations had been reduced by upsets and other accidents to enough musty flour for ten days, plenty of coffee, and a few dried apples. The bacon had spoiled. Most of the scientific instruments were in the bottom of the river. One boat was destroyed. The men were wet to the skin and unable to make a fire. In this plight they entered the Grand Canyon, somewhere in whose depths a great cataract had been reported.

The story of the passage is too long to tell here. Chilled, hungry, and worn, they struggled through it. Often they were obliged to let their boats down steep rapids by ropes, and clamber after them along the slippery precipices. Often there was nothing to do but to climb into their boats and run down long foaming slants around the corners of which death, perhaps, awaited. Many times they were upset and barely escaped with their lives. With no wraps or clothing that were not soaked with water, there were nights when they could not sleep for the cold.

So the days passed and the food lessened to a few handfuls of wet flour. The dangers increased; some falls were twenty feet in height. Finally three of the men determined to desert; they believed they could climb the walls and that their chances would be better with the Indians than with the canyon. Powell endeavored to dissuade them, but they were firm. He offered to divide his flour with them, but this they refused.

These men, two Howlands, brothers, and William Dunn, climbed the canyon walls and were killed by Indians. Two or three days later Powell and the rest of his party emerged below the Grand Canyon, where they found food and safety.

Taught by the experience of this great adventure, Powell made a second trip two years later which was a scientific achievement. Later on he became Director of the United States Geological Survey.

Since then, the passage of the Grand Canyon has been made several times. R. B. Stanton made it in 1889 in the course of a survey for a proposed railroad through the canyon; one of the leaders of the party was drowned.

V

The history of the Grand Canyon has been industriously collected. It remains for others to gather the legends. It is enough here to quote from Powell the Indian story of its origin.

"Long ago," he writes, "there was a great and wise chief who mourned the death of his wife, and would not be comforted until Tavwoats, one of the Indian gods, came to him and told him his wife was in a happier land, and offered to take him there that he might see for himself, if, upon his return, he would cease to mourn. The great chief promised. Then Tavwoats made a trail through the mountains that intervene between that beautiful land, the balmy region of the great West, and this, the desert home of the poor Numa. This trail was the canyon gorge of the Colorado. Through it he led him; and when they had returned the deity exacted from the chief a promise that he would tell no one of the trail. Then he rolled a river into the gorge, a mad, raging stream, that should engulf any that might attempt to enter thereby."

VI

The bill creating the Grand Canyon National Park passed Congress early in 1919, and was signed by President Wilson on February 26. This closed an intermittent campaign of thirty-three years, begun by President Harrison, then senator from Indiana, in January, 1886, to make a national park of the most stupendous natural spectacle in the world. Politics, private interests, and the deliberation of governmental procedure were the causes of delay. A self-evident proposition from the beginning, it illustrates the enormous difficulties which confront those who labor to develop our national-parks system. The story is worth the telling.

Senator Harrison's bill of 1886 met an instant response from the whole nation. It called for a national park fifty-six miles long and sixty-nine miles wide. There was opposition from Arizona and the bill failed. In 1893 the Grand Canyon National Forest was created. In 1898, depredations and unlawful seizures of land having been reported, the Secretary of the Interior directed the Land-Office to prepare a new national-park bill. In 1899 the Land-Office reported that the bill could not be drawn until the region was surveyed. It took the Geological Survey five years to make the survey. The bill was not prepared because meantime it was discovered that the Atlantic and Pacific Railroad, now the Santa Fé, owned rights which first must be eliminated.

Failing to become a national park, President Roosevelt proclaimed the Grand Canyon a national monument in 1908. In 1909 a bill was introduced entitling Ralph H. Cameron to build a scenic railway along the canyon rim, which created much adverse criticism and failed. In 1910 the American Scenic and Historic Preservation Society proposed a bill to create the Grand Canyon a national park of large size. The Geological Survey, to which it was referred, recommended a much smaller area. By the direction of President Taft, Senator Flint introduced a national-park bill which differed from both suggestions. The opposition of grazing interests threw it into the hands of conferees. In 1911 Senator Flint introduced the conferees' bill, but it was opposed by private interests and failed.

Meantime the country became aroused. Patriotic societies petitioned for a national park, and the National Federation of Women's Clubs began an agitation. The Department of the Interior prepared a map upon which to base a bill, and for several years negotiated with the Forest Service, which administered the Grand Canyon as a national monument, concerning boundaries. Finally the boundaries were reduced to little more than the actual rim of the canyon, and a bill was prepared which Senator Ashurst introduced in February, 1917. It failed in committee in the House owing to opposition from Arizona. It was the same bill, again introduced by Senator Ashurst in the new Congress two months later, which finally passed the House and became a law in 1919; but it required a favoring resolution by the Arizona legislature to pave the way.

Meantime many schemes were launched to utilize the Grand Canyon for private gain. It was plastered thickly with mining claims, though the Geological Survey showed that it contained no minerals worth mining; mining claims helped delay. Schemers sought capital to utilize its waters for power. Railroads were projected. Plans were drawn to run sightseeing cars across it on wire cables. These were the interests, and many others, which opposed the national park.

XVII

THE RAINBOW OF THE DESERT

ZION NATIONAL MONUMENT, SOUTHERN UTAH. AREA, 120
SQUARE MILES

WHEN, in the seventies, Major J. W. Powell, the daring adventurer of the Grand Canyon, faced Salt Lake City on his return from one of his notable geological explorations of the southwest, he laid his course by a temple of rock "lifting its opalescent shoulders against the eastern sky." His party first sighted it across seventy miles of a desert which "rose in a series of Cyclopean steps." When, climbing these, they had seen the West Temple of the Virgin revealed in the glory of vermilion body and shining white dome, and had gazed between the glowing Gates of Little Zion into the gorgeous valley within, these scenery-sated veterans of the Grand Canyon and the Painted Desert passed homeward profoundly impressed and planning quick return.

No wonder that Brigham Young, who had visited it many years before with a party of Mormons seeking a refuge in event of Indian raids or of exile from their Zion, Salt Lake City, had looked upon its glory as prophetic, and named it Little Zion.

Geologists found the spot a fruitful field of study. They found it also a masterpiece of desert beauty.

"Again we are impressed with the marvellous beauty of outline, the infinite complication of these titanic buttes," wrote F. S. Dellenbaugh, topographer of the Powell party, on his second visit. "It is doubtful if in this respect the valley has its equal. Not even the Grand Canyon offers a more varied spectacle; yet all is welded together in a superb ensemble."

"Nothing can exceed the wondrous beauty of Little Zion Canyon," wrote C. E. Dutton. "In its proportions it is about equal to Yosemite, but in the nobility and beauty of its sculptures there is no comparison. It is Hyperion to a Satyr. No wonder the fierce Mormon zealot who named it was reminded of the Great Zion on which his fervid thoughts were bent, of 'houses not built with hands, eternal in the heavens.'"

And Doctor G. K. Gilbert, whose intimate study of its recesses has become a geological classic, declared it "the most wonderful defile" that it had been even his experienced fortune to behold.

Technical literature contains other outbursts of enthusiastic admiration, some of eloquence, hidden, however, among pages so incomprehensible to the average lover of the sublime in Nature that the glory of Little Zion was lost in its very discovery. So remote did it lie from the usual lines of travel and traffic that, though its importance resulted in its conservation as a national monument in 1909, it was six or seven years more before its fame as a spectacle of the first order began to get about. The tales of adventurous explorers, as usual, were discounted. It was not until agencies seeking new tourist attractions sent parties to verify reports that the public gaze was centred upon the canyon's supreme loveliness.

To picture Zion one must recall that the great plateau in which the Virgin River has sunk these canyons was once enormously higher than now. The erosion of hundreds of thousands, or, if you please, millions of years, has cut down and still is cutting down the plateau. These "Cyclopean steps," each step the thickness of a stratum or a series of strata of hardened sands, mark progressive stages in the decomposition of the whole.

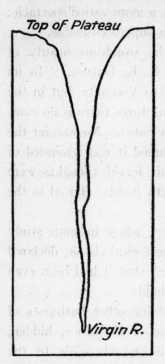

Little Zion Canyon is an early stage in Nature's process of levelling still another sandstone step, that is all; this one fortunately of many gorgeous hues. From the top of this layer we may look down thousands of vertical feet into the painted canyon whose river still is sweeping out the sands that Nature chisels from the cliffs; or from the canyon's bottom we may look up thousands of feet to the cliffed and serrated top of the doomed plateau. These ornate precipices were carved by trickling water and tireless winds. These fluted and towered temples of master decoration were disclosed when watery chisels cut away the sands that formerly had merged them with the ancient rock, just as the Lion of Lucerne was disclosed for the joy of the world when Thorwaldsen's chisel chipped away the Alpine rock surrounding its unformed image.

The colors are even more extraordinary than the forms. The celebrated Vermilion Cliff, which for more than a hundred miles streaks the desert landscape with vivid red, here combines spectacularly with the White Cliff, another famous desert feature—two thousand feet of the red surmounted by a thousand feet of the white. These constitute the body of color.

But there are other colors. The Vermilion Cliff rests upon the so-called Painted Desert stratum, three hundred and fifty feet of a more insistent red relieved by mauve and purple shale. That in turn rests upon a hundred feet of brown conglomerate streaked with gray, the grave of reptiles whose bones have survived a million years or more. And that rests upon the greens and grays and yellows of the Belted Shales.

Nor is this all, for far in the air above the wonderful White Cliff rise in places six hundred feet of drab shales and chocolate limestones intermixed with crimsons whose escaping dye drips in broad vertical streaks across the glistening white. And even above that, in places, lie remnants of the mottled, many-colored beds of St. Elmo shales and limestones in whose embrace, a few hundred miles away, lie embedded the bones of many monster dinosaurs of ages upon ages ago.

Through these successive layers of sands and shales and limestones, the deposits of a million years of earth's evolution, colored like a Roman sash, glowing in the sun like a rainbow, the Virgin River has cut a vertical section, and out of its sides the rains of centuries of centuries have detached monster monoliths and temples of marvellous size and fantastic shape, upon whose many-angled surfaces water and wind have sculptured ten thousand fanciful designs and decorations.

The way in to this desert masterpiece of southern Utah is a hundred miles of progressive preparation. From railroad to canyon there is not an unuseful mile or hour. It is as if all were planned, step by step, to make ready the mind of the traveller to receive the revelation with fullest comprehension.

To one approaching who does not know the desert, the motion-picture on the screen of the car-window is exciting in its mystery. These vast arid bottom-lands of prehistoric Lake Bonneville, girded by mountain groups and ranges as arid as the sands from which they lift their tawny sides, provoke suggestive questions of the past.

In this receptive mood the traveller reaches Lund and an automobile. The ride to Cedar City, where he spends the night, shows him the sage-dotted desert at close range. His horizon is one of bare, rugged mountains. In front of him rise the "Cyclopean steps" in

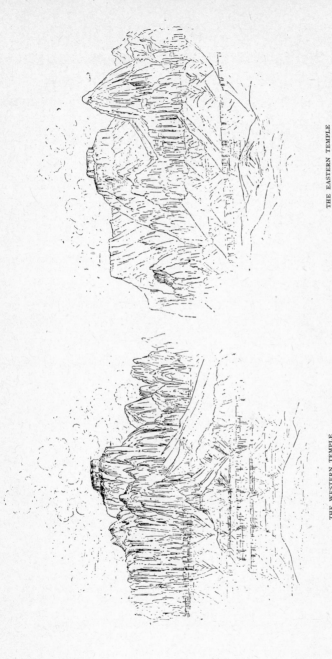

THE WESTERN TEMPLE   THE EASTERN TEMPLE

OUTLINES OF THE WESTERN AND EASTERN TEMPLES, ZION NATIONAL MONUMENT

From drawings by William H. Holmes

long, irregular, deeply indented sweeps. The vivid Pink Cliff, which, had it not long since been washed away from Little Zion, would have added another tier of color to its top, here, on the desert, remains a distant horizon. The road climbs Lake Bonneville's southern shore, and, at Cedar City, reaches the glorified sandstones.

From Cedar City to the canyon one sweeps through Mormon settlements founded more than sixty years ago, a region of stream-watered valleys known of old as Dixie. The road is part of the Arrowhead Trail, once in fact a historic trail, now a motor-highway between Salt Lake and Los Angeles. The valleys bloom. Pomegranates, figs, peaches, apricots, melons, walnuts, and almonds reach a rare perfection. Cotton, which Brigham Young started here as an experiment in 1861, is still grown. Lusty cottonwood-trees line the banks of the little rivers. Cedars dot the valleys and cover thickly the lower hills. And everywhere, on every side, the arid cliffs close in. The Pink Cliff has been left behind, but the Vermilion Cliff constantly appears. The White Cliff enters and stays. Long stretches of road overlie one and another colored stratum; presently the ground is prevailingly red, with here and there reaches of mauve, yellow, green, and pink.

Cedar City proves to be a quaint, straggling Mormon village with a touch of modern enterprise; south of Cedar City the villages lack the enterprise. The houses are of a gray composition resembling adobe, and many of them are half a century old and more. Dilapidated square forts, reminders of pioneer struggles with the Indians, are seen here and there. Compact Mormon churches are in every settlement, however small. The men are bearded, coatless, and wear baggy trousers, suggestive of Holland. Bronzed and deliberate women, who drive teams and work the fields with the men, wear old-fashioned sunbonnets. Many of these people have never seen a railroad-train. Newspapers are scarce and long past date. Here Mormonism of the older fashion is a living religion, affecting the routine of daily life.

Dixie is a land of plenty, but it is a foreign land. It is reminiscent, with many differences, of an Algerian oasis. The traveller is immensely interested. Somehow these strange primitive villages, these simple, earnest, God-fearing people, merge into unreality with the desert, the sage-dotted mountains, the cedar-covered slopes, the blooming valleys, the colored sands, and the vivid cliffs.

Through Bellevue, Toquerville, the ruins of Virgin City, Rockville, and finally to Springdale winds the road. Meantime the traveller has speeded south under the Hurricane Cliff, which is the ragged edge left when all the land west of it sank two thousand feet during some geologic time long past. He reaches the Virgin River where it emerges from the great cliffs in whose recesses it is born, and whence it carries in its broad muddy surge the products of their steady disintegration.

From here on, swinging easterly up-stream, sensation hastens to its climax. Here the Hurricane Cliff sends aloft an impressive butte painted in slanting colors and capped with black basalt. Farther on a rugged promontory striped with vivid tints pushes out from the southern wall nearly to the river's brink. The cliffs on both sides of the river are carved from the stratum which geologists call the Belted Shales. Greenish-grays, brownish-yellows, many shades of bright red, are prominent; it is hard to name a color or shade which is not represented in its horizontal bands. "The eye tires and the mind flags in their presence," writes Professor Willis T. Lee. "To try to realize in an hour's time the beauty and variety of detail here presented is as useless as to try to grasp the thoughts expressed in whole rows of volumes by walking through a library."

Far up the canyon which North Creek pushes through this banded cliff, two towering cones of glistening white are well named Guardian Angels—of the stream which roars between their feet. Eagle Crag, which Moran painted, looms into view. On the south appears the majestic massing of needle-pointed towers which Powell named the Pinnacles of the Virgin. The spectacular confuses with its brilliant variations.

At the confluence of the Virgin River and its North Fork, known of old as the Parunuweap and the Mukuntuweap, the road sweeps northward up the Mukuntuweap. There have been differing reports of the meaning of this word, which gave the original name to the national monument. It has been popularly accepted as meaning "Land of God," but John R. Wallis, of St. George, Utah, has traced it to its original Indian source. Mukuntuweap, he writes, means "Land of the Springs," and Parunuweap "Land of the Birds."

Reaching Springdale, at the base of the Vermilion Cliff, the traveller looks up-stream to the valley mouth through which the river emerges from the cliffs, and a spectacle without parallel meets his eye. Left of the gorgeous entrance rises the unbelievable West Temple of the Virgin, and, merging with it from behind, loom the lofty Towers of the Virgin. Opposite these, and back from the canyon's eastern brink, rises the loftier and even more majestic East Temple of the Virgin. Between them he sees a perspective of red and white walls, domes, and pinnacles which thrills him with expectation.

And so, fully prepared in mind and spirit, awed and exultant, he enters Zion.

Few natural objects which have been described so seldom have provoked such extravagant praise as the West Temple. It is seen from a foreground of gliding river, cotton-wood groves, and talus slopes dotted with manzanita, sage, cedars, and blooming cactus. From a stairway of mingled yellows, reds, grays, mauves, purples, and chocolate brown, it springs abruptly four thousand feet. Its body is a brilliant red. Its upper third is white. It has the mass and proportions, the dignity and grandeur, of a cathedral. It is supremely difficult to realize that it was not designed, so true to human conception are the upright form and mass of its central structure, the proportioning and modelling of its extensive wings and buttresses. On top of the lofty central rectangle rests, above its glistening white, a low squared cap of deepest red. It is a temple in the full as well as the noblest sense of the word.

The East Temple, which rises directly opposite and two miles back from the rim, is a fitting companion. It is a thousand feet higher. Its central structure is a steep truncated cone capped like the West Temple. Its wings are separated half-way down, one an elongated pyramid and the other a true cone, both of magnificent size and bulk but truly proportioned to the central mass. Phrase does not convey the suggestion of architectural calculation in both of these stupendous monuments. One can easily believe that the Mormon prophet in naming them saw them the designed creations of a personal deity.

A more definite conception of Nature's gigantic processes follows upon realization that these lofty structures once joined across the canyon, stratum for stratum, color for color. The rock that joined them, disintegrated by the frosts and rains, has passed down the muddy current of the Virgin, down the surging tide of the Colorado, through the Grand Canyon, and into the Pacific. Some part of these sands doubtless helped to build the peninsula of Lower California.

Passing the gates the traveller stands in a trench of nearly perpendicular sides more than half a mile deep, half a mile wide at the bottom, a mile wide from crest to crest. The proportions and measurements suggest Yosemite, but there is little else in common. These walls blaze with color. On the west the Streaked Wall, carved from the White Cliff, is stained with the drip from the red and drab and chocolate shales and limestones not yet wholly washed from its top. It is a vivid thing, wonderfully eroded. Opposite is the Brown Wall, rich in hue, supporting three stupendous structures of gorgeous color, two of which are known as the Mountain of the Sun and the Watchman. Together they are the Sentinels. Passing these across a plaza apparently broadened for their better presentation rise on the west the Three Patriarchs, Yosemite-like in form, height, and bulk, but not in personality or color. The brilliance of this wonder-spot passes description.

Here the canyon contracts, and we come to the comfortable hotel-camp, terminal of the automobile journey. It is on the river side in a shady alcove of the east wall near a spring. Here horses may be had for exploration.

A mile above the camp stands one of the most remarkable monoliths of the region. El Gobernador is a colossal truncated dome, red below and white above. The white crown is heavily marked in two directions, suggesting the web and woof of drapery. Directly opposite, a lesser monolith, nevertheless gigantic, is suggestively if sentimentally called Angel's Landing. A natural bridge which is still in Nature's

From a photograph by Douglas White

EL GOBERNADOR, ZION NATIONAL MONUMENT

Three thousand feet high; the lower two thousand feet is a brilliant red, the upper thousand
feet is white

workshop is one of the interesting spectacles of this vicinity. Its splendid arch is fully formed, but the wall against which it rests its full length remains, broken through in one spot only. How many thousands or hundreds of thousands of years will be required to wipe away the wall and leave the bridge complete is for those to guess who will.

Here also is the valley end of a wire cable which passes upward twenty-five hundred feet to cross a break in the wall to a forest on the mesa's top. Lumber is Dixie's most hardly furnished need. For years sawn timbers have been cabled down into the valley and carted to the villages of the Virgin River.

In some respects the most fascinating part of Little Zion is still beyond. A mile above El Gobernador the river swings sharply west and doubles on itself. Raspberry Bend is far nobler than its name implies, and the Great Organ which the river here encircles exacts no imaginative effort. Beyond this the canyon narrows rapidly. The road has long since stopped, and soon the trail stops. Presently the river, now a shrunken stream, concealing occasional quicksands, offers the only footing. The walls are no less lofty, no less richly colored, and the weary traveller works his difficult way forward.

There will come a time if he persists when he may stand at the bottom of a chasm more than two thousand feet deep and, nearly touching the walls on either side, look up and see no sky.

"At the water's edge the walls are perpendicular,"

writes Doctor G. K. Gilbert, of the U. S. Geological Survey, who first described it, "but in the deeper parts they open out toward the top. As we entered and found our outlook of sky contracted—as we had never before seen it between canyon cliffs—I measured the aperture above, and found it thirty-five degrees. We had thought this a minimum, but soon discovered our error. Nearer and nearer the walls approached, and our strip of blue narrowed down to twenty degrees, then ten, and at last was even intercepted by the overhanging rocks. There was, perhaps, no point from which, neither forward nor backward, could we discover a patch of sky, but many times our upward view was completely cut off by the interlocking of the walls, which, remaining nearly parallel to each other, warped in and out as they ascended."

Here he surprises the secret of the making of Zion.

"As a monument of denudation, this chasm is an example of downward erosion by sand-bearing water. The principle on which the cutting depends is almost identical with that of the marble saw, but the sand grains, instead of being embedded in rigid iron, are carried by a flexible stream of water. By gravity they have been held against the bottom of the cut, so that they should make it vertical, but the current has carried them, in places, against one side or the other, and so far modified the influence of gravity that the cut undulates somewhat in its vertical section, as well as in its horizontal."

This, then, is how Nature began, on the original

ZION CANYON FROM THE RIM

THE THREE PATRIARCHS, ZION CANYON

These red-and-white structures rise more than two thousand feet above the canyon floor

surface of the plateau, perhaps with the output of a spring shower, to dig this whole mighty spectacle for our enjoyment to-day. We may go further. We may imagine the beginning of the titanic process that dug the millions of millions of chasms, big and little, contributing to the mighty Colorado, that dug the Grand Canyon itself, that reduced to the glorified thing it now is the enormous plateau of our great southwest, which would have been many thousands of feet higher than the highest pinnacle of Little Zion had not erosion more than counteracted the uplifting of the plateau.

Little else need be said to complete this picture. The rains and melting snows of early spring produce mesa-top torrents which pour into the valley and hasten for a period the processes of decorating the walls and levelling the plateau. So it happens that waterfalls of power and beauty then enrich this wondrous spectacle. But this added beauty is not for the tourist, who may come in comfort only after its disappearance.

But springs are many. Trickling from various levels in the walls, they develop new tributary gorges. Gushing from the foundations, they create alcoves and grottos which are in sharp contrast with their desert environment, enriching by dampness the colors of the sandstone and decorating these refreshment-places with trailing ferns and flowering growths. In these we see the origin of the Indian name, Mukuntuweap, Land of the Springs.

The Indians, however, always stood in awe of Little Zion. They entered it, but feared the night.

In 1918 President Wilson changed the name from
Mukuntuweap to Zion. At the same time he greatly
enlarged the reservation. Zion National Monument
now includes a large area of great and varied desert
magnificence, including the sources and canyons of
two other streams besides Mukuntuweap.

XVIII

HISTORIC MONUMENTS OF THE SOUTHWEST

ELEVEN national monuments in the States of
Arizona, New Mexico, and Colorado illustrate
the history of our southwest from the times when prehistoric man dwelt in caves hollowed in desert precipices down through the Spanish fathers' centuries of
self-sacrifice and the Spanish explorers' romantic search
for the Quivira and the Seven Cities of Cibola.

The most striking feature of the absorbing story
of the Spanish occupation is its twofold inspiration.
Hand in hand the priest and the soldier boldly invaded
the desert. The passion of the priest was the saving
of souls, and the motive of the soldier was the greed
of gold. The priest deprecated the soldier; the soldier
despised the priest. Each used the other for the
realization of his own purposes. The zealous priest,
imposing his religion upon the shrinking Indian, did
not hesitate to invoke the soldier's aid for so holy a
purpose; the soldier used the gentle priest to cloak
the greedy business of wringing wealth from the frugal
native. Together, they hastened civilization.

Glancing for a moment still further back, the
rapacious hordes already had gutted the rich stores of
Central America and the northern regions of South
America. The rush of the lustful conqueror was as-

tonishingly swift. Columbus himself was as eager for gold as he was zealous for religion. From the discovery of America scarcely twenty years elapsed before Spanish armies were violently plundering the Caribbean Islands, ruthlessly subjugating Mexico, overrunning Venezuela, and eagerly seeking tidings of the reputed wealth of Peru. The air was supercharged with reports of treasure, and no reports were too wild for belief; myths, big and little, ran amuck. El Dorado, the gilded man of rumor, became the dream, then the belief, of the times; presently a whole nation was conceived clothed in dusted gold. The myth of the Seven Cities of Cibola, each a city of vast treasure, the growth of years of rumor, seems to have perfected itself back home in Spain. The twice-born myth of Quivira, city of gold, which cost thousands of lives and hundreds of thousands of Spanish ducats, lives even to-day in remote neighborhoods of the southwest.

Pizarro conquered Peru in 1526; by 1535, with the south looted, Spanish eyes looked longingly northward. In 1539 Fray Marcos, a Franciscan, made a reconnaissance from the Spanish settlements of Sonora into Arizona with the particular purpose of locating the seven cities. The following year Coronado, at his own expense, made the most romantic exploration in human history. Spanish expectation may be measured by the cost of this and its accompanying expedition by sea to the Gulf of California, the combined equipment totalling a quarter million dollars of American money of to-day. Coronado took two hundred and

sixty horsemen, sixty foot-soldiers, and more than a
thousand Indians. Besides his pack-animals he led a
thousand spare horses to carry home the loot.

He sought the seven cities in Arizona and New
Mexico, and found the pueblo of Zuñi, prosperous but
lacking its expected hoard of gold; he crossed Colorado
in search of Quivira and found it in Kansas, a wretched
habitation of a shiftless tribe; their houses straw, he
reported, their clothes the hides of cows, meaning
bison. He entered Nebraska in search of the broad
river whose shores were lined with gold—the identical
year, curiously, in which De Soto discovered the Mississippi. Many were the pueblos he visited and many
his adventures and perils; but the only treasure he
brought back was his record of exploration.

This was the first of more than two centuries of
Spanish expeditions. Fifty years after Coronado, the
myth of Quivira was born again; thereafter it wandered
homeless, the inspiration of constant search, and finally settled in the ruins of the ancient pueblo of Tabirá,
or, as Bandelier has it, Teypaná, New Mexico; the
myth of the seven cities never wholly perished.

It is not my purpose to follow the fascinating fortunes of Spanish proselyting and conquest. I merely
set the stage for the tableaux of the national monuments.

I

The Spaniards found our semiarid southwest dotted thinly with the pueblos and its canyons hung with the cliff-dwellings of a large and fairly prosperous population of peace-loving Indians, who hunted the deer and the antelope, fished the rivers, and dry-farmed the mesas and valleys. Not so advanced in the arts of civilization as the people of the Mesa Verde, in Colorado, nevertheless their sense of form was patent in their architecture, and their family life, government, and religion were highly organized. They were worshippers of the sun. Each pueblo and outlying village was a political unit.

Let us first consider those national monuments which touch intimately the Spanish occupation.

Gran Quivira National Monument

Eighty miles southeast of Albuquerque, in the hollow of towering desert ranges, lies the arid country which Indian tradition calls the Accursed Lakes. Here, at the points of a large triangle, sprawl the ruins of three once flourishing pueblo cities, Abo, Cuaray, and Tabirá. Once, says tradition, streams flowed into lakes inhabited by great fish, and the valleys bloomed; it was an unfaithful wife who brought down the curse of God.

When the Spaniards came these cities were at the flood-tide of prosperity. Their combined population was large. Tabirá was chosen as the site of the mission whose priests should trudge the long desert trails and minister to all.

Undoubtedly, it was one of the most important of the early Spanish missions. The greater of the two churches was built of limestone, its outer walls six feet thick. It was a hundred and forty feet long and forty-eight feet wide. The present height of the walls is twenty-five feet.

The ancient community building adjoining the church, the main pueblo of Tabirá, has the outlines which are common to the prehistoric pueblos of the entire southwest and persist in general features in modern Indian architecture. The rooms are twelve to fifteen feet square, with ceilings eight or ten feet high. Doors connect the rooms, and the stories, of which there are three, are connected by ladders through trapdoors. It probably held a population of fifteen hundred. The pueblo has well stood the rack of time; the lesser buildings outside it have been reduced to mounds.

The people who built and inhabited these cities of the Accursed Lakes were of the now extinct Piro stock. The towns were discovered in 1581 by Francisco Banchez de Chamuscado. The first priest assigned to the field was Fray Francisco de San Miguel, this in 1598. The mission of Tabirá was founded by Francisco de Acevedo about 1628. The smaller church was built then; the great church was built in 1644, but was never fully finished. Between 1670 and 1675 all three native cities and their Spanish churches were wiped out by Apaches.

Charles F. Lummis, from whom some of these historical facts are quoted, has been at great pains to trace the wanderings of the Quivira myth. Bandelier mentions an ancient New Mexican Indian called Tio Juan Largo, who told a Spanish explorer about the middle of the eighteenth century that Quivira was Tabirá. Otherwise history is silent concerning the process by which the myth finally settled upon that historic city, far indeed from its authentic home in what now is Kansas. The fact stands, however, that as late as the latter half of the eighteenth century the name Tabirá appeared on the official map of New Mexico. When and how this name was lost and the famous ruined city with its Spanish churches accepted as Gran Quivira perhaps never will be definitely known.

"Mid-ocean is not more lonesome than the plains, nor night so gloomy as that dumb sunlight," wrote Lummis in 1893, approaching the Gran Quivira across the desert. "The brown grass is knee-deep, and even this shock gives a surprise in this hoof-obliterated land. The bands of antelope that drift, like cloud shadows, across the dun landscape suggest less of life than of the supernatural. The spell of the plains is a wondrous thing. At first it fascinates. Then it bewilders. At last it crushes. It is intangible but resistless; stronger than hope, reason, will—stronger than humanity. When one cannot otherwise escape the plains, one takes refuge in madness."

This is the setting of the "ghost city" of "ashen hues," that "wraith in pallid stone," the Gran Quivira.

EL MORRO NATIONAL MONUMENT

Due west from Albuquerque, New Mexico, not far from the Arizona boundary, El Morro National Monument conserves a mesa end of striking beauty upon whose cliffs are graven many inscriptions cut in passing by the Spanish and American explorers of more than two centuries. It is a historical record of unique value, the only extant memoranda of several expeditions, an invaluable detail in the history of many. It has helped trace obscure courses and has established important departures. To the tourist it brings home, as nothing else can, the realization of these grim romances of other days.

El Morro, the castle, is also called Inscription Rock. West of its steepled front, in the angle of a sharp bend in the mesa, is a large partly enclosed natural chamber, a refuge in storm. A spring here betrays the reason for El Morro's popularity among the explorers of a semidesert region. The old Zuñi trail bent from its course to touch this spring. Inscriptions are also found near the spring and on the outer side of the mesa facing the Zuñi Road.

For those acquainted with the story of Spanish exploration this national monument will have unique interest. To all it imparts a fascinating sense of the romance of those early days with which the large body of Americans have yet to become familiar. The popular story of this romantic period of American history, its poetry and its fiction remain to be written.

The oldest inscription is dated February 18, 1526. The name of Juan de Oñate, later founder of Santa Fe, is there under date of 1606, the year of his visit to the mouth of the Colorado River. One of the latest Spanish inscriptions is that of Don Diego de Vargas, who in 1692 reconquered the Indians who rebelled against Spanish authority in 1680.

The reservation also includes several important community houses of great antiquity, one of which perches safely upon the very top of El Morro rock.

CASA GRANDE NATIONAL MONUMENT

In the far south of Arizona not many miles north of the boundary of Sonora, there stands, near the Gila River, the noble ruin which the Spaniards call Casa Grande, or Great House. It was a building of large size situated in a compound of outlying buildings enclosed in a rectangular wall; no less than three other similar compounds and four detached clan houses once stood in the near neighborhood. Evidently, in prehistoric days, this was an important centre of population; remains of an irrigation system are still visible.

The builders of these prosperous communal dwellings were probably Pima Indians. The Indians living in the neighborhood to-day have traditions indicated by their own names for the Casa Grande, the Old House of the Chief and the Old House of Chief Morning Green. "The Pima word for green and blue is the

CASA GRANDE NATIONAL MONUMENT

PREHISTORIC CAVE HOMES IN THE BANDELIER NATIONAL MONUMENT
The holes worn by erosion have been enlarged for doors and windows

same," Doctor Fewkes writes me. "Russell trans-
lates the old chief's name Morning Blue, which is the
same as my Morning Green. I have no doubt Morning Glow is also correct, no doubt nearer the Indian
idea which refers to sun-god. This chief was the son
of the Sun by a maid, as was also Tcuhu-Montezuma,
a sun-god who, legends say, built Casa Grande."

Whatever its origin, the community was already
in ruins when the Spaniards first found it. Kino identified it as the ruin which Fray Marcos saw in 1539
and called Chichilticalli, and which Coronado passed
in 1540. The early Spanish historians believed it an
ancestral settlement of the Aztecs.

Its formal discovery followed a century and a half
later. Domingo Jironza Petriz de Cruzate, governor
of Sonora, had directed his nephew, Lieutenant Juan
Mateo Mange, to conduct a group of missionaries into
the desert, where Mange heard rumors from the natives
of a fine group of ruins on the banks of a river which
flowed west. He reported this to Father Eusebio
Francisco Kino, the fearless and famous Jesuit missionary among the Indians from 1687 to 1711; in November, 1694, Kino searched for the ruins, found them,
and said mass within the walls of the Casa Grande.

This splendid ruin is built of a natural concrete
called culeche. The external walls are rough, but are
smoothly plastered within, showing the marks of human hands. Two pairs of small holes in the walls
opposite others in the central room have occasioned
much speculation. Two look east and west; the others,

also on opposite walls, look north and south. Some persons conjecture that observations were made through them of the solstices, and perhaps of some star, to establish the seasons for these primitive people. "The foundation for this unwarranted hypothesis," Doctor Fewkes writes, "is probably a statement in a manuscript by Father Font in 1775, that the 'Prince,' 'chief' of Casa Grande, looked through openings in the east and west walls 'on the sun as it rose and set, to salute it.' The openings should not be confused with smaller holes made in the walls for placing iron rods to support the walls by contractors when the ruin was repaired."

TUMACACORI NATIONAL MONUMENT

One of the best-preserved ruins of one of the finest missions which Spanish priests established in the desert of the extreme south of Arizona is protected under the name of the Tumacacori National Monument. It is fifty-seven miles south of Tucson, near the Mexican border. The outlying country probably possessed a large native population.

The ruins are most impressive, consisting of the walls and tower of an old church building, the walls of a mortuary chapel at the north end of the church, and a surrounding court with adobe walls six feet high. These, like all the Spanish missions, were built by Indian converts under the direction of priests, for the Spanish invaders performed no manual labor. The walls of the church are six feet thick and plastered

TUMACACORI MISSION

From a photograph by T. H. Bate

MONTEZUMA CASTLE

within. The belfry and the altar-dome are of burned brick, the only example of brick construction among the early Spanish missions. There is a fine arched doorway.

For many reasons, this splendid church is well worth a visit. It was founded and built about 1688 by Father Eusebio Francisco Kino, and was known as the Mission San Cayetano de Tumacacori. About 1769 the Franciscans assumed charge, and repaired and elaborated the structure. They maintained it for about sixty years, until the Apache Indians laid siege and finally captured it, driving out the priests and dispersing the Papagos. About 1850 it was found by Americans in its present condition.

Navajo National Monument

The boundary-line which divides Utah from Arizona divides the most gorgeous expression of the great American desert region. From the Mesa Verde National Park on the east to Zion National Monument on the west, from the Natural Bridges on the north to the Grand Canyon and the Painted Desert on the south, the country glows with golden sands and crimson mesas, a wilderness of amazing and impossible contours and indescribable charm.

Within this region, in the extreme north of Arizona, lie the ruins of three neighboring pueblos. Richard Wetherill, who was one of the discoverers of the famous cliff-cities of the Mesa Verde, was one of the party which found the Kit Siel (Broken Pottery) ruin in 1894 within a long crescent-shaped cave in the side of a glowing red sandstone cliff; in 1908, upon information given by a Navajo Indian, John Wetherill, Professor Byron Cumming, and Neil Judd located Betatakin (Hillside House) ruin within a crescent-shaped cavity in the side of a small red canyon. Twenty miles west of Betatakin is a small ruin known as Inscription House upon whose walls is a carved inscription supposed to have been made by Spanish explorers who visited them in 1661.

While these ruins show no features materially differing from those of hundreds of other more accessible pueblo ruins, they possess quite extraordinary beauty because of their romantic location in cliffs of striking color in a region of mysterious charm.

II

But the Indian civilization of our southwest began very many centuries before the arrival of the Spaniard, who found, besides the innumerable pueblos which were crowded with busy occupants, hundreds of pueblos which had been deserted by their builders, some of them for centuries, and which lay even then in ruins.

The desertion of so many pueblos with abundant pottery and other evidences of active living is one of the mysteries of this prehistoric civilization. No doubt, with the failure of water-supplies and other changing physical conditions, occasionally communities sought better living in other localities, but it is certain that many of these desertions resulted from the raids of the wandering predatory tribes of the plains, the Querechos of Bandelier's records, but usually mentioned by him and others by the modern name of Apaches. These fierce bands continually sought to possess themselves of the stores of food and clothing to be found in the prosperous pueblos. The utmost cruelties of the Spanish invaders who, after all, were ruthless only in pursuit of gold, and, when this was lacking, tolerant and even kindly in their treatment of the natives, were nothing compared to the atrocities of these Apache Indians, who gloried in conquest.

Of the ruins of pueblos which were not identified with Spanish occupation, six have been conserved as national monuments.

THE BANDELIER NATIONAL MONUMENT

Many centuries before the coming of the Spaniards, a deep gorge on the eastern slope of the Sierra de los Valles, eighteen miles west of Santa Fe, New Mexico, was the home of a people living in caves which they hollowed by enlarging erosional openings in the soft volcanic sides of nearly perpendicular cliffs. The work was done with pains and skill. A small entrance, sometimes from the valley floor, sometimes reached by ladder, opened into a roomy apartment which in many cases consisted of several connecting rooms. These apartments were set in tiers or stories, as in a modern flat-house. There were often two, sometimes three, floors. They occurred in groups, probably representing families or clans, and some of these groups numbered hundreds. Seen to-day, the cliff-side suggests not so much the modern apartment-house, of which it was in a way the prehistoric prototype, as a gigantic pigeon-house.

In time these Indians emerged from the cliff and built a great semicircular pueblo up the valley, surrounded by smaller habitations. Other pueblos, probably still later in origin, were built upon surrounding mesas. All these habitations were abandoned perhaps centuries before the coming of the Spaniards. The gorge is known as the Rito de la Frijoles, which is the Spanish name of the clear mountain-stream which flows through it. Since 1916 it has been known as the Bandelier National Monument, after the late Adolf Francis Bandelier, the distinguished archæologist of the southwest.

The valley is a place of beauty. It is six miles long and nowhere broader than half a mile; its entrance scarcely admits two persons abreast. Its southern wall is the slope of a tumbled mesa, its northern wall the vertical cliff of white and yellowish pumice in which the caves were dug. The walls rise in crags and pinnacles many hundreds of feet. Willows, cottonwoods, cherries, and elders grow in thickets along the streamside, and cactus decorates the wastes. It is reached by automobile from Santa Fe.

This national monument lies within a large irregular area which has been suggested for a national park because of the many interesting remains which it encloses. The Cliff Cities National Park, when it finally comes into existence, will include among its exhibits a considerable group of prehistoric shrines of great value and unusual popular interest.

"The Indians of to-day," writes William Boone Douglass, "guard with great tenacity the secrets of their shrines. Even when the locations have been found they will deny their existence, plead ignorance of their meaning, or refuse to discuss the subject in any form." Nevertheless, they claim direct descent from the prehistoric shrine-builders, many of whose shrines are here found among others of later origin.

CHACO CANYON NATIONAL MONUMENT

For fourteen miles, both sides of a New Mexican canyon sixty-five miles equidistant from Farmington and Gallup are lined with the ruins of very large and prosperous colonies of prehistoric people. Most of the buildings were pueblos, many of them containing between fifty and a hundred rooms; one, known to-day as Pueblo Bonito, must have contained twelve hundred rooms.

These ruins lie in their original desolation; little excavation, and no restoration has yet been done. Chaco Canyon must have been the centre of a very large population. For miles in all directions, particularly westward, pueblos are grouped as suburbs group near cities of to-day.

It is not surprising that so populous a desert neighborhood required extensive systems of irrigation. One of these is so well preserved that little more than the repair of a dam would be necessary to make it again effective.

MONTEZUMA CASTLE NATIONAL MONUMENT

Small though it is, Montezuma Castle is justly one of the most celebrated prehistoric ruins in America. Its charming proportions, and particularly its commanding position in the face of a lofty precipice, make it a spectacle never to be forgotten. It is fifty-four miles from Prescott, Arizona.

This structure was a communal house which originally contained twenty-five rooms. The protection of the dry climate and of the shallow cave in which it stands has well preserved it these many centuries. Most of the rooms are in good condition. The timbers, which plainly show the hacking of the dull primeval stone axes, are among its most interesting exhibits. The building is crescent-shaped, sixty feet in width and about fifty feet high. It is five stories high, but the fifth story is invisible from the front because of the high stone wall of the façade. The cliff forms the back wall of the structure.

Montezuma's Castle is extremely old. Its material is soft calcareous stone, and nothing but its sheltered position could have preserved it. There are many ruined dwellings in the neighborhood.

Tonto National Monument

Four miles east of the Roosevelt Dam and eighty miles east of Phœnix, Arizona, are two small groups of cliff-dwellings which together form the Tonto National Monument. The southern group occupies a cliff cavern a hundred and twenty-five feet across. The masonry is above the average. The ceilings of the lower rooms are constructed of logs laid lengthwise, upon which a layer of fibre serves as the foundation for the four-inch adobe floor of the chamber overhead.

There are hundreds of cliff-dwellings which exceed this in charm and interest, but its nearness to an attraction like the Roosevelt Dam and glimpses of it which the traveller catches as he speeds over the Apache Trail make it invaluable as a tourist exhibit. Thousands who are unable to undertake the long and often arduous journeys by trail to the greater ruins, can here get definite ideas and a hint of the real flavor of prehistoric civilization in America.

Walnut Canyon National Monument

Thirty cliff-dwellings cling to the sides of picturesque Walnut Canyon, eight miles from Flagstaff, Arizona. They are excellently preserved. The largest contains eight rooms. The canyon possesses unusual beauty because of the thickets of locust which fringe the trail down from the rim. One climbs down ladders to occasional ruins which otherwise are inaccessible. Because of its nearness to Flagstaff several thousand persons visit this reservation yearly.

Gila Cliffs National Monument

Fifty miles northeast of Silver City, New Mexico, a deep rough canyon in the west fork of the Gila River contains a group of four cliff-dwellings in a fair state of preservation. They lie in cavities in the base of an overhanging cliff of grayish-yellow volcanic rock which at one time apparently were closed by protecting walls. When discovered by prospectors and hunters about 1870, many sandals, baskets, spears, and cooking utensils were found strewn on the floors. Corn-cobs are all that vandals have left.

XIX

DESERT SPECTACLES

THE American desert, to eyes attuned, is charged with beauty. Few who see it from the car-window find it attractive; most travellers quickly lose interest in its repetitions and turn back to their novels. A little intimacy changes this attitude. Live a little with the desert. See it in its varied moods—for every hour it changes; see it at sunrise, at midday, at sunset, in the ghostly night, by moonlight. Observe its life—for it is full of life; its amazing vegetation; its varied outline. Drink in its atmosphere, its history, its tradition, its romance. Open your soul to its persuading spirit. Then, insensibly but swiftly, its flavor will enthrall your senses; it will possess you. And once possessed, you are charmed for life. It will call you again and again, as the sea calls the sailor and the East its devotees.

This alluring region is represented in our national parks system by reservations which display its range. The Zion National Monument, the Grand Canyon, and the Mesa Verde illustrate widely differing phases. The historical monuments convey a sense of its romance. There remain a few to complete the gamut of its charms.

THE RAINBOW BRIDGE NATIONAL MONUMENT

Imagine a gray Navajo desert dotted with purple sage; huge mesas, deep red, squared against the gray-blue atmosphere of the horizon; pinnacles, spires, shapes like monstrous bloody fangs, springing from the sands; a floor as rough as stormy seas, heaped with tumbled rocks, red, yellow, blue, green, grayish-white, between which rise strange yellowish-green thorny growths, cactus-like and unfamiliar; a pathless waste, strewn with obsidian fragments, glaring in the noon sun, more confusing than the crooked mazes of an ancient Oriental city.

Imagine shapeless masses of colored sandstone, unclimbable, barring the way; acres of polished mottled rock tilted at angles which defy crossing; unexpected canyons whose deep, broken, red and yellow precipices force long detours.

And everywhere color, color, color. It pervades the glowing floor, the uprising edifices. The very air palpitates with color, insistent, irresistible, indefinable.

This is the setting of the Rainbow Bridge.

Scarcely more than a hundred persons besides Indians, they tell me, have seen this most entrancing spectacle, perhaps, of all America. The way in is long and difficult. There are only two or three who know it, even of those who have been there more than once, and the region has no inhabitants to point directions among the confusing rocks. There is no water, nor any friendly tree.

ROOSEVELT PARTY IN MONUMENT VALLEY

RAINBOW BRIDGE IN FULL PERSPECTIVE

The day's ride is wearying in the extreme in spite of its fascinations. The objective is Navajo Mountain, which, strange spectacle in this desert waste, is forested to its summit with yellow pine above a surrounding belt of juniper and pinyon, with aspen and willows, wild roses, Indian paint-brush, primrose, and clematis in its lower valleys. Below, the multicolored desert, deep cut with the canyons which carry off the many little rivers.

Down one of these wild and highly colored desert canyons among whose vivid tumbled rocks your horses pick their course with difficulty, you suddenly see a rainbow caught among the vivid bald rocks, a slender arch so deliciously proportioned, so gracefully curved among its sharp surroundings, that your eye fixes it steadfastly and your heart bounds with relief; until now you had not noticed the oppression of this angled, spine-carpeted landscape.

From now on nothing else possesses you. The eccentricity of the going constantly hides it, and each reappearance brings again the joy of discovery. And at last you reach it, dismount beside the small clear stream which flows beneath it, approach reverently, overwhelmed with a strange mingling of awe and great elation. You stand beneath its enormous encircling red and yellow arch and perceive that it is the support which holds up the sky. It is long before turbulent emotion permits the mind to analyze the elements which compose its extraordinary beauty.

Dimensions mean little before spectacles like this.

To know that the span is two hundred and seventy-eight feet may help realization at home, where it may be laid out, staked and looked at; it exceeds a block of Fifth Avenue in New York. To know that the apex of the rainbow's curve is three hundred and nine feet above your wondering eyes means nothing to you there; but to those who know New York City it means the height of the Flatiron Building built three stories higher. Choose a building of equal height in your own city, stand beside it and look up. Then imagine it a gigantic monolithic arch of entrancing proportions and fascinating curve, glowing in reds and yellows which merge into each other insensibly and without form or pattern. Imagine this fairy unreality outlined, not against the murk which overlies cities, but against a sky of desert clarity and color.

All natural bridges are created wholly by erosion. This was carved from an outstanding spur of Navajo sandstone which lay crosswise of the canyon. Originally the stream struck full against this barrier, swung sideways, and found its way around the spur's free outer edge. The end was merely a matter of time. Gradually but surely the stream, sand-laden in times of flood, wore an ever-deepening hollow in the barrier. Finally it wore it through and passed under what then became a bridge. But meantime other agencies were at work. The rocky wall above, alternately hot and cold, as happens in high arid lands, detached curved, flattened plates. Worn below by the stream, thinned above by the destructive processes of wind and temperature, the window enlarged. In time the Rainbow Bridge evolved in all its glorious beauty. Not far away is another natural bridge well advanced in the making.

The Rainbow Bridge was discovered in 1909 by William Boone Douglass, Examiner of Surveys in the General Land Office, Santa Fe. Following is an abstract of the government report covering the discovery:

"The information had come to Mr. Douglass from a Paiute Indian, Mike's Boy, who later took the name of Jim, employed as flagman in the survey of the three great natural bridges of White Canyon. Seeing the white man's appreciation of this form of wind and water erosion, Jim told of a greater bridge known only to himself and one other Indian, located on the north side of the Navajo Mountain, in the Paiute Indian reservation. Bending a twig of willow in rainbow-shape, with its ends stuck in the ground, Jim showed what his bridge looked like.

"An effort was made to reach the bridge in December. Unfortunately Jim could not be located. On reaching the Navajo trading-post, Oljato, nothing was known of such a bridge, and the truth of Jim's statement was questioned.

"The trip was abandoned until August of the following year, when Mr. Douglass organized a second party at Bluff, Utah, and under Jim's guidance, left for the bridge. At Oljato the party was augmented by Professor Cummings, and a party of college students, with John Wetherill as packer, who were excavating ruins in the Navajo Indian Reservation. As the uninhabited and unknown country of the bridge was reached, travel became almost impossible. All equipment, save what was absolutely indispensable, was discarded. The whole country was a maze of box canyons, as though some turbulent sea had suddenly solidified in rock. Only at a few favored points could the canyon walls be scaled even by man, and still fewer where a horse might clamber. In the sloping sandstone ledges footholds for the horses must be cut, and even then they fell, until their loss seemed certain. After many adventures the party arrived at 11 o'clock, A. M., August 14, 1909.

"Jim had indeed made good. Silhouetted against a turquoise sky was an arch of rainbow shape, so delicately proportioned that it seemed as if some great sculptor had hewn it from the rock. Its span of 270 feet bridged a stream of clear, sparkling water, that flowed 310 feet below its crest. The world's greatest natural bridge had been found as Jim had described it. Beneath it, an ancient altar bore witness to the fact that it was a sacred shrine of those archaic people, the builders of the weird and mysterious cliff-castles seen in the Navajo National Monument.

"The crest of the bridge was reached by Mr. Douglass and his three assistants, John R. English, Jean F. Rogerson, and Daniel Perkins, by lowering themselves with ropes to the south abutment, and climbing its arch. Probably they were the first human beings to reach it.

"No Indian name for the bridge was known, except such descriptive generic terms as the Paiute 'The space under a horse's belly between its fore and hind legs,' or the 'Hole in the rock' (nonnezoshi) of the Navajo, neither of which was deemed appropriate. While the question of a name was still being debated, there appeared in the sky, as if in answer, a beautiful rainbow, the 'Barahoni' of the Paiutes.

"The suitability of the name was further demonstrated by a superstition of the Navajos. On the occasion of his second visit, the fall of the same year, Mr. Douglass had as an assistant an old Navajo Indian named White Horse, who, after passing under the bridge, would not return, but climbed laboriously around its end. On being pressed for an explanation, he would arch his hand, and through it squint at the sun, solemnly shaking his head. Later, through the assistance of Mrs. John Wetherill, an experienced Navajo linguist, Mr. Douglass learned that the formations of the type of the bridge were symbolic rainbows, or the sun's path, and one passing under could not return, under penalty of death, without the utterance of a certain prayer, which White Horse had forgotten. The aged Navajo informant would not reveal the prayer for fear of the 'Lightning Snake.'"

If your return from Rainbow Bridge carries you through Monument Valley with its miles of blazing red structures, memory will file still another amazing sensation. Some of its crimson monsters rise a thousand feet above the grassy plain.

NATURAL BRIDGES NATIONAL MONUMENT

Not many miles north of the Rainbow Bridge, fifty miles from Monticello in southern Utah, in a region not greatly dissimilar in outline, and only less colorful, three natural bridges of large size have been conserved under the title of the Natural Bridges National Monument. Here, west of the Mesa Verde, the country is characterized by long, broad mesas, sometimes crowned with stunted cedar forests, dropping suddenly into deep valleys. The erosion of many thousands of centuries has ploughed the surface into winding rock-strewn canyons, great and small. Three of these canyons are crossed by bridges stream-cut through the solid rock.

The largest, locally known as the Augusta Bridge, is named Sipapu, Gate of Heaven. It is one of the largest natural bridges in the world, measuring two hundred and twenty-two feet in height, with a span of two hundred and sixty-one feet. It is a graceful and majestic structure, so proportioned and finished that it is difficult, from some points of view, to believe it the unplanned work of natural forces. One crosses it on a level platform twenty-eight feet wide.

The other two, which are nearly its size, are found within five miles. The Kachina, which means Guardian Spirit, is locally called the Caroline Bridge. The Owachomo, meaning Rock Mound, is locally known as the Edwin Bridge. The local names celebrate persons who visited them soon after they were first discovered by Emery Knowles in 1895.

They may be reached by horse and pack-train from Monticello, or Bluff, Utah. One of the five sections of the reservation conserves two large caves.

Dinosaur National Monument

The Age of Reptile developed a wide variety of monsters in the central regions of the continent from Montana to the Gulf of Mexico. The dinosaurs of the Triassic and Jurassic periods sometimes had gigantic size, the Brontosaurus attaining a length of sixty feet or more. The femur of the Brachiosaurus exceeded six feet; this must have been the greatest of them all.

The greater dinosaurs were herbivorous. The carnivorous species were not remarkable for size; there were small leaping forms scarcely larger than rabbits. The necessity for defense against the flesh-eaters developed, in the smaller dinosaurs, extremely heavy armor. The stegosaur carried huge plates upon his curved back, suggesting a circular saw; his long powerful tail was armed with sharp spikes, and must have been a dangerous weapon. Dinosaurs roamed all over what is now called our middle west.

In those days the central part of our land was warm and swampy. Fresh-water lagoons and sluggish streams were bordered by low forests of palms and ferns; one must go to the tropics to find a corresponding landscape in our times. The waters abounded in reptiles and fish. Huge winged reptiles flew from cover to cover. The first birds were evolving from reptilian forms.

The absorbing story of these times is written in the rocks. The life forms were at their full when the sands were laid which to-day is the wide-spread layer of sandstone which geologists call the Morrison formation. Erosion has exposed this sandstone in several parts of the western United States, and many have been the interesting glimpses it has afforded of that strange period so many millions of years ago.

In the Uintah Basin of northwestern Utah, a region of bad lands crossed by the Green River on its way to the Colorado and the Grand Canyon, the Morrison strata have been bent upward at an angle of sixty degrees or more and then cut through, exposing their entire depth. The country is extremely rough and bare. Only in occasional widely separated bottoms has irrigation made farming possible; elsewhere nothing grows upon the bald hillsides.

Here, eighteen miles east of the town of Vernal, eighty acres of the exposed Morrison strata were set aside in 1915 as the Dinosaur National Monument. These acres have already yielded a very large collection of skeletons. Since 1908 the Carnegie Museum of Pittsburgh has been gathering specimens of the greatest importance. The only complete skeleton of a dinosaur ever found was taken out in 1909. The work of quarrying and removal is done with the utmost care. The rock is chiselled away in thin layers, as no one can tell when an invaluable relic may be found. As fast as bones are detached, they are covered with plaster of Paris and so wrapped that breakage becomes impossible. Two years were required to unearth the skeleton of a brontosaurus.

The extraordinary massing of fossil remains at this point suggests that floods may have swept these animals from a large area and lodged their bodies here, where they were covered with sands. But it also is possible that this spot was merely a favorite feeding-ground. It may be that similarly rich deposits lie hidden in many places in the wide-spread Morrison sandstone which some day may be unearthed. The bones of dinosaurs have been found in the Morrison of Colorado near Boulder.

PETRIFIED FOREST NATIONAL MONUMENT

For a hundred and twenty-five or thirty miles southwest of the Grand Canyon, the valley of the Little Colorado River is known as the Painted Desert. It is a narrow plain of Carboniferous and Triassic marls, shales, sandstones, and conglomerates, abounding in fossils, the most arid part of Arizona; even the river's lower reaches dry up for a part of each year. But it is a palette of brilliant colors; it will be difficult to name a tint or shade which is not vividly represented in this gaudy floor and in the strata of the cliffs which define its northern and eastern limits. Above and beyond these cliffs lies that other amazing desert, the Navajo country, the land of the Rainbow Bridge and the Canyon de Chelly.

I have mentioned the Painted Desert because it is shaped like a long narrow finger pointed straight

at the Petrified Forests lying just beyond its touch.
Here the country is also highly colored, but very differently. Maroon and tawny yellow are the prevailing tints of the marls, red and brown the colors of the
sandstones. There is a rolling sandy floor crisscrossed
with canyons in whose bottoms grow stunted cedars
and occasional cottonwoods. Upon this floor thousands of petrified logs are heaped in confusion. In
many places the strong suggestion is that of a log jam
left stranded by subsiding floods. Nearly all the logs
have broken into short lengths as cleanly cut as if
sawn, the result of succeeding heat and cold.

Areas of petrified wood are common in many parts
of the Navajo country and its surrounding deserts.
The larger areas are marked on the Geological Survey
maps, and many lesser areas are mentioned in reports.
There are references to rooted stumps. The three
groups in the Petrified Forest National Monument,
near the town of Adamana, Arizona, were chosen for
conservation because they are the largest and perhaps
the finest; at the time, the gorgeously colored logs
were being carried away in quantities to be cut up into
table-tops.

As a matter of fact, these are not forests. Most
of these trees grew upon levels seven hundred feet or
more higher than where they now lie and at unknown
distances; floods left them here.

The First Forest, which lies six miles south of
Adamana, contains thousands of broken lengths.
One unbroken log a hundred and eleven feet long

THE PETRIFIED FOREST OF ARIZONA

Showing the formation in colored strata. The logs seen on the ground grew upon a level seven
hundred feet higher

PETRIFIED TRUNK FORMING A BRIDGE OVER A CANYON

The trunk is 111 feet long. The stone piers were built to preserve it

bridges a canyon forty-five feet wide, a remarkable spectacle. In the Second Forest, which lies two miles and a half south of that, and the Third Forest, which is thirteen miles south of Adamana and eighteen miles southeast of Holbrook, most of the trunks appear to lie in their original positions. One which was measured by Doctor G. H. Knowlton of the Smithsonian Institution was more than seven feet in diameter and a hundred and twenty feet long. He estimates the average diameters at three or four feet, while lengths vary from sixty to a hundred feet.

The coloring of the wood is variegated and brilliant. "The state of mineralization in which most of this wood exists," writes Professor Lester F. Ward, paleobotanist, "almost places them among the gems or precious stones. Not only are chalcedony, opals, and agates found among them, but many approach the condition of jasper and onyx." "The chemistry of the process of petrifaction or silicification," writes Doctor George P. Merrill, Curator of Geology in the National Museum, "is not quite clear. Silica is ordinarily looked upon as one of the most insoluble of substances. It is nevertheless readily soluble in alkaline solutions—*i. e.*, solutions containing soda or potash. It is probable that the solutions permeating these buried logs were thus alkaline, and as the logs gradually decayed their organic matter was replaced, molecule by molecule, by silica. The brilliant red and other colors are due to the small amount of iron and manganese deposited together with the silica, and superoxydized as the trunks are exposed to the air. The most brilliant colors are therefore to be found on the surface."

The trees are of several species. All those identified by Doctor Knowlton were Araucaria, which do not now live in the northern hemisphere. Doctor E. C. Jeffrey, of Harvard, has described one genus unknown elsewhere.

To get the Petrified Forest into full prospective it is well to recall that these shales and sands were laid in water, above whose surface the land raised many times, only to sink again and accumulate new strata. The plateau now has fifty-seven hundred feet of altitude.

"When it is known," writes Doctor Knowlton, "that since the close of Triassic times probably more than fifty thousand feet of sediments have been deposited, it is seen that the age of the Triassic forests of Arizona can only be reckoned in millions of years —just how many it would be mere speculation to attempt to estimate. It is certain, also, that at one time the strata containing these petrified logs were themselves buried beneath thousands of feet of strata of later ages, which have in places been worn away sufficiently to expose the tree-bearing beds. Undoubtedly other forests as great or greater than those now exposed lie buried beneath the later formations."

A very interesting small forest, not in the reservation, lies nine miles north of Adamana.

Papago Saguaro National Monument

The popular idea of a desert of dry drifting sand unrelieved except at occasional oases by evidences of life was born of our early geographies, which pictured the Sahara as the desert type. Far different indeed is our American desert, most of which has a few inches of rainfall in the early spring and grows a peculiar flora of remarkable individuality and beauty. The creosote bush seen from the car-windows shelters a few grasses which brown and die by summer, but help to color the landscape the year around. Many low flowering plants gladden the desert springtime, and in the far south and particularly in the far southwest are several varieties of cactus which attain great size. The frequenter of the desert soon correlates its flora with its other scenic elements and finds all rich and beautiful.

In southwestern Arizona and along the southern border of California this strange flora finds its fullest expression. Here one enters a new fairy-land, a region of stinging bushes and upstanding monsters lifting ungainly arms to heaven. In 1914, to conserve one of the many rich tracts of desert flora, President Wilson created the Papago Saguaro National Monument a few miles east of Phœnix, Arizona. Its two thousand and fifty acres include fine examples of innumerable desert species in fullest development.

Among these the cholla is at once one of the most fascinating and the most exasperating. It belongs

to the prickly pear family, but there resemblance
ceases. It is a stocky bush two or three feet high
covered with balls of flattened powerful sharp-pointed
needles which will penetrate even a heavy shoe. In
November these fall, strewing the ground with spiny
indestructible weapons. There are many varieties of
chollas and all are decorative. The tree cholla grows
from seven to ten feet in height, a splendid showy
feature of the desert slopes, and the home, fortress,
and sure defense for all the birds who can find nest-
room behind its bristling breastwork.

The Cereus thurberi, the pipe-organ, or candela-
brum cactus, as it is variously called, grows in thick
straight columns often clumped closely together, a
picturesque and beautiful creation. Groups range
from a few inches to many feet in height. One clump
of twenty-two stems has been reported, the largest
stem of which was twenty feet high and twenty-two
inches in diameter.

Another of picturesque appeal is the bisnaga or
barrel cactus, of which there are many species of many
sizes. Like all cacti, it absorbs water during the brief
wet season and stores it for future use. A specimen
the size of a flour-barrel can be made to yield a couple
of gallons of sweetish but refreshing water, whereby
many a life has been saved in the sandy wastes.

But the desert's chief exhibit is the giant saguaro,
the Cereus giganteus, from which the reservation got
its name. This stately cactus rises in a splendid green
column, accordion-plaited and decorated with star-

like clusters of spines upon the edges of the plaits. The larger specimens grow as high as sixty or seventy feet and throw out at intervals powerful branches which bend sharply upward; sometimes there are as many as eight or nine of these gigantic branches.

No towering fir or spreading oak carries a more princely air. A forest of giant saguaro rising from a painted desert far above the tangle of creosote-bush, mesquite, cholla, bisnaga, and scores of other strange growths of a land of strange attractions is a spectacle to stir the blood and to remember for a lifetime.

COLORADO NATIONAL MONUMENT

On the desert border of far-western Colorado near Grand Junction is a region of red sandstone which the erosion of the ages has carved into innumerable strange and grotesque shapes. Once a great plain, then a group of mesas, now it has become a city of grotesque monuments. Those who have seen the Garden of the Gods near Colorado Springs can imagine it multiplied many times in size, grotesqueness, complexity, and area; such a vision will approximate the Colorado National Monument. The two regions have other relations in common, for as the Garden of the Gods flanks the Rockies' eastern slopes and looks eastward to the great plains, so does the Colorado National Monument flank the Rockies' western desert. Both are the disclosure by erosion of similar strata of red sandstone which may have been more or less continuous before the great Rockies wrinkled. lifted, and burst upward between them.

The rock monuments of this group are extremely highly colored. They rise in several neighboring canyons and some of them are of great height and fantastic design. One is a nearly circular column with a diameter of a hundred feet at the base and a height of more than four hundred feet.

Caves add to the attractions, and there are many springs among the tangled growths of the canyon floors. There are cedars and pinyon trees. The region abounds in mule-deer and other wild animals.

Capulin Mountain National Monument

After the sea-bottom which is now our desert southwest rose for the last time and became the lofty plateau of to-day, many were the changes by which its surface became modified. Chief of these was the erosion which has washed its levels thousands of feet below its potential altitude and carved it so remarkably. But it also became a field of wide-spread volcanic activity, and lavas and obsidians are constantly encountered among its gravels, sands, and shales. Many also are the cones of dead volcanoes.

Capulin Mountain in northeastern New Mexico near the Colorado line is a very ancient volcano which retains its shape in nearly perfect condition. It was made a national monument for scientific reasons, but it also happily rounds out the national parks' exhibit of the influences which created our wonderful southwest. Its crater cone is composed partly of lava flow, partly of fine loose cinder, and partly of cemented volcanic ash. It is nearly a perfect cone.

Capulin rises fifteen hundred feet from the plain to an altitude of eight thousand feet. Its crater is fifteen hundred feet across and seventy-five feet deep. To complete the volcanic exhibit many blister cones are found around its base. It is easily reached from two railroads or by automobile.

XX

THE MUIR WOODS AND OTHER NATIONAL
MONUMENTS

NATIONAL monuments which commemorate history, conserve forests, and distinguish conspicuous examples of world-making dot other parts of the United States besides the colorful southwest. Their variety is great and the natural beauty of some of them unsurpassed.

Their number should be much greater. Every history-helping exploration of the early days, from Cortreal's inspection of the upper Atlantic coast in 1501 and Ponce de Leon's exploration of Florida eleven years later, from Cabrillo's skirting of the Pacific coast in 1542 and Vancouver's entrance into Puget Sound in 1792, including every early expedition from north and south into the country now ours and every exploration of the interior by our own people, should be commemorated, not by a slab of bronze or marble, but by a striking and appropriate area set apart as a definite memorial of the history of this nation's early beginnings.

These areas should be appropriately located upon or overlooking some important or characteristic landmark of the explorations or events which they commemorated, and should have scenic importance sufficient to attract visitors and impress upon them the stages of the progress of this land from a condition of wilderness to settlement and civilization.

Nor should it end here. The country is richly endowed, from the Atlantic to the Pacific, with examples of Nature's amazing handicraft in the making of this continent, the whole range of which should be fully expressed in national reservations.

Besides these, examples of our northeastern forests, the pines of the southern Appalachians, the everglades of Florida, the tangled woodlands of the gulf, and other typical forests which perchance may have escaped the desolation of civilization, should be added to the splendid forest reserves of the national parks of the West, first-grown as Nature made them, forever to remain untouched by the axe.

Thus will the national parks system become the real national museum for to-day and forever.

There follows a brief catalogue of the slender and altogether fortuitous beginnings of such an exhibit.

Muir Woods National Monument

One of the last remaining stands of original redwood forest easily accessible to the visitor is the Muir Woods in California. It occupies a picturesque canyon on the slope of Mount Tamalpais, north of the Golden Gate and opposite San Francisco, from which it is comfortably reached by ferry and railroad. It was rescued from the axe by William Kent of California, who, jointly with Mrs. Kent, gave it to the nation as an exhibit of the splendid forest which once crowded the shores of San Francisco Bay. It is named after John Muir, to whom this grove was a favorite retreat for many years.

It exhibits many noble specimens of the California redwood, Sequoia sempervirens, cousin of the giant sequoia. Some of them attain a height of three hundred feet, with a diameter exceeding eighteen feet. They stand usually in clusters, or family groups, their stems erect as pillars, their crowns joined in a lofty roof, rustling in the Pacific winds, musical with the songs of birds. Not even in the giant sequoia groves of the Sierra have I found any spot more cathedral-like than this. Its floor is brown and sweet-smelling, its aisles outlined by the tread of generations of worshippers. Its naves, transepts, alcoves, and sanctuaries are still and dim, yet filled mysteriously with light.

The Muir Woods is a grove of noble redwoods, but it is much more. Apart from its main passages, in alcove, gateway, and outlying precinct it is an exhibit of the rich Californian coast forest. The Douglas fir here reaches stately proportions. Many of the western oaks display their manifold picturesqueness. A hundred lesser trees and shrubs add their grace and variety. The forest is typical and complete. Though small in scope it is not a remnant but naturally blends into its surroundings. The shaded north hill slopes carry the great trees to the ridge line; the southern slope exhibits the struggle for precedence with the

From a photograph by Tibbitts

CATHEDRAL ISLE OF THE MUIR WOODS

mountain shrubs. At the lower end one bursts out into the grass country and the open hills. Every feature of the loveliest of all forests is at hand: the valley floor with its miniature trout-stream overhung with fragrant azaleas; the brown carpet interwoven with azaleas and violets. There is the cool decoration of many ferns.

The straight-growing redwoods compel a change of habit in the trees that would struggle toward a view of the sky. Mountain-oaks and madrona are straight-trunked and clear of lower branches. There is rivalry of the strong and protection for the weak.

The grove is, in truth, a complete expression in little of Nature's forest plan. The characteristics of the greater redwood forests which require weeks or months to compass and careful correlation to bring into perspective, here are exhibited within the rambling of a day. The Muir Woods is an entity. Its meadow borders, its dark ravines, its valley floor, its slopes and hilltops, all show fullest luxuriance and perfect proportion. The struggle of the greater trees to climb the hills is exemplified as fully as in the great exhibits of the north, which spread over many miles of hill slope; here one may see its range in half an hour.

The coloring, too, is rich. The rusty foliage and bark, the brighter green of the shrubs, the brown carpet, the opal light, stirs the spirit. The powerful individuality of many of its trees is the source of never-ending pleasure. There is a redwood upon the West Fork which has no living base, but feeds, vampire-like, through another's veins; or, if you prefer the figure of family dependence so strikingly exemplified in these woods, has been rescued from destruction by a brother. The base of this tree has been completely girdled by fire. Impossible to draw subsistence from below, it stands up from a burned, naked, slender foundation. But another tree fell against it twenty-five or thirty feet above the ground, in some far past storm, and lost its top; this tree pours its sap into the veins of the other to support its noble top. The twin cripples have become a single healthy tree.

One of the most striking exhibits of the Muir Woods is its tangle of California laurel. Even in its deepest recesses, the bays, as they are commonly called, reach great size. They sprawl in all directions, bend at sharp angles, make great loops to enter the soil and root again; sometimes they cross each other and join their trunks; in one instance, at least, a large crownless trunk has bent and entered head first the stem of still a larger tree.

There are greater stands of virgin redwoods in the northern wilderness of California which the ruthless lumberman has not yet reached but is approaching fast; these are inland stands of giants, crowded like battalions. But there is no other Muir Woods, with its miniature perfection.

DEVIL'S POSTPILE NATIONAL MONUMENT

Southeast of craggy Lyell, mountain climax and eastern outpost of the Yosemite National Park, the

Muir Trail follows the extravagantly beautiful beginnings of the Middle Fork of the San Joaquin River
through a region of myriad waters and snow-flecked
mountains. Banner Peak, Ritter Mountain, Thousand Island Lake, Volcanic Ridge, Shadow Lake—
national park scenery in its noblest expression, but not
yet national park.

A score of miles from Lyell, the trail follows the
river into a volcanic bottom from whose forest rises the
splendid group of pentagonal basaltic columns which
was made a national monument in 1911 under the title
of the Devil's Postpile. Those who know the famous
Giant's Causeway of the Irish coast will know it in
kind, but not in beauty.

The enormous uplift which created the Sierra was
accompanied on both its slopes by extensive volcanic
eruptions, the remains of which are frequently visible
to the traveller. The huge basaltic crystals of the
Devil's Postpile were a product of this volcanic out-
pouring; they formed deep within the hot masses
which poured over the region for miles around. Their
upper ends have become exposed by the erosion of the
ages by which the cinder soil and softer rock around
them have been worn away.

The trail traveller comes suddenly upon this
splendid group. It is elevated, as if it were the front
of a small ridge, its posts standing on end, side by
side, in close formation. Below it, covering the front
of the ridge down to the line of the trail, is an enormous talus mass of broken pieces. The appropriate-

ness of the name strikes one at the first glance. This is really a postpile, every post carefully hewn to pattern, all of nearly equal length. The talus heap below suggests that his Satanic Majesty was utilizing it also as a woodpile, and had sawn many of the posts into lengths to fit the furnaces which we have been taught that he keeps hot for the wicked.

Certainly it is a beautiful, interesting, and even an imposing spectacle. One also thinks of it as a gigantic organ, whose many hundred pipes rise many feet in air. Its lofty position, seen from the viewpoint of the trail, is one of dignity; it overlooks the pines and firs surrounding the clearing in which the observer stands. The trees on the higher level scarcely overtop it; in part, it is outlined against the sky.

"The Devil's Postpile," writes Professor Joseph N. LeConte, Muir's successor as the prophet of the Sierra, "is a wonderful cliff of columnar basalt, facing the river. The columns are quite perfect prisms, nearly vertical and fitted together like the cells of a honeycomb. Most of the prisms are pentagonal, though some are of four or six sides. The standing columns are about two feet in diameter and forty feet high. At the base of the cliff is an enormous basalt structure, but, wherever the bed-rock is exposed beneath the pumice covering, the same formation can be seen."

An error in the proclamation papers made the official title of this monument the Devil Postpile, and thus it must legally appear in all official documents.

The reservation also includes the Rainbow Fall of the San Juan River, one of the most beautiful waterfalls of the sub-Sierra region, besides soda springs and hot springs. This entire reservation was originally included in the Yosemite National Park, but was cut out by an unappreciative committee appointed to revise boundaries. It is to be hoped that Congress will soon restore it to its rightful status.

DEVIL'S TOWER NATIONAL MONUMENT

A structure similar in nature to the Devil's Postpile, but vastly greater in size and sensational quality, forms one of the most striking natural spectacles east of the Rocky Mountains. The Devil's Tower is unique. It rises with extreme abruptness from the rough Wyoming levels just west of the Black Hills. It is on the banks of the Belle Fourche River, which later, encircling the Black Hills around the north, finds its way into the Big Cheyenne and the Missouri.

This extraordinary tower emerges from a rounded forested hill of sedimentary rock which rises six hundred feet above the plain; from the top of that the tower rises six hundred feet still higher. It is visible for a hundred miles or more in every direction. Before the coming of the white man it was the landmark of the Indians. Later it served a useful purpose in guiding the early explorers.

To-day it is the point which draws the eye for many miles. The visitor approaching by automobile sees it hours away, and its growth upon the horizon as he approaches is not his least memorable experience. It has the effect at a distance of an enormous up-pointing finger which has been amputated just below the middle joint. When near enough to enable one to distinguish the upright flutings formed by its closely joined pentagonal basaltic prisms, the illusion vanishes. These, bending inward from a flaring base, straighten and become nearly perpendicular as they rise. Now, one may fancy it the stump of a tree more than a hundred feet in diameter whose top imagination sees piercing the low clouds. But close by, all similes become futile; then the Devil's Tower can be likened to nothing but itself.

This column is the core of a volcanic formation which doubtless once had a considerably larger circumference. At its base lies an immense talus of broken columns which the loosening frosts and the winter gales are constantly increasing; the process has been going on for untold thousands of years, during which the softer rock of the surrounding plains has been eroded to its present level.

One may climb the hill and the talus. The column itself cannot be climbed except by means of special apparatus. Its top is nearly flat and elliptical, with a diameter varying from sixty to a hundred feet.

PINNACLES NATIONAL MONUMENT

Forty miles as the crow flies east of Monterey, California, in a spur of the low Coast Range, is a region which erosion has carved into many fantastic

From a photograph by N. H. Darton THE DEVIL'S TOWER

From a photograph by Tibbits PINNACLES NATIONAL MONUMENT

shapes. Because of its crowded pointed rocks, it has been set apart under the title of the Pinnacles National Monument. For more than a century and a quarter it was known as Vancouver's Pinnacles because the great explorer visited it while his ships lay at anchor in Monterey Bay, and afterward described it in his "Voyages and Discoveries." It is unfortunate that the historical allusion was lost when it became a national reservation.

Two deep gorges, bordered by fantastic walls six hundred to a thousand feet high, and a broad semi-circular, flower-grown amphitheatre, constitute the central feature. Deep and narrow tributary gorges furnish many of the curious and intricate forms which for many years have made the spot popular among sightseers. Rock masses have fallen upon the side walls of several of these lesser gorges, converting them into picturesque winding tunnels and changing deep alcoves into caves which require candles to see.

It is a region of very unusual interest and charm.

SHOSHONE CAVERN NATIONAL MONUMENT

On the way to the Yellowstone National Park by way of the Wyoming entrance at Cody, and three miles east of the great Shoshone Dam, a limestone cave has been set apart under the title of the Shoshone Cavern National Monument. The way in is rough and precipitous and, after entering the cave, a descent by rope is necessary to reach the chambers of unusual beauty. One may then journey for more than a mile through galleries some of which are heavily incrusted with crystals.

LEWIS AND CLARK CAVERN NATIONAL MONUMENT

Approaching the crest of the Rockies on the Northern Pacific Railroad, the Lewis and Clark Cavern is passed fifty miles before reaching Butte. Its entrance is perched thirteen hundred feet above the broad valley of the Jefferson River, which the celebrated explorers followed on their westward journey; it overlooks fifty miles of their course.

The cavern, which has the usual characteristics of a limestone cave, slopes sharply back from its main entrance, following the dip of the strata. Some of its vaults are decorated in great splendor. The depredations of vandals were so damaging that in 1916 its entrance was closed by an iron gate.

This cavern is the only memorial of the Lewis and Clark expedition in the national parks system; there is no record that the explorers entered it or knew of its existence.

Two hundred and thirty miles east of the Cavern, Clark inscribed his name and the date, July 25, 1806, upon the face of a prominent butte known as Pompey's Pillar. This would have been a far more appropriate monument to the most important of American explorations than the limestone cave. In fact, the Department of the Interior once attempted to have it proclaimed a national monument; the fact that it lay within an Indian allotment prevented. The entire course of this great expedition should be marked at significant points by appropriate national monuments.

WIND CAVE NATIONAL PARK

In the southwestern corner of South Dakota, on the outskirts of the Black Hills, is one of the most interesting limestone caverns of the country. It was named Wind Cave because, with the changes of temperature during the day, strong currents of wind blow alternately into and out of its mouth. It has many long passages and fine chambers gorgeously decorated. It is a popular resort.

The United States Biological Survey maintains a game-preserve.

JEWEL CAVE NATIONAL MONUMENT

Northwest of Wind Cave, thirteen miles west and south of Custer, South Dakota boasts another limestone cavern of peculiar beauty, through whose entrance also the wind plays pranks. It is called Jewel Cave because many of its crystals are tinted in various colors, often very brilliantly. Under torchlight the effect is remarkable.

Connecting chambers have been explored for more than three miles, and there is much of it yet unknown.

OREGON CAVES NATIONAL MONUMENT

In the far southwestern corner of Oregon, about thirty miles south of Grant's Pass, upon slopes of coast mountains and at an altitude of four thousand feet, is a group of large limestone caves which have been set apart by presidential proclamation under the title of the Oregon Caves National Monument. Locally they are better known as the Marble Halls of Oregon.

There are two entrances at different levels, the passages and chambers following the dip of the strata. A considerable stream, the outlet of the waters which dissolved these caves in the solid limestone, passes through. The wall decorations, and, in some of the chambers, the stalagmites and stalactites, are exceedingly fine. The vaults and passages are unusually large. There is one chamber twenty-five feet across whose ceiling is believed to be two hundred feet high.

MOUNT OLYMPUS NATIONAL MONUMENT

For sixty miles or more east and west across the Olympian Peninsula, which is the forested northwestern corner of Washington and the United States between Puget Sound and the Pacific Ocean, stretch the Olympian Mountains. The country is a rugged wilderness of tumbled ranges, grown with magnificent forests above which rise snowy and glaciered summits. Its climax is Mount Olympus, eight thousand one hundred feet in altitude, rising about twenty-five miles equidistant from the Strait of Juan de Fuca upon the north and the Pacific Ocean upon the west.

The entire peninsula is extremely wild. It is skirted by a road along its eastern and part of its northern edges, connecting the water-front towns. Access to the mountain is by arduous trail. The reservation contains nine hundred and fifty square miles. Although possessing unusual scenic beauty, it was reserved for the purpose of protecting the Olympic elk, a species peculiar to the region. Deer and other wild animals also are abundant.

WHEELER NATIONAL MONUMENT

High under the Continental Divide in southwestern Colorado near Creede, a valley of high altitude, grotesquely eroded in tufa, rhyolite, and other volcanic rock, is named the Wheeler National Monument in honor of Captain George Montague Wheeler, who conducted geographical explorations between 1869 and 1879. Its deep canyons are bordered by lofty pinnacles of rock. It is believed that General John C. Fremont here met the disaster which drove back his exploring-party of 1848, fragments of harness and camp equipment and skeletons of mules having been found.

VERENDRYE NATIONAL MONUMENT

The first exploration of the northern United States east of the Rocky Mountains is commemorated by the Verendrye National Monument at the Old Crossing of the Missouri River in North Dakota. Here rises Crowhigh Butte, on the Fort Berthold Indian Reservation, an eminence commanding a wide view in every direction.

Verendrye, the celebrated French explorer, started from the north shore of Lake Superior about 1740 and passed westward and southward into the regions of the great plains. He or his sons, for the records of their journeys are confusing, passed westward into Montana along a course which Lewis and Clark paralleled in 1806, swung southward in the neighborhood of Fort Benton, and skirted the Rockies nearly to the middle of Wyoming, passing within a couple of hundred miles of the Yellowstone National Park.

Crowhigh Butte is supposed to have given the Verendryes their first extensive view of the upper Missouri. The butte was long a landmark to guide early settlers to Old Crossing.

SULLY'S HILL NATIONAL PARK

Congress created the Sully's Hill National Park in North Dakota in 1904 in response to a local demand. Its hills and meadows constitute a museum of practically the entire flora of the State. The United States Biological Survey maintains there a wild-animal preserve for elk, bison, antelope, and other animals representative of the northern plains.

SITKA NATIONAL MONUMENT

On Baranoff Island, upon the southeastern shore of Alaska, is a reservation known as the Sitka National Monument which commemorates an important episode in the early history of Alaska. On this tract, which lies within a mile of the steamboat-landing at Sitka, formerly stood the village of the Kik-Siti Indians who, in 1802, attacked the settlement of Sitka

and massacred the Russians who had established it.
Two years later the Russians under Baranoff recovered
the settlement from the Indians, contrary to the active
opposition of Great Britain, and established the title
which they afterward transferred to the United States.
Graves of some of those who fell in the later battle
may be seen.

The reservation is also a fine exhibit of the forest
and flora of the Alexander Archipelago.   Sixteen totem-
poles remain from the old native days.

OLD KASAAN NATIONAL MONUMENT

Remains of the rapidly passing native life of the
Alexander Archipelago on the southeast coast of Alaska
are conserved in the Old Kasaan National Monument
on the east shore of Prince of Wales Island.   The village of Old Kasaan, occupied for many years by the
Hydah tribe and abandoned a decade or more ago,
contains several community houses of split timber,
each of which consists of a single room with a common
fireplace in the middle under a smoke-hole in the centre
of the roof.   Cedar sleeping-booths, each the size of an
ordinary piano-box, are built around the wall.

The monument also possesses fifty totem-poles,
carved and richly colored.

Of the thirty-six national monuments, twenty-
four are administered by the National Parks Service,
ten by the Department of Agriculture, and two by
the War Department.   Congress made the assign-

ments to the Department of Agriculture on the theory that, as these monuments occurred in forests, they could be more cheaply administered by the Forest Service; but, as many of the other monuments and nearly all the national parks also occur in forests, the logic is not apparent, and these monuments suffer from disassociation with the impetus and machinery of the National Park Service.

The Big Hole Battlefield National Monument, about fifty-five miles southwest of Butte, Montana, was assigned to the War Department because a battle took place there in 1877 between a small force of United States troops and a large force of Indians.

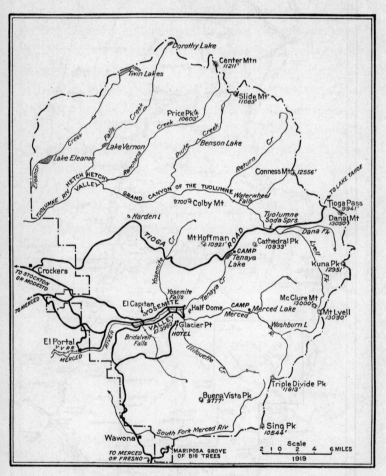

MAP OF YOSEMITE NATIONAL PARK, CALIFORNIA

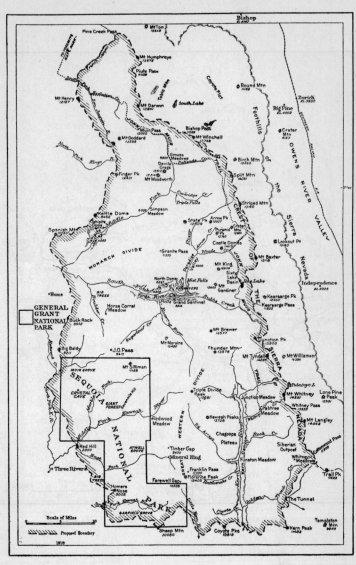

PROPOSED ROOSEVELT NATIONAL PARK AND THE SEQUOIA AND
GENERAL GRANT NATIONAL PARKS, CALIFORNIA

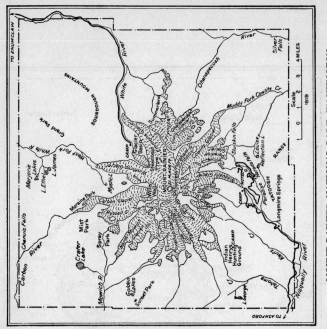

MOUNT RAINIER NATIONAL PARK, WASHINGTON

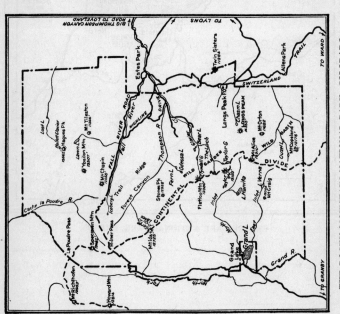

THE ROCKY MOUNTAIN NATIONAL PARK, COLORADO

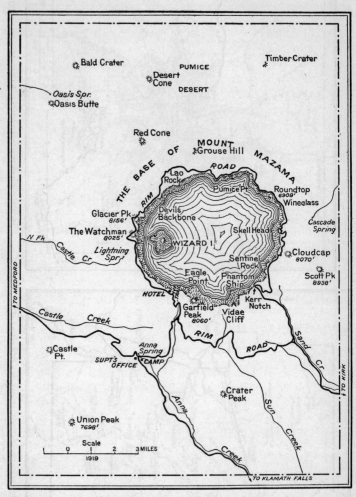

CRATER LAKE NATIONAL PARK, OREGON

The map contains the following labels:

Bald Crater

Timber Crater

PUMICE

Desert Cone

DESERT

Oasis Spr.
Oasis Butte

Red Cone

MOUNT

Grouse Hill

MAZAMA

THE BASE OF

ROAD

RIM

Lao Rock

Pumice Pt.

Roundtop
6909'

Wineglass

Glacier Pk.
8156'

Devils Backbone

Cascade Spring

The Watchman
8025'

N Fk

Castle Cr.

Lightning Spr.

Skell Head

Cloudcap
8070'

WIZARD I.

Sentinel Rock

Scott Pk
8938'

Eagle Point

Phantom Ship

TO MEDFORD

HOTEL

Kerr Notch

Castle   Creek

Garfield Peak
8060'

Vidae Cliff

RIM   ROAD

Sand Cr.

Castle Pt.

Anna Spring

SUPT'S OFFICE

CAMP

TO KIRK

Union Peak
7698'

Crater Peak

Anna

Sun   Creek

Scale

0   1   2   3 MILES

1919

Creek

TO KLAMATH FALLS

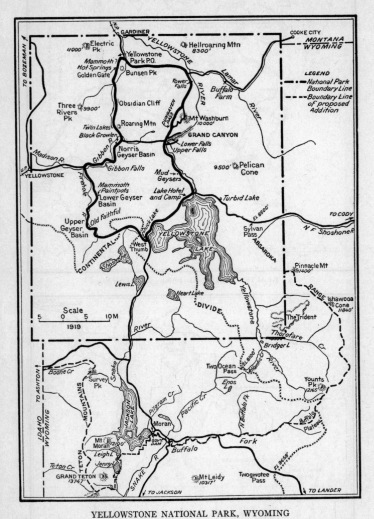

YELLOWSTONE NATIONAL PARK, WYOMING

The proposed Jackson Hole addition is enclosed by a broken line south of boundary

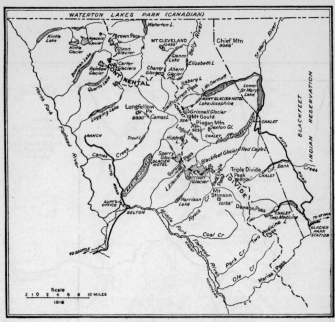

GLACIER NATIONAL PARK, MONTANA

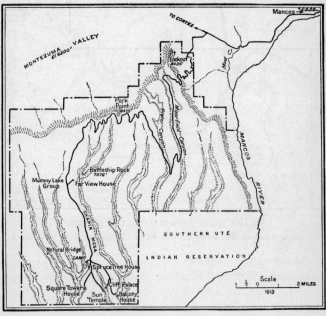

MESA VERDE NATIONAL PARK, COLORADO

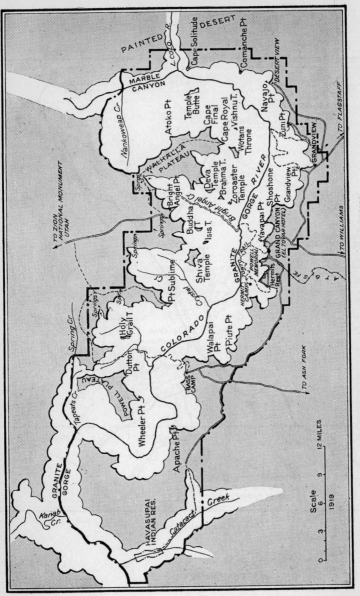

GRAND CANYON NATIONAL PARK, ARIZONA

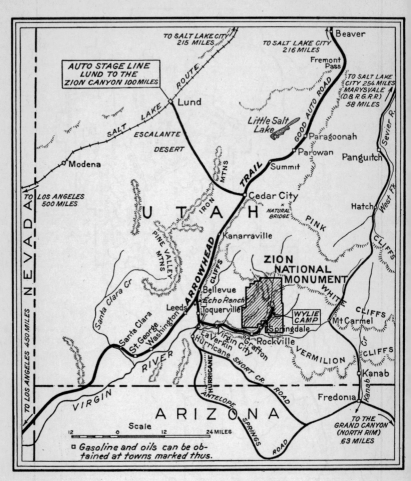

ZION NATIONAL MONUMENT, UTAH

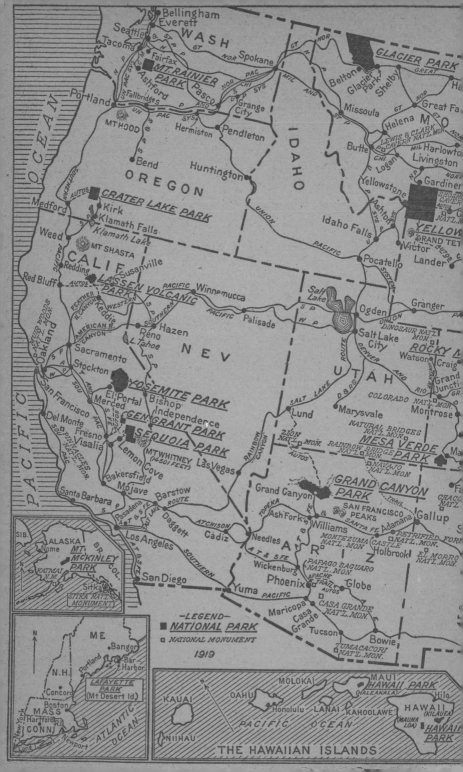